Advanced Financial Accounting

Advanced Financial Accounting

Dr. Anoop Pant

RANDOM
RANDOM PUBLICATIONS
NEW DELHI (INDIA)

Advanced Financial Accounting

ISBN 978-93-5111-393-5

Published in 2014 in India by

RANDOM PUBLICATIONS

4376-A/4B, Gali Murari Lal, Ansari Road
New Delhi-110 002
Phone : +91-11-43580356, +91-11-23289044
e-mail: randomexports@gmail.com, sales@randompublications.com, info@randompublications.com

Reprinted 2023

Type Setting by : Keystoneprintads, Delhi-110051
Printed at : Replika Press Pvt. Ltd.

Preface

Financial accounting is the field of accountancy concerned with the preparation of financial statements for decision makers, such as stockholders, suppliers, banks, employees, government agencies, owners, and other stakeholders. Financial capital maintenance can be measured in either nominal monetary units or units of constant purchasing power. The central need for financial accounting is to reduce the various principal-agent problems, by measuring and monitoring the agents' performance and thereafter reporting the results to interested users.

Financial accounting is used to prepare accounting data for people outside the organisation or for those, who are not involved in the mundane administration of the company. Management accounting, provides accounting information to help managers make decisions to manage and enhance the business. In short, financial accounting is the process of summarising financial data, which is taken from an organisation's accounting records and publishing it in the form of annual or quarterly reports, for the benefit of people outside the organisation. Financial accounting is governed not only by local standards but also by international accounting standard.

Financial accounting generates some key documents, which includes profit and loss account, patterning the method of business traded for a specific period and the balance sheet that provides a statement, showing mode of trade in business for a specific period. It records financial transactions showing both the inflows and outflows of money from sales, wages etc. Financial accounting empowers the managers and aids them in managing more efficiently by preparing standard financial information, which includes monthly management report tracing the costs and profits against budgets, sales and investigations of the cost.

In India, the Accounting Standards Board (ASB) was constituted by the Institute of Chartered Accountants of India (ICAI) on 21st April 1977, which performs the functions of formulating accounting standards. Accurate and reliable financial information is the lifeline of commerce and investing.

Presently, there are two sets of accounting standards accepted for international use namely, the U.S., Generally Accepted Accounting Principles (GAAP) and the International Financial Reporting Standards (IFRS). India is yet to implement IFRS and is in the process of adopting the globally accepted International Financial Reporting Standards (IFRS) by 2011.

While the book is aimed at advanced level accounting degree students in tertiary institutions, it is a useful primer for practitioners who wish to reinforce their knowledge of rapidly changing accounting standards.

I thank all members of my team who have helped in the preparation of the book. My special thanks go to "Random Publications" who have published the book.

– Dr. Anoop Pant

Contents

1

Accounting

WHAT IS ACCOUNTING

This is not an easy question. What do you think accounting is? The scope and definition of accounting changes throughout time. In general, it is argued that accounting is concerned with the provision of information about the position and performance of an enterprise that is useful to a wide range of potential users in making decisions.

Historically, this information has been financial, but accounting is increasingly being used to address the 'triple-bottom-line' of social and environmental, as well as economic, concerns. In this part, we focus on financial uses of accounting but you can study social and environmental reporting, Auditing. Similarly, in this course the types of enterprises that as suggested, focus on are businesses whose aim is to make profit or otherwise to increase their owners' wealth.

However, it is important to remember that other types of enterprises such as charities, other non-government organisations, and public sector bodies such as schools, universities, hospitals, and local and national government, also use accounting. You can also find out more about accounting for these types of enterprises, Auditing. The decisions that users of accounting information make may be economic or legal in nature. Economic decisions are concerned with the allocation of resources, for example, whether to sell or invest in a business, or invest in the equipment to manufacture a new product.

'Legal' decisions are concerned with determining whether managers have made a good job of running a business on the owners' behalf (stewardship), and how much managers should be paid, or they concern matters such as how much tax a business should pay, or whether a business has broken the terms of its borrowing agreements. Users of accounting information are usually thought of as individuals, but there is also a social role for accounting, and it can be regarded as a 'public good' which aims to improve the allocation of scarce resources for the welfare of society in general.

A BRIEF HISTORY

Accounting originally served a stewardship function, as a result of the separation of ownership and control of resources. First wealthy landowners, and later company shareholders, hired managers or 'stewards' to run their properties and businesses. The landowners and shareholders owned the resources, but the stewards and managers controlled them. As the business owners could not always be on hand to watch their stewards or managers perform their duties, they required the stewards to make regular reports on their activities, using accounting to prepare the figures. This is what we call financial reporting. The separation of ownership and control has grown wider and wider throughout the last century, as companies increased in number, and became larger and more complicated.

Their owners became an increasingly distant and diverse body, often buying and selling shares on stock exchanges with no direct dealings with the company at all. As the opportunities to hide or manipulate information have therefore also increased, financial reporting by businesses to their owners has required more and more regulation. Step by step with the increased demand for financial reporting, demand has arisen for independent audits to check the reported information. Recent accounting and auditing scandals such as that involving Enron and Arthur Andersen have thrown the problems with financial reporting into the spotlight. Alongside the growth in financial reporting, has been the development of the use of accounting for the benefit of the business managers themselves. The practice of using accounting information as a direct aid to management arose later than financial reporting, but is no less important. Increasing business complexity and changes to the economic environment have meant that more and more sophisticated systems of collecting and recording information are required. In contrast to financial accounting, this information is used to help make decisions about the future, not just report on past events.

Different types of information, and different tools with which to analyse it, are required. Finally, as accounting has been recognised as a social science, the impact of the use of accounting information (whether as and aid to management, or for financial reporting purposes) on the employees of the business has been widely explored. Managers or employees who are paid salary bonuses based on figures provided by accounting systems may change their actions as a result of the incentives (or disincentives!) this provides.

THE CHANGING ROLE OF ACCOUNTING

Accounting is shaped by the environment in which it operates. As a result, accounting systems vary from country to country. The most obvious differences concern financial reporting, as this is the area where there are most likely to be rules and regulations in place. One of the most important issues affecting the development of accounting today is the need for internationally comparable financial information and the drive for harmonisation of accounting practices. Many businesses operate globally and face costs of having to prepare financial reports in different ways to satisfy different regulators. Also, investors from one country may wish to buy shares in or make loans to businesses in another country. These investors need to be able to compare all businesses fairly in order to decide where to invest their funds. In order for businesses all over the world to be treated similarly and reduce their reporting costs, different accounting regimes need to agree a common set of rules.

As you can imagine, this is a difficult process, and one that is dominated by a handful of the most influential bodies. The management uses of accounting information are also developing. Businesses face increasingly complex decisions in an increasingly complex world. Advances in technology create both new markets, and new tools and capacities for recording and analysing data. For instance, the increasing importance of social and environmental reporting means that accountants need to develop new ways of collecting, classifying and measuring non-financial data. This information may include the levels of pollutants emitted by a factory, or whether the factory meets health and safety standards. Some businesses are choosing to report this kind of information in order to avoid negative publicity or to gain business from 'green' consumers (or finance from 'ethical' investors).

There is also an increasing demand for government and public sector bodies to be held accountable to tax-payers and citizens for their actions. For example, schools publish their examination results, and hospitals their waiting lists. Although social and environmental reporting are outside the scope of this unit, thinking about these issues helps us to understand the changing nature of accounting throughout time.

TOWARDS A DEFINITION OF ACCOUNTING

Perhaps the best way of thinking about the role and development of accounting is to consider the functions that accounting information performs. Not all of these functions have been expected or required of accounting at all times in the past, and it is likely that additional functions will be demanded in the future. Therefore, if accounting is defined by the functions it performs, you can see that this definition changes through time. The earliest roles of accounting information were to measure and record financial transactions and provide information for stewardship purposes.

At present, accounting is generally viewed as serving the following functions:

- *Recording*: accounting systems supply a means of recording data so as to enable the production of reports or for use in calculations. For example, for the preparation of financial statements, the calculation of performance indicators on which managerial bonuses are based, or for costing inventory.

- *Classification*: accounting systems assist in categorising data so as to enable the production of reports or for use in calculations. For example, identifying whether an item is an asset or an expense, or which costs should be included in inventory.
- *Measurement*: accounting systems quantify data so as to enable the production of reports or for use in calculations. For example, determining how much profit a business has earned in a year, or the value of a piece of machinery.
- *Stewardship*: accounting systems provide information which enables owners to determine how funds entrusted to managers have been used by them, and to what ends.
- *Information for decisions*: accounting systems provide information which enables users to make decisions about the future. For example, to assist investors or managers in deciding how to allocate their limited resources.
- *Monitoring and control*: accounting systems provide information which enables management to monitor performance, and take corrective action if necessary.
- *Performance evaluation and compensation*: accounting systems provide information on the performance of different individuals and parts of the business in order to determine how much managers and employees should be rewarded, just as to the terms of their contracts.
- *Communication*: accounting systems provide a means by which information is transmitted to users. For example, to external users via the financial statements, or to internal users via the budget-setting process.

These functions can be divided into two types. The first three functions concern the production of accounting information. The last five functions concern the uses of the information produced.

ACCOUNTING THEORY AND PRACTICE

The nature of any theory is to provide a logical basis for the practice or procedure to which the theory is applied. Accounting theory has evolved over a long passage of time during which substantial changes in human behaviour and market structures have taken place. There are two main types of accounting theory that impact the practice of accounting. Normative theory concerns how things should be done. For example, ideas about the meaning of economic income can influence the way in which regulators decide that accounting systems should measure profit. In contrast, positive accounting theory tries to explain why things are the way they are. For example, why managers choose a particular accounting method over another, or choose not to invest in research and development activities. For policy-makers to make changes to accounting systems, they not only need to know what they are trying to achieve (*i.e.* they need to form an opinion as to the desired outcome), they also need to understand why people are currently behaving differently and how any changes will affect them. They will refer to normative theory for the former, and positive theory for the latter.

Positive accounting theory is tested by gathering and analysing data. Usually, researchers either study a single organisation in great depth over a long period of time, or they collect a smaller amount of data about a much larger number of organisations. Analysing a single organisation may mean that the research findings are not generalisable to other organisations. However, analysing a large number of organisations to reach conclusions about the 'average' organisation, does not tell you very much about individual cases.

ACCOUNTING INFORMATION AND ITS USES

We have seen that financial reporting provides information to users who are not normally involved in actually running the organisation. These users are external to the business. They include actual and potential shareholders, lenders and other investors. They may also include customers, suppliers, the government, and the general public. We have also seen that management use accounting information themselves. Directors, other managers, and employees are internal to the business, and use information to make economic decisions (for example, which new product to manufacture, or what price to charge to a new customer).

External users may wish to make both economic decisions (for example, whether or not to invest their money in the business by buying shares) and legal/stewardship decisions (for example, the government needs to calculate how much tax to charge, and shareholders need to determine how well the managers have performed in managing their funds). These different types of decisions require different types of information.

There is usually a trade-off between:

- Relevant information (that can influence decisions about the future or confirm the outcome of a past transaction); and
- Reliable information.

Economic decisions need forward-looking information. This information is unlikely to be reliable as no one has a crystal ball that can predict the future with total accuracy! Legal and stewardship decisions need information about the past. It is usually important that this information is very reliable, as getting it wrong may result in fines and penalties.

NATURE OF ACCOUNTING SYSTEMS

An accounting system is a process whereby a specific output is produced by a given input. In an information accounting system, data is processed to provide information. Data is a collection of unprocessed facts, while information is data or facts that have been processed into a meaningful form.

In the normal course of events, a business undertaking will enter into a large variety of transactions. The details of a particular transaction are referred to as transaction data. The term transaction data therefore refers to the facts that completely describe a specific transaction.

The aim of an accounting system is to record the transaction data and then to process this data to provide information that is ultimately collected in the financial and management reports of the enterprise. There are two stages in the development of an accounting system, namely systems analysis and system design. A good accounting system must comply with at least the following fundamental requirements. The system must provide decision–makers with timely and accurate information relevant to the responsibilities and requirements; the internal control measures must be adequate to ensure the protection of assets and the provision of reliable information and the system must be sufficiently flexible to accommodate changes in the volume of activities and in the operating procedures without requiring drastic modifications.

A thorough knowledge of the activities of the undertaking and its information and control requirements is an essential prerequisite for the development of an effective accounting system that meets the necessary criteria. The procedure of surveying the undertaking's activities and information and control requirements is known as system analysis. In the system's design process the system is designed to comply with the specifications determined by systems analysis. Initial transactions are recorded in source documents and the in journals and finally they are classified and stored in ledger accounts. The processed information is extracted from the ledger accounts for drawing up the financial reports. The design of any accounting system within this framework comprises of, planning the procedures just as to which the system will function, the design of the source documents, journals, ledger accounts and final reports and finally the design of the necessary internal control measures. From a management information point of view it is important that the information needs of a user are determined and that the accounting report meets these needs. Rapid development in the field of computer accounting has led to the effectiveness of the accounting process, enabling more usable, more accurate and more timely output of accounting data. Efficiency increases as the value of the system increases in relation to the cost thereof. Computerised systems have made the accountants job in designing the accounting process that much easier than the manual systems of days gone by.

TYPES OF ACCOUNTING

Accounting is believed to be one of the most important elements in the business world where money is almost everything. It is termed as a process in which finances of an organization are recorded for further assessment. By employing the purpose of accounting and this process of financial management, businesses are able to determine if they are earning profits or going in losses.

In contrary to a common misconception, the practice of accountancy was carried out even in the early ages. It is only with new types of accounting and Information Technology (IT) that it has advanced to a greater level. The principles of accounting are the basis of carrying out the accounting process. Let us get to know about the general types of accounting in the industry.

COMMON TYPES OF ACCOUNTING

Financial Accounting

For carrying out this type of accounting, professionals use guidelines laid down by certain financial institutions such as the Securities and Exchange Commission (SEC) and the International Accounting Standards Committee (IASC). A financial accountant is handed over the responsibility to assess financial conditions which would help companies determine further steps in investments.

Management Accounting

Management accounting is one of the most important types of accounting careers. It deals with studying, analyzing, and recording the financial aspects of business firms. Few of the sub sections of this field of accounting are asset management, internal auditing, financial planning and budgeting, etc. Professionals working in management accounting really need to be adept in using related computer accounting software for data management.

Governmental Accounting

As the name suggests, governmental accounting is a field that relates to financial management of the federal, state or regional government. It is concentrated more on providing data management services instead of earning profits. An accountant employed in this sector usually looks after the audits, budgeting, and financial management of government facilities.

Fiduciary Accounting

The task of fiduciary accounting is normally handed over to a trustee or an administrator in a non profit organization or a specific community. This accounting is likely to be administrated or initiated by the court. A fiduciary accountant performs traditional accounting duties like record maintenance, financial assessment, and even asset management.

National Income Accounting

National income accounting is associated with the social and economic factors of a nation, unlike just the financial management in a company. It covers a much broader scope which eventually gives out results such as the purchasing capacity of a country per year. The use of national income accounting also enables a country to find out the market value of goods and services manufactured in the country for a specific time period.

Project Accounting

Project accounting is very much similar to management accounting. However, both types of accounting are conducted in business; it is only that project accounting is concerned with the financial advancements on a particular project. It is believed to be a very effective tool in project management. This helps organizations to schedule the deliverables in accordance with the project progress reports.

OTHER TYPES OF ACCOUNTING

Private or Industrial Accounting

This type of accounting refers to accounting activity that is limited only to a single firm. A private accountant provides his skills and services to a single employer and receives salary on an employer-employee basis. The term private is applied to the accountant and the accounting service he renders. The term is used when an employer-employee type of relationship exists even though the employer is some case is a public corporation.

Public Accounting

Public accounting refers to the accounting service offered by a public accountant to the general public. When a practitioner-client relationship exists, the accountant is referred to as a public accountant. Public accounting is considered to be more professional than private accounting. Both certified and non certified public accountants can provide public accounting services. Certified accountants can be single practitioners or by partnership ranging in size from two to hundreds of members. The scope of these accounting firms can include local, national and international clientele.

Governmental Accounting

Governmental accounting refers to accounting for a branch or unit of government at any level, may it be federal, state, or local. Governmental accounting is very similar to conventional accounting methods. Both the governmental and conventional accounting methods use the double-entry system of accounting and journals and ledgers. The object of government accounting units is to give service rather than make profits. Since profit motive cannot be used as a measure of efficiency in government units, other control measures must be developed. To enhance control, special funds accounting is used. Governmental units can use the services of both private and public accountant just as any business entity.

Fiduciary Accounting

Fiduciary accounting lies in the notion of trust. This type of accounting is done by a trustee, administrator, executor, or anyone in a position of trust. His work is to keep the records and prepares the reports. This may be authorized by or under the jurisdiction of a court of law. The fiduciary accountant should seek out and control all property subject to the estate or trust. The concept of proprietorship that is common in the usual types of accounting is non-existent or greatly modified in fiduciary accounting.

National Income Accounting

National income accounting uses the economic or social concept in establishing accounting rather than the usual business entity concept. The national income accounting is responsible in providing the public an estimate of the nation's annual purchasing power. The GNP or the gross national product is a related term, which refers to the total market value of all the goods and services produced by a country within a given period of time, usually a calendar year.

ACCOUNTING EQUATION

The accounting equation represents the basic equation associated with double-entry accounting. Essentially, the accounting equation establishes the formula for representing the relationship that exists between assets, liabilities, and net worth. As the most common of all balance sheet equations, the accounting equation is also fundamental to learning how to properly read and utilize a balance sheet.

For the purposes of understanding how the accounting equation works, it is important to have some grasp of what is meant by each of the three basic components in the equation. Assets refer to the worth of goods or products in the possession of the owner. Liabilities represent the amount of cash or resources that were borrowed in order to acquire the assets. Net worth is the financial worth of the individual, less any outstanding debts to outside entities. Essentially, the point of the accounting equation is to arrive at this final component of net worth, or as it is sometimes referred to, the equity.

To show the way that the accounting equation works to determine net worth, assume that an investor currently has a net worth of two thousand dollars, with no current liabilities. The owner chooses to acquire a new asset for the amount of one thousand dollars. In order to acquire the asset, the owner chose to use five hundred dollars of assets that were already in his or her possession, and then borrow five hundred dollars to complete the purchase. Assuming there is no depreciation associated with the acquired asset, the owner now has control of assets worth a total of three thousand Rupees (₹). However, he or she now has liabilities in the amount of five hundred Rupees (₹). This will result in a net worth of two thousand, five hundred Rupees (₹).

As long as the sum of the net worth and the liabilities equal the assets, all is well in the accounting process. Simply speaking, the accounting equation shows that net worth is determined by taking the value of current assets in hand and subtracting the value of any current liabilities. When it comes to use of the accounting equation as the foundational balance sheet equation, this means that the bottom line on the balance sheet will always show the net worth of the individual or entity.

As long as the final net worth figure and the amount of liabilities balance with the assets, all is well. However, if the combination of liabilities and net worth does not equal the total of the assets, there is something wrong in the accounting process, and an investigation to uncover the origin of the imbalance should take place immediately.

GENERALLY ACCEPTED ACCOUNTING PRINCIPLES

Generally Accepted Accounting Principles (GAAP) is a term used to refer to the standard framework of guidelines for financial accounting used in any given jurisdiction which are generally known as Accounting Standards. GAAP includes the standards, conventions, and rules accountants follow in recording and summarizing transactions, and in the preparation of financial statements.

The term "GAAP" is an abbreviation for Generally Accepted Accounting Principles (GAAP). GAAP is a codification of how CPA firms and corporations prepare and present their business income and expense, assets and liabilities on their financial statements. GAAP is not a single accounting rule, but rather the aggregate of many rules on how to account for various transactions.

When preparing financial statements prepared using GAAP, most American corporations and other business entities use the many rules of how to report business transactions based upon the various GAAP rules. This provides for consistency in the reporting of companies and businesses so that financial analysis, Banks, Shareholders and the SEC can have all reporting companies preparing their financial statements using the same rules and reporting procedures. This allows for an "Apple to Apple" comparison of any corporation or business entity with another. Thus, if Company A reports ₹1,000,000 of net income, using GAAP, than the public and other users of financial statements can compare that net income to another company that is reporting ₹500,000 of net income, using GAAP.

The rules and procedures for reporting under GAAP are complex and have developed over a long period of time. Currently there are more than 150 "pronouncements" as to how to account for different types of transactions, ranging from how to report regular income from the sale of goods, and its related inventory values, to accounting for incentive stock option distributions. By using consistent principles, all companies reporting under GAAP report these transactions on their financial statements in a consistent manner.

The various rules and pronouncements come from the Financial Accounting Standards Board (FASB) which is a non-profit organization that the accounting profession has created to promulgate the rules of GAAP reporting and to amend the rules of GAAP reporting as occasion requires. The more recent pronouncements come as Statements of the Financial Accounting Board.

Changes in the GAAP rules can carry tremendous impact upon American business. For example, when FASB stopped requiring banks to mark their assets (loans) to the lower of cost or market (*i.e.* value of a foreclosed home loan). the effect on a bank's "net worth" as defined by GAAP can change dramatically. While generally neutral, there is some pressure on the FASB to yield to industry or political pressure when it makes its rules. Nonetheless, since all companies report using the same set of rules, know the rules of GAAP reporting can tell the user of financial statements a great deal. The study of accounting, in large part, entails learning the many rules and promulgations set forth by FASB and how to apply those rules to actual business events.

GAAP is slowly being phased out in favour of the International Accounting Standards as the global business becomes more pervasive. GAAP applies only to United States financial reporting and thus an American company reporting under GAAP might show different results if it was compared to a British company, that uses the International Standards. While there is tremendous similarity in between GAAP and the International Rules. the differences can lead a financial statement user to incorrectly believe that company A made more money than company B simply because they report using different rules. The move towards International Standards seeks to eliminate this kind of disparity.

Financial Accounting is information that must be assembled and reported objectively. Third-parties who must rely on such information have a right to be assured that the data are free from bias and inconsistency, whether deliberate or not. For this reason, financial accounting relies on certain standards or guides that are called "Generally Accepted Accounting Principles" (GAAP).

Principles derive from tradition, such as the concept of matching. In any report of financial statements (audit, compilation, review, etc.), the preparer/auditor must indicate to the reader whether or not the information contained within the statements complies with GAAP.

- *Principle of regularity*: Regularity can be defined as conformity to enforced rules and laws.
- *Principle of consistency*: This principle states that when a business has once fixed a method for the accounting treatment of an item, it will enter all similar items that follow in exactly the same way.
- *Principle of sincerity*: This principle, the accounting unit should reflect in good faith the reality of the company's financial status.

- *Principle of the permanence of methods*: This principle aims at allowing the coherence and comparison of the financial information published by the company.
- *Principle of non-compensation*: One should show the full details of the financial information and not seek to compensate a debt with an asset, a revenue with an expense, etc.
- *Principle of prudence*: This principle aims at showing the reality "as is": one should not try to make things look prettier than they are. Typically, a revenue should be recorded only when it is *certain* and a provision should be entered for an expense which is *probable.*
- *Principle of continuity*: When stating financial information, one should assume that the business will not be interrupted. This principle mitigates the principle of prudence: assets do not have to be accounted at their disposable value, but it is accepted that they are at their historical value.
- *Principle of periodicity*: Each accounting entry should be allocated to a given period, and split accordingly if it covers several periods. If a client pre-pays a subscription (or lease, etc.), the given revenue should be split to the entire time-span and not counted for entirely on the date of the transaction.
- *Principle of Full Disclosure/Materiality*: All information and values pertaining to the financial position of a business must be disclosed in the records.
- *Principle of Utmost Good Faith*: All the information regarding to the firm should be disclosed to the insurer before the insurance policy is taken.

INTERNATIONAL ACCOUNTING STANDARDS AND RULES

Many countries use or are converging on the International Financial Reporting Standards (IFRS), established and maintained by the International Accounting Standards Board. In some countries, local accounting principles are applied for regular companies but listed or large companies must conforms to IFRS, so statutory reporting is comparable internationally, across jurisdictions.

ACCOUNTING CONVENTIONS

The most commonly encountered convention is the "historical cost convention". This requires transactions to be recorded at the price ruling at the time, and for assets to be valued at their original cost. Under the "historical cost convention", therefore, no account is taken of changing prices in the economy.

MONETARY MEASUREMENT

Accountants do not account for items unless they can be quantified in monetary terms. Items that are not accounted for (unless someone is prepared to pay something for them) include things like workforce skill, morale, market leadership, brand recognition, quality of management etc.

SEPARATE ENTITY

This convention seeks to ensure that private transactions and matters relating to the owners of a business are segregated from transactions that relate to the business.

REALISATION

With this convention, accounts recognise transactions (and any profits arising from them) at the point of sale or transfer of legal ownership—rather than just when cash actually changes hands. For example, a company that makes a sale to a customer can recognise that sale when the transaction is legal—at the point of contract. The actual payment due from the customer may not arise until several weeks (or months) later—if the customer has been granted some credit terms.

MATERIALITY

An important convention. As we can see from the application of accounting standards and accounting policies, the preparation of accounts involves a high degree of judgement. Where decisions are required about the appropriateness of a particular accounting judgement, the "materiality" convention suggests that this should only be an issue if the judgement is "significant" or "material" to a user of the accounts. The concept of "materiality" is an important issue for auditors of financial accounts.

DOUBLE ENTRY SYSTEM

The double entry system of bookkeeping owes its origin to an Italian merchant named Lucas Pacioli who wrote the first book on *double entry bookkeeping* entitled "Decomputis et Scripturis". It was published in Venice in 1544. All modern methods of accounting are simply adaptation of the system invented by that ancient pioneer.

DEFINITION AND EXPLANATION

The double entry theory of bookkeeping can be defined as the system of recording transactions having two fundamental aspects—one involving the receiving of a benefit and the other to giving the benefit—in the same set of books. In this theory, as the two fold aspects of each transaction are recorded, the name "double entry" has been given to this system. Every transaction involves two fold aspects *e.g.,* an aspect of receiving and an aspect of giving. One who receives is a debtor (Dr) and one who gives is a creditor (Cr). Under the double entry system, both the aspects of giving and receiving are recorded in terms of accounts. The account which receives the benefit is debited and the account which gives the benefit is credited. It is the ultimate result of this system that every debit must have corresponding credit and vice versa and on any particular day the total of the debit entries and the credit entries on the various accounts must be equal.

ADVANTAGES OF DOUBLE ENTRY SYSTEM

The main advantages of double entry theory of book–keeping are as follows:

- Trial balance can be drawn up on any day to prove the arithmetical accuracy of record.
- The nominal sides of transactions being recorded: it is possible to prepare Trading and Profit and Loss Account from which the Gross Profit and Net Profit made by the business during a particular period can be easily ascertained.
- As all personal accounts of debtors and creditors as well as real accounts are kept, it is possible to prepare Balance Sheet.
- The transactions being recorded in the most scientific and systematic way gives the most reliable information of business.
- It prevents fraud by rendering any alteration in any account more difficult.
- It enables the trader to compare the different items, such as sales, purchases, opening stock and closing stock of one period with similar items of preceding period and the trader may thus know whether his business is progressing or not.

DISADVANTAGES OF DOUBLE ENTRY SYSTEM

The following are the main disadvantages of this system:

- This system requires the maintenance of a number of books of accounts which is not practical in small concerns.
- The system is costly because a number of records are to be maintained.
- There is no guarantee of absolute accuracy of the books of accounts inspite of agreement of the trial balance.

2

Understanding the Financial Accounting

FINANCIAL STATEMENT ELEMENTS

Although the content, presentation, and basis of accounting may vary just as to the reporting requirements of Statement 34, the basic elements of the financial statements remain the same.

The major elements of the financial statements (*i.e.*, assets, liabilities, fund balance/net assets, revenues, expenditures, and expenses) including the proper accounting treatments and disclosure requirements.

However, the narrative does not exhaustively discuss all reporting requirements that school districts may face. School district personnel, therefore, should refer to the actual GASB statements or other definitive sources for detailed disclosure requirements and reporting formats.

ASSETS

Assets are defined as a probable future economic benefits obtained or controlled by a particular entity as a result of past transactions or events.

The following typically represent the major asset categories:

- Cash and Investments
- Receivables
- Prepaid Items
- Inventory
- Capital Assets

Cash and Investments

Cash and investments often represent a large portion of the assets on a government's balance sheet. Because of the importance of these assets, proper management based on sound investment policies and strategies is vital. The investment of excess funds is often governed by statute. Many state governments have adopted legal frameworks that restrict the investment activities of local governments, including school districts. These restrictions often place limitations on the types of investments allowed, regulate procedures used to manage investments, and require governing bodies to institute certain review procedures. The following discussion about cash and investments does not show all the possible investment scenarios that a local government might use. However, the following five general rules may protect a school district from problems related to investment decisions.

- For public funds, the investment objectives have traditionally been safety of principal first, then liquidity, followed by yield.
- All investments should be made with consideration of the district's cash requirements and cash flows.
- The district must understand the investment instrument, the investment mechanics, and the associated risk of the investment. Knowing the factors and variables that affect the market value of each investment will help the district determine investment policies and strategies.
- School district personnel should know with whom they are dealing before purchasing an investment. This means researching any financial institutions or brokers/dealers that the district uses.
- Proper protection of investments includes acquiring legal ownership or custody of securities. It also includes ensuring that deposits have been properly insured and collateralized.

Certain words in common usage have more limited definitions when they are used for accounting and financial reporting.

Within the context of governmental accounting, the following definitions describe the specific content of accounts used by governmental entities:

- Cash is considered to be the most liquid (readily available) asset owned by an entity and represents readily available cash held by the organization.
- Cash equivalents are short-term, highly liquid investments (readily convertible to known amounts of cash) that are so near to maturity that they present an insignificant risk of changes in value resulting from changes in interest rates.

Generally only investments with original maturities of three months or less qualify under this definition. Items commonly considered cash equivalents are treasury bills, commercial document, short-term deposits in financial institutions, and money market funds. However, investments that qualify as cash equivalents are not all required to be treated as cash equivalents. Therefore, an entity should establish a policy concerning the classification of qualified investments as cash equivalents, which may be no more liberal than the authoritative definition except under pooling of cash and investments. The policy must be disclosed in the notes to the financial statements.

- Investments are defined as securities and similar assets acquired primarily to earn income or profit. A security is a transferable financial instrument that evidences ownership or creditor status.

Securities that are often held by or pledged to school districts generally include U.S. Treasury bills, notes, and bonds; federal agency and instrumentality obligations; direct obligations of a state or its agencies; commercial document; negotiable and non-negotiable certificates of deposit; fully collateralized repurchase agreements; and prime domestic bankers' acceptances.

The pooling of cash and investments provides several advantages, including better physical custody and control, enhanced investment opportunities, and ease of operations. It may also simplify custody, collection, and disbursements. In certain instances, the pooling of cash and investments may be prohibited in contractual clauses such as bond indentures or through legal restrictions. If the school district pools cash for investment purposes, the resulting pooled cash and investments may qualify as a cash equivalent for participating funds, even though some of the pooled investments would not individually meet that definition.

Financial Statement Presentation and Disclosure

The complexity and range of investment potential and the large amounts of cash and other assets present in most governmental units emphasize the need to carefully capture and present these data in usable form. Cash and investment balances are segregated into individual funds and, depending on contractual requirements, may be classified as restricted assets. If a fund overdraws its share of a pooled cash account, the overdraft should be reported as a liability of that fund. Fund overdrafts of this type should be reported as inter fund payables and receivables.

Disclosures for cash and investments normally include, in addition to the GASB Statement 3 disclosures, the valuation basis of investments (*e.g.*, investments are stated at fair value that approximates market). Changes in fair value are included as a component of investment income.

The detailed disclosure requirements for cash and investments have been established in GASB Statement 3, Deposits with Financial Institutions, Investments (including Repurchase Agreements), and Reverse Repurchase Agreements; GASB Statement 28, Accounting and Financial Reporting for Securities Lending Transactions; and GASB Statement 31, Accounting and Financial Reporting for Certain Investments and for External Investment Pools. These GASB statements and the entity's external auditor should both be consulted regarding disclosure requirements for cash and investments.

Receivables

Receivables usually arise as a result of revenue transactions.

The following are the main sources of revenues for school districts that would result in outstanding receivables:

- Property taxes

- State and federal grants
- Intergovernmental revenues (due from other governmental entities)
- Interest income

The accounting for revenues and related accounts receivable in governmental entities depends on the type of fund in which the revenue is recorded. Because governmental funds use the modified accrual basis of accounting, governmental fund revenues should be recognized in the accounting period in which they become susceptible to accrual, that is, when they become both measurable and available to finance expenditures of the fiscal period. "Available" refers to the collectibility of the receivable within the current period or soon enough thereafter to be used to pay for liabilities of the current period.

A general criterion for availability is 60 days, although a longer or shorter period may be used, except for property taxes in which the maximum period may not be more than 60 days. The availability period will be disclosed in the notes. Each entity should adopt a revenue accrual policy that implements the susceptibility to accrual criterion and applies it consistently. This policy should also be disclosed in the notes to the financial statements. Proprietary funds use the accrual basis of accounting to determine when revenues and related receivables should be recorded. Revenues are recognized when they are earned, that is, when the earnings process is complete and an exchange has taken place.

GASB Statements 33, Accounting and Financial Reporting for Non-exchange Transactions, and 36, Recipient Reporting for Certain Shared Non-exchange Revenues, may have an impact on a governmental entity's reporting of revenues related to certain non-exchange transactions. Entities should consult the statements and their external auditors to determine the impact.

Property Taxes Receivable

Property taxes are generally assessed to finance expenditures of a specific fiscal year. On the assessment date or levy date, the property taxes become a lien against the assessed property. Property taxes should be recorded in the governmental funds by using the modified accrual basis of accounting (recorded when they are both measurable and available).

The amount of the property taxes receivable is based on the assessed value of the property, the current property tax rate, and an estimate of the uncollectible portion. When taxes are levied, the revenue and related receivable should be recognized, net of estimated uncollectible amounts. A receivable is usually recognized at the time an enforceable legal claim arises. The revenue is usually recognized in the first period in which the use of the revenues is permitted or required. If taxes that are levied to finance a subsequent fiscal period are collected in the current period, the amount collected should be recorded as deferred revenue. In the next fiscal year, a journal entry will be recorded to recognize the revenue amount that was collected in advance. In the fund financial statements, when property taxes are delinquent but expected to be collected, they should be reported as deferred revenues if it is estimated that the taxes will not be available to pay current obligations of the governmental fund. This situation indicates that the delinquent property taxes are not expected to be collected within 60 days of the close of the fiscal year, although a shorter availability period may be used.

Due from State

This receivable represents amounts from state resources that exceed the amounts received during the fiscal year for which the school district has met all eligibility requirements. A district should also use the measurable and available criteria that are consistent with the modified accrual basis of accounting in the governmental funds to record revenues due from the state. Revenue due from the state for which all eligibility requirements were met during the fiscal year, and which is expected to be received within the availability period (*e.g.*, 60 days) from the financial statement date, should be recorded as a receivable using this account.

Due from Federal Agencies

This account represents amounts for which all eligibility requirements have been met by a district under a federal financial assistance programme that are expected to be available to finance current liabilities. Such revenues are usually accounted for in special revenue funds using the measurable and available criteria, as appropriate for a modified accrual-based fund. If this is an expenditure-driven grant, revenues may be recognized only to the extent that expenditures have been incurred.

Due from Other Governments or Agencies

In some instances, districts become eligible for revenue from other local governments or agencies through grant programmes or by providing services. The receivable earned from such revenue should be recorded only if it also meets the measurable and available criteria.

Thus, when the revenue has been earned under the grant programme or the services have been provided, the district should recognize the revenues and receivables for the amount earned. In addition, if the amount of an outstanding receivable at the end of a fiscal year is not expected to be collected within the availability period (*e.g.*, 60 days) from the financial statement date, the district should record a deferred revenue for the outstanding amount.

Accrued Interest Receivable

Accrued interest represents the amount of interest at the end of an accounting period on all cash accounts and investments held at that date. Accrued interest should be computed for all investments and cash accounts held by the government that generate interest earnings regardless of the expected payment date.

Inventory

Governmental accounting generally requires that amounts spent to purchase goods be recorded as an expenditure at the time of the purchase. An exception to this general rule is made for inventory. If the amount of inventory on hand at year-end is significant, the value of such inventory should be recorded as an asset. This is considered the "Purchase Method" whereupon fund balance is reserved for the amount of inventory. Inventory may also be recorded as an expenditure when it is consumed rather than when it is purchased. Under the "Consumption Method," purchase transactions are first recorded in the inventory account. As inventory is actually used, an entry to recognize the expenditure is posted to the appropriate accounts. This method is required for the proprietary funds.

It is not uncommon for school districts to have a relatively high level of inventory at the end of the fiscal year, since this often coincides with the start of a new school year. In addition to the balance sheet presentation, note disclosure regarding the method of accounting for inventory should be made. Districts often distribute inventoried supplies to schools prior to fiscal year-end to accommodate the beginning of the new academic school year. Such inventories may either be included in inventory at year-end or be expensed in the year of distribution.

For the entity-wide statements, the consumption method must be used. If the purchase method is used in the governmental funds and the consumption method produces a different result, the difference should be included in the reconciliations of governmental funds to governmental activities. Inventories in school districts generally represent goods that are insignificant individually, but are significant as a whole.

These items may be described as follows:

- Consumable goods that have a relatively short shelf life. Common examples are office supplies, document, computer supplies, building and maintenance supplies, and science lab supplies.
- Items that are expected to be used within a short time, including cafeteria foods such as commodities received from the United States Department of Agriculture (USDA).
- Tangible personal property that is durable but does not meet the entity's criteria for capitalization as an asset.

The accounting for inventory can be broken down into two general areas:

1. Monitoring and valuation of inventory
2. Accounting for transactions related to inventory

For internal control purposes, these two functions should be performed by individuals (or departments, if the district is of sufficient size) that are organizationally independent. The results of the two processes should then be reconciled by personnel external to these functions.

This segregation of duties will improve the internal controls over inventory and may mitigate the risks of theft or defalcation.

Accounting for and Control of Inventory

Governmental entities have several options for physical counts of inventory. Independent auditors are required by generally accepted auditing procedures to conduct physical observations of inventories at least annually when such inventories are material to the district's operations.

The physical observations should be conducted as of the balance sheet date or as of a single date that is within a reasonable time before or after the balance sheet date.

The independent auditor is usually present at the time of the inventory to assess the effectiveness of the inventory-taking procedures and to determine the reliance that the independent auditor can place on the entity's representations relating to the physical condition and quantities of the inventory.

The most common physical inventory count methods are:

- Cycle counts,
- Full counts taken at fiscal year-end, and
- Full counts taken at times other than fiscal year-end.

Accounting for Commodities

School districts that receive federal commodities during the year should recognize the fair value as revenue in the period when all eligibility requirements are met (typically, when the commodities are received). (Guide to Implementation of GASB Statement 34 and Related Pronouncements Q&A, Q152). Because the federal agricultural commodity programme involves purpose restrictions in the use of the resources, the value of inventory remaining on hand at fiscal year-end should be reflected as a reservation of fund balance/restriction of net assets..

However, there may be instances in which resources are transmitted before the eligibility requirements are met. These resources would be reflected by the recipient as deferred revenues.

Pension Assets

The advanced funding of pension plans is an intangible asset, which is recognized by an employer for contributions to a pension plan, which were greater than pension expense. This asset will be amortized against the pension costs of the employer when due.

Capital Assets

Governmental entities are responsible for accounting for, controlling, and reporting both current and capital assets.

Capital assets have certain properties that distinguish them from other types of assets:

- Tangible or intangible in nature
- Long-lived (have a life longer than one year)
- Of a significant value at the time of purchase or acquisition
- Reasonably identified and controlled through a physical inventory system

Capital assets may include the following:

- Land and land improvements
- Easements
- Buildings and building improvements
- Vehicles
- Machinery and equipment
- Technological assets such as computers and network equipment
- Works of art and historical treasures
- Infrastructure
- Software

The emphasis in governmental accounting for capital assets is on control and accountability. A variety of data relating to an entity's capital assets must be maintained to ensure control and accountability over them:

- Quantity and types of assets
- Location of assets
- Life expectancy of assets

Capital asset records are necessary to demonstrate accountability for the custody and maintenance of individual items and to assist in projecting future requirements. All capital transactions for the acquisition of capital assets should be controlled through a well-defined authorization procedure. If the budget does not authorize the purchase of specific items, approval power, subject to specific monetary limits, should be assigned to the chief administrator or to a person designated by the chief administrator. The entity should adopt policies to govern this situation even if it has not been an issue in the past.

Basis of Capital Assets

Capital assets are included in the financial records at cost. In some situations, the purchase or acquisition documents may not be available for capital assets already on hand. If reliable historical records are not available, an estimate or appraisal of the original cost based on other information, such as price index levels at time of acquisition, may be used. The intent of such valuation is to record a fair value at the date of acquisition and not expend excessive resources in ascertaining exact costs. If capital assets are acquired by gift, then the fair value on the date received is the appropriate amount to include in the capital asset records.

Capital assets may be acquired by several methods:

- Purchase
- Lease-purchase
- Construction
- Tax foreclosures
- Gifts and contributions

All capital assets acquired in some manner other than gift are recorded at the cost necessary to place the asset in service. Capital assets arising from gifts or donations are recorded at their estimated fair value at the time of receipt.

Capital Asset Reporting

GASB Statement 34 establishes reporting requirements for general government capital assets. Previously, financial statement presentation for capital assets of the general government was limited to the general fixed asset account group in the combined balance sheet. No depreciation was recognized on these assets.

However, Statement 34 establishes the following new reporting requirements for capital assets:

- Depreciable capital assets should be reported in the Statement of Net Assets (a government wide statement) at historical cost, net of accumulated depreciation.
- The historical cost should include the ancillary charges necessary to place the asset into its intended location and condition for use, including freight and transportation charges, site preparation costs, and professional fees that directly relate to the acquisition of the asset.
- Depreciable capital assets may be reported on the face of the Statement of Net Assets as a single item or by major class.
- Significant non-depreciable capital assets that are inexhaustible, such as land, certain non-depreciable site improvements, and infrastructure assets reported using the modified approach should be reported separately from depreciable capital assets on the statement of net assets. GASB has defined an inexhaustible capital asset as one whose economic benefit or service is used up so slowly that its estimated useful life is extraordinarily long. Construction-in-progress should be included with non-depreciable capital assets in the Statement of Net Assets.
- Accumulated depreciation may be reported on the face of the Statement of Net Assets, parenthetically or as a separate line item

reducing capital assets. However, regardless of the statement presentation in the Statement of Net Assets, the notes to the financial statements should disclose balances and changes in accumulated depreciation for the period by major asset class, as well as information regarding depreciation methods used.

Capitalization Thresholds, Estimated Useful Lives, and Depreciation Methods for Capital Assets

Given the new requirements in Statement 34 to depreciate general capital assets, governments must establish a range of policies regarding capitalization thresholds for capital assets, estimates for useful lives, and depreciation methods.

Statement 34 does not prescribe policies for any of these areas; however, note disclosure is required. Management is granted discretion to determine appropriate policies for control purposes in accordance with the laws and regulations under which the entity operates.

Some states have established specific regulations surrounding capital assets; therefore, school districts should consult state sources in establishing new policies.

Capitalization Thresholds

Capitalization threshold refers to the dollar value threshold at which purchases of assets will be capitalized in the financial records of the governmental entity rather than be recorded as an expenditure/expense at the time of purchase.

Many assets having useful lives greater than one year do not have values that are material to the entity's financial statements. Additionally, the costs of tagging, tracking, and accounting for numbers of immaterial items may be considered excessive by the entity. As a result, many local governments establish capitalization thresholds that exclude reporting these items as capital assets and instead rely on systems other than the financial management system for tracking and control purposes (*e.g.*, PC inventories, building equipment lists, maintenance systems).

In determining an appropriate capitalization threshold, entities should consider the following factors:

- Total value of all capital assets
- Impact of the new/revised capitalization threshold on values reported in the statement of net assets
- Value of any related debt (financial statement presentations may be misleading if significant assets acquired through debt are excluded by the capitalization threshold)
- Costs associated with tracking and reporting assets
- Applicable state or federal requirements (typically for grant funds)

Several resources exist to guide governmental entities in making informed decisions related to asset capitalization thresholds, including industry guidelines for specific assets, state auditors' and comptrollers' guidelines for state agencies, and the implementation guide produced by the Association of School Business Officials.

Finally, local governmental entities should review applicable state and federal requirements related to asset capitalization in determining appropriate policies.

For example, the federal government uses a dollar threshold of ₹5,000 for federal grant management purposes. This threshold may have an impact on an entity's policies, particularly as it relates to capital assets that are acquired with federal grant funds.

Estimated Useful Lives

The estimated useful life of an asset is the period (of months or years) that the asset will be used for the purpose for which it was purchased. In determining the estimated useful life of an asset, consideration must be given to the asset's present condition and intended use, maintenance policy, and how long the asset is expected to meet service and technology standards.

School districts may use general guidelines obtained from professional or industry organizations, information on comparable assets of other school districts/governments, and internal historical data.

The determination of appropriate estimated useful lives is a management decision that is affected by a number of factors:

- Experience with asset management
- Plans for asset use
- Property management practices
- Asset maintenance practices
- Applicable federal or state regulations

Many sources of information on estimated useful lives are available to assist in establishing appropriate policies in this area.

These sources include, but are not limited to the following:

- GASB Statement 34 implementation guides issued by state education agencies and other key state agencies, including state auditors and comptrollers. Many of these agencies have web sites that contain information about the useful lives of various asset classes in the state.
- Statement 34 Implementation Guide for schools issued by ASBO, International. This guide discusses capitalization policies and depreciation methods at length.

A periodic reassessment of the estimated useful lives of capital assets may be appropriate. Any change in the useful life of a capital asset should be applied prospectively in accordance with Accounting Principles Board Opinion 20.

Depreciation Methods

GASB Codification Section 1400.113 states that "depreciation expense should be measured by allocating the net cost of depreciable assets (historical cost less estimated salvage value) over their estimated useful lives in a systematic and rational manner."

Although GASB requires governmental entities to depreciate capital assets (other than non-exhaustible assets), the Statement does not prescribe the method. As a result, depreciation methods are a management decision that should be based on the resources necessary to determine the various calculations and the capabilities of asset management systems. In addition to composite or group methods, any established depreciation method may be used (*e.g.*, straight-line, sum-of the-years' digits, or double-declining balance).

Depreciation may be calculated for individual assets or it may be determined for:

- Class of assets,
- Network of assets, or
- Subsystem of a network.

The depreciation method can vary for different categories of assets. To simplify the calculations involved, the composite method may be used to calculate depreciation expense. It is applied to a group of similar assets or dissimilar assets in the same class, using the same depreciation rate, but not across classes of assets.

The estimated life for the group may be based on the individual weighted average, the simple average of the useful lives of the assets in the group, or the weighted average or assessment of the life of the group as a whole. This method assumes no salvage value for assets; therefore, it simplifies the calculations and the recording of asset dispositions.

Works of Art and Historical Treasures

Works of art, historical treasures, and similar assets are a special class of capital assets that may require developing a specific capitalization and depreciation policy.

These assets are defined as items held singly or in collections that meet all of the following conditions:

- Held for public exhibition, education, or research in furtherance of public service, rather than financial gain.
- Protected, kept unencumbered, cared for, and preserved.
- Subject to an organization policy that requires the proceeds from sales of collection items to be used to acquire other items for collections.

Historical buildings, monuments, and fountains are capital assets that may qualify as works of art, historical treasures, or similar assets if they meet the requirements above. School districts that have collections meeting the criteria above may choose not to capitalize these collections of works of art or historical treasures. Depreciation is not required for those capitalized collections or individual items that are considered to be inexhaustible. Inexhaustible collections of individual works of art or historical treasures are those with extraordinarily long useful lives. Because of their cultural, aesthetic, or historical value, the holder of the asset applies efforts to protect and preserve the asset in a manner greater than that for similar assets without such cultural, aesthetic, or historical value.

Technology Assets

Technology-related assets are a class of capital assets that may require special treatment and reporting by school districts based on local or state reporting and accountability requirements or policies. Although technology assets are not dissimilar from other capital assets such as vehicles or furniture and fixtures, the resources dedicated to the installation and ongoing support and use of technology by school districts have resulted in an increased level of interest by policymakers and citizens related to the use of resources dedicated to these purposes.

Thus, many school districts have instituted special accounting and reporting practices associated with expenditures for technology-related assets. To facilitate the proper accounting and reporting of technology expenditures by school districts.

School districts should account for technology-related expenditures just as to the following principles:

- Expenditures related to the technology and media-related activities that support instruction should be segregated from those associated with administrative technology.
- Expenditures associated with purchased services to support technology should be distinguished from other types of purchased and professional services. Expenditure object codes 351 and 352 have been established for this purpose.
- Expenditures associated with the rental of computer and other technology equipment should be distinguished from other types of rentals. Expenditure object code 443 has been established for this purpose.
- Communications expenditures should include all costs associated with voice, data, and video communications charges regardless of the media used.
- Technology supplies should be segregated from other types of supplies. Expenditure object code 650 has been established for this purpose.
- Purchases of technology capital equipment should be specifically

tracked for analysis purposes. Expenditure object codes 734 and 735 have been established for this purpose.

Using these codes to account for and report on technology-related costs will allow school districts to

- Capture information on both instructional and administrative technology costs and
- Accumulate the total expenditures associated with technology for operating purposes and capital purchases.

Many of the key issues related to tracking and reporting on technology-related costs, school districts will still need to establish capitalization and depreciation policies for technology assets.

School districts should capitalize only those technology assets that meet their local policies in this area. Non-capital technology purchases should be treated as supplies for reporting purposes.

Infrastructure Assets

Infrastructure assets are long-lived capital assets that are normally stationary in nature and that can be maintained for a significantly greater number of years than most capital assets.

Infrastructure assets include:

- Roads,
- Bridges,
- Drainage systems,
- Water and sewer systems, and
- Lighting systems.

Parking lots and related lighting systems may be defined by the entity as part of the associated building, rather than as infrastructure. Most school districts have no or an immaterial amount of infrastructure assets.

Reporting Requirements

Infrastructure assets have several reporting requirements:

- Governmental entities are required to capitalize and report major general infrastructure assets that were acquired in fiscal years ending after June 30, 1980, or that received major renovations, restorations, or improvements during that period. Governments with revenues of less than ₹10 million (annually) are not required to report their infrastructure assets retroactively.
- Prospective reporting of general infrastructure assets is required for all entities at the date of implementation of Statement 34.

Statement 34 defines major general infrastructure at the network or subsystem level on the basis of the following criteria:

- The cost or estimated cost of the subsystem is expected to be at least 5 per cent of the total cost of all general capital assets reported in the first fiscal year ending after June 15, 1999. OR

- The cost or estimated cost of the network is expected to be at least 10 per cent of the total cost of all general capital assets reported in the first fiscal year ending after June 15, 1999.
- The reporting of non-major networks is encouraged, but not required.

In determining when to implement the retroactive infrastructure asset reporting requirements, governmental entities should consider the value of any related debt that will be reflected in the Statement of Net Assets.

Valuation of Infrastructure Assets

Infrastructure assets are reported at historical cost or estimated historical cost. If a determination of the historical cost is not viable because of incomplete records, an estimated historical cost may be determined in the following ways:

- Using standard costing, which relies on available records from the period of acquisition to estimate asset cost. These records may include historical documents such as invoices for similar assets and vendor catalogs from the acquisition period.
- Calculating the current replacement cost of a similar asset and deflating this cost back by using price-level indexes to the year or average year of acquisition.

Depreciation of Infrastructure Assets

GASB Statement 34 allows two distinct approaches to reporting infrastructure assets in the Statement of Net Assets. The standard approach requires governmental entities to capitalize all major infrastructure assets and depreciate them over their useful lives. This approach does not differ from the accounting and reporting treatment of other types of capital assets. Alternatively, entities may elect to use a modified approach to infrastructure asset reporting under a specific set of conditions.

The modified approach allows governmental entities to capitalize assets yet avoid the depreciation of their eligible infrastructure assets if they meet two criteria:

1. The entity has a qualifying asset management system that
   - Has an up-to-date inventory of infrastructure;
   - Performs consistent and complete condition assessments every three years, the results of which are summarized using a measurement scale; and
   - Can estimate, on an annual basis, the cost to maintain and preserve the infrastructure assets at the disclosed condition level.
2. The entity documents that the eligible infrastructure assets are being preserved approximately at or above a condition level established and disclosed by the government.

The modified approach is not limited to general infrastructure assets, that is, infrastructure assets associated with governmental activities. Eligible infrastructure assets of enterprise funds that were previously depreciated may also be reported using the modified approach. If entities choose the modified approach for reporting general infrastructure assets, they are required to present information on condition and on estimated versus actual maintenance as required supplementary information (RSI). If the governmental entities report eligible infrastructure assets using the modified approach, additional schedules and disclosures are required as RSI.

Entities should consult their external auditors and the detailed disclosure requirements outlined in Statement 34 to determine policy decisions concerning the modified approach of infrastructure asset reporting.

LIABILITIES

Liabilities represent financial obligations of an entity to transfer assets or provide services to other entities in the future as a result of past transactions or events. Although governments are required to record liabilities in the period in which they are incurred, it is necessary to distinguish between obligations that represent fund liabilities, which are amounts that are due and payable, from unmatured long-term indebtedness, which represents a general long-term liability.

GASB Interpretation No. 6, Recognition and Measurement of Certain Liabilities and Expenditures in Governmental Fund Financial Statements, provides that governmental fund liabilities include those that are due and payable in full when incurred. Additionally, the matured portion of long-term indebtedness to the extent that it is expected to be liquidated with expendable available financial resources should also be recorded as a fund liability. This applies to the matured portions of formal debt issues as well as to other forms of general long-term indebtedness, such as compensated absences, capital leases, and claims and judgments. The unmatured portion of the long-term indebtedness represents a general long-term liability.

Interpretation No. 6 clarifies financial reporting guidance relative to governmental funds. Because proprietary funds use an accrual basis of accounting for liability recognition, all obligations of the fund should be reflected as fund liabilities. The following sub-section identifies the primary obligations typical of most governments.

ACCOUNTS PAYABLE

Accounts payable are those liabilities incurred in the normal course of business for which goods or services have been received but payment has not been made as of the end of the fiscal year.

SALARIES AND RELATED BENEFITS PAYABLE

Expenditures should be recorded and reported in the period in which the liability has been incurred. Therefore, unpaid salaries and related benefits that have not yet been paid at the close of the accounting period should be accrued.

DUE TO/FROM OTHER FUNDS

Each fund is a separate self-balancing set of accounts. Therefore, amounts due to/from other funds generally arise from inter fund loans or inter fund services used/inter fund services provided between funds. For instance, one fund may make an advance to another fund, or one fund may provide services to another without payment at the time the services are provided. Although inter fund receivables and liabilities may be classified as current or non-current depending on the terms for repayment, all such transactions must be reflected as fund receivables and liabilities. The advancing fund should reserve fund balance for the non-current portion of amounts due from another fund.

COMPENSATED ABSENCES

Statement provides guidance for the accounting and financial reporting of compensated absences on both a short-term and a long-term basis. Compensated absences include future vacations, sick leave, sabbatical leave, and other leave benefits.

The need for a governmental entity to accrue a liability for vacation leave or other similar compensated absences is based on the following criteria:

- The government's obligation relating to employees' rights to receive compensations for future absences is attributable to employees' services already rendered.
- It is probable that the entity will compensate employees for the benefits through paid time off or some other means (*e.g.*, cash payments at termination or retirement).

Requirements for accruing a liability for sick leave or similar compensated absences is attributed to services already rendered and it is probable that payment will be made at termination. Therefore, sick leave benefits that have been earned but will only be used as sick leave should not be accrued. Liabilities for compensated absences should be calculated at the end of each fiscal year and adjusted (and recorded) to current salary rates, unless payment will be made at rates other than the current salary rate. This liability also includes the employer's share of social security and Medicare taxes as well as others.

A fund liability for the governmental funds may be recorded only when amounts are due and payable. Any liability not due and payable is recorded as a government wide liability. For proprietary funds, all of the liability is a fund liability.

DEFERRED COMPENSATION AND PENSION PLANS

A deferred compensation plan allows employees to defer the receipt of a portion of their salary and, therefore, the associated tax liability on that salary. Authorization for deferred compensation plans is established by the Internal Revenue Service (IRS).

Employees of many school districts participate in statewide retirement systems. However, districts may establish deferred compensation plans and other pension plans at their discretion, some of which are locally funded. School districts may also provide pension benefits to employees through locally funded pension plans.

Locally funded pension plans should be accounted for in a Pension and Other Employee Benefits Trust Fund. If the school district has significant administrative or fiduciary responsibility for a deferred compensation plan, such as managing the plan's investments, a pension and other employee benefits trust fund should be used. This is not the case for most school districts. If a governmental entity does not have significant administrative or fiduciary responsibility, the plan should not be reported in the entity's funds.

DEBT

Governmental entities borrow money on a short-term basis either to meet operating cash needs or in anticipation of long-term borrowing at later dates. School districts usually borrow money on a long-term basis to finance capital acquisitions or construction or infrastructure improvements. Borrowings may also occur for the initial funding of a risk-retention programme, the payment of a claim or judgment, or the financing of an accumulated operating deficit.

Short-term debt obligations and long-term debt obligations are defined (based on the initial maturity of the obligation) as follows:

- Short-term obligations are loans, negotiable notes, time-bearing warrants, or leases with a duration of 12 months or less, regardless of whether they extend beyond the fiscal year. Using the current financial resources measurement focus, short-term debt should be reflected in the balance sheet of the governmental fund that must repay the debt. The presentation of the liability on the balance sheet of a governmental fund implies that the debt is current and will require the use of current financial resources. Bond anticipation notes may be classified as long-term debt if the criteria of FASB Statement No. 6, Classification of Short-Term Obligations Expected to be Refinanced, are met.
- Long-term obligations are loans, negotiable notes, time-bearing warrants, bonds, or leases with a duration of more than 12 months. Non-current obligations that will be repaid from revenues generated by proprietary funds should be recorded in the related proprietary fund, whereas non-current obligations to be repaid from governmental funds should be reported only on the government wide statement of net assets.

The following sub-section concentrates on long-term debt presentation in different types of funds and the related accounting requirements and disclosures.

It is organized as follows:

- Recording of long-term liabilities in different types of funds
- Types of debt instruments
- Extinguishment of debt

Long-Term Liabilities in Governmental Funds

long-term fund liabilities and general long-term liabilities. Long-term liabilities of proprietary funds and fiduciary funds should be accounted for in those funds and presented in the fund financial statements. Long-term liabilities for the proprietary funds, but not the fiduciary funds, should also be reported in the government wide statements. However, general long-term liabilities of the entity should be accounted for and reported only in the government wide statement of net assets.

BONDS

- General obligation bonds are issued for the construction or acquisition of major capital assets. The security pledged for the bonds is the general taxing power of the government. General obligation bonds are usually either term bonds, which are due in total on a single date, or serial bonds, which are repaid in periodic installments over the life of the issue.
- Revenue bonds are issued to acquire, purchase, construct, or improve major capital facilities. The revenue generated by the facility or the activity supporting the facility is pledged as security for the repayment of the debt.

Other Types of Debt

- Tax anticipation notes and other revenue anticipation notes are often issued to pay current operating expenditures prior to the receipt of the revenues. The proceeds from the revenue sources are pledged as security for the notes.
- Installment financing may be used for either constructing or acquiring property. The security for the financing is the property being acquired or constructed.
- Leases are agreements between two parties that convey the use of property for a specified period of time. A lease must be classified as capital if it meets the criteria of FASB Statement 13, Accounting for Leases, or as operating if it does not qualify as a capital lease. Capital leases are considered to be debt financing; operating leases are not. Capital leases are in substance an acquisition of an asset.

This determination is made using the following criteria:

- The ownership of the property transfers to the lessee at the end of the lease term, or
- The lease contains a bargain purchase option, or
- The lease term is equal to 75 per cent or more of the estimated useful life of the leased property, or
- At the inception of the lease, the present value of the minimum lease payments is equal to 90 per cent or more of the fair value of the leased property.

When a lease satisfies one of the criteria above, an asset and a liability should be recorded. If the lease obligation is incurred by a governmental fund, the asset and the liability will be reported in the government wide statement of net assets. The initial value of the asset should be recorded as the lesser of the fair value of the leased property or the present value of the net minimum lease payments.

Generally accepted accounting principles require governmental entities to disclose a range of information related to both capital and operating leases in the annual financial statements. The GASB Codification should be consulted for detailed disclosure requirements.

Extinguishment of Debt

GASB has established a range of accounting and reporting requirements for debt refundings. These requirements are presented primarily in GASB Codification Section D20 and GASB Statement 23, Accounting and Financial Reporting for Refundings of Debt Reported by Proprietary Activities. The extinguishment of debt is the reacquisition or calling of the debt or the removal of the debt prior to or at the maturity of the debt.

When debt is extinguished, the entity either has no further legal responsibilities under the original debt agreement or continues to be legally responsible for the debt but the extinguishment is considered an in-substance defeasance (retirement).

GASB Statement 23 concludes that debt is considered to be extinguished when one of the following criteria is met:

- The debtor pays the creditor and is relieved of all its obligations with respect to the debt, or
- The debtor is legally released as the primary obligor under the debt either judicially or by the creditor, and it is probable that the debtor will not be required to make future payments with respect to the debt under the guarantees, or
- The debtor irrevocably places cash or other assets with an escrow agent in a trust to be used solely for satisfying scheduled payments of both interest and principal of the defeased debt, and the possibility that the debtor will be required to make future payments on that

debt is remote. In this circumstance, usually referred to as "in-substance defeasance," debt is extinguished even though the debtor is not legally released as the primary obligor under the debt obligation.

The most common method of debt extinguishment is an advance refunding.

Advance Refunding

In an advance refunding transaction, new debt is issued to provide funds to pay principal and interest on old, outstanding debt as it becomes due, or at an earlier call date. An advance refunding occurs before the maturity or call date of the old debt, and the proceeds of the new debt are invested until the maturity or call date.

Debt may be advance refunded for a variety of reasons, including to:

- Take advantage of lower interest rates,
- Extend maturity dates,
- Revise payment schedules, or
- Remove or modify restrictions contained in the old debt agreements.

Some advance refundings are intended to achieve short-term budgetary savings by extending debt service requirements further into the future. In these cases, total debt service requirements over the life of the new debt may be more or less than total service requirements over the life of the existing debt. Advance refundings undertaken for other reasons, such as to remove undesirable covenants of the old debt, may also result in higher or lower total debt service requirements.

It may be necessary in an advance refunding to issue new debt in an amount greater than the old debt. In these cases, savings may still result if the total new debt service requirements (interest and principal payment) are less than the old debt service requirements. Most advance refundings result in defeasance of debt.

Debt Defeasance

Defeasance of debt can be either legal or in-substance. A legal defeasance occurs when debt is legally satisfied on the basis of certain provisions in the debt instrument even though the debt is not actually paid. An in-substance defeasance occurs when debt is considered defeased for accounting and financial reporting purposes even though a legal defeasance has not occurred. When debt is defeased, it is no longer reported as a liability on the face of the balance sheet; only the new debt, if any, is presented in the financial statements.

Debt is considered defeased in-substance for accounting and financial reporting purposes if the school district irrevocably places cash or other assets with an escrow agent in a trust to be used solely for satisfying scheduled payments of both interest and principal of the defeased debt and when the possibility that the debtor will be required to make future payments on that debt is considered remote. The trust that is created should be restricted to monetary assets that are essentially risk-free as to the amount, timing, and collection of interest and principal.

Certain disclosures are required on defeasance of debt. GASB Codification Section D20.111 requires that a general description of the transaction should be provided in the notes to the financial statements in the year of refunding and that the disclosure should include at a minimum the following:

- The difference between the cash flows required to service the old debt and the cash flows required to service the new debt and complete the refunding.
- The economic gain or loss resulting from the transaction.

FUND BALANCE/NET ASSETS

FUND FINANCIAL STATEMENTS

Within governmental funds, equity is reported as fund balance; proprietary and fiduciary fund equity is reported as net assets. Fund balance and net assets are the difference between fund assets and liabilities reflected on the balance sheet or statement of net assets. Because of the current financial resources measurement focus of governmental funds, fund balance is often considered a measure of available expendable financial resources. This is a particularly important measure in the general fund because it reflects the primary functions of the government and includes both state aid and local tax revenues.

The relative amount of unreserved fund balance reflected in the general fund is used by rating agencies as a measure of financial strength of the government. Declines in the amount of unreserved fund balance may signal deterioration in the financial condition of the entity.

Governmental fund balances are categorized as follows:

- Reserved
- Unreserved
  - Designated
  - Undesignated

Reserved Fund Balances

Reservations of fund balance should be used in governmental financial reporting to identify the portion that is:

- Not available for appropriation or expenditure (*e.g.*, reserve for inventories, reserve for long-term receivables) and/or
- Legally earmarked by external parties or entities for a specific future use, that is, a legal restriction on the use of assets (*e.g.*, reserve for encumbrances).

The amount and nature of the reservation of fund balance should be disclosed on the face of the financial statements. The description may need to be supplemented by disclosure in the notes to the financial statements.

Examples of reservations of fund balance follow:

- Inventories
- Debt service
- Endowments
- Prepaid items
- Outstanding encumbrances
- Construction
- Federal and state programmes

The aggregate fund balance in the debt service fund is legally reserved for the payment of bonded indebtedness and is not available for other purposes until all bonded indebtedness is liquidated.

The fund balance of the capital projects fund reflects an amount designated for construction and major renovation projects, and it usually represents unexpended proceeds from the sale of bonds that have restricted uses. However, in all instances in which the name of the fund communicates the legal segregation, the fund balance should be reported as unreserved.

Unreserved Fund Balances

Unreserved fund balance is the difference between the total and reserved fund balance. It has two components: designated and undesignated. The unreserved fund balance of the general fund represents the balance available for legal appropriation and expenditure for general operating expenditures. Prudent financial management requires accumulating a sufficient undesignated, unreserved fund balance in the general fund representing available expendable financial resources to meet the net cash outflows during the fiscal year.

Designated, Unreserved Fund Balances

Portions of fund balance may be designated by management to reflect tentative plans or commitments of governmental resources. Designations generally reflect board action to earmark the balance for purposes that will be fulfilled at a later time, but specific board action is not required.

Designations represent planned actions, rather than actual commitments. Because they typically arise from internal actions (management decisions) rather than actions external to the entity (encumbrances), designations are reported as part of unreserved fund balance.

The amount and nature of the designation should be explained in a:

- Separate line of the balance sheet,
- Parenthetical comment, or
- Note to the financial statements.

Designations may be related to:

- Construction or other capital expenditures,
- Claims and judgments, or
- Self-insurance contingencies.

Undesignated, Unreserved Fund Balances

Undesignated, unreserved fund balance is the difference between total fund balance and the portion that is reserved and designated. This is the balance available for legal appropriation and expenditure if a government budgets on a GAAP basis for its governmental funds.

Within proprietary and fiduciary fund statements of net assets, net asset balances are classified into three components:

1. Invested in capital assets, net of related debt represents the net amount invested in capital assets (original cost, net of accumulated depreciation, and capital-related debt).
2. Restricted represents the amount of net assets for which limitations have been placed by creditors, grantors, contributors, laws, and regulations. For example, school districts that account for food services within an enterprise fund may have restrictions related to certain proceeds or commodities imposed by the USDA. Internal actions through enabling legislation and constitutional provisions may also lead to restricted net assets.
3. Unrestricted is the amount of net assets that is not restricted or invested in capital assets, net of related debt.

GOVERNMENT WIDE FINANCIAL STATEMENTS: STATEMENT OF NET ASSETS

The difference between an entity's assets and liabilities in the Statement of Net Assets represents its net assets.

Net assets have three components:

1. Invested in capital assets, net of related debt
2. Restricted net assets
3. Unrestricted net assets

REVENUES

The accounting and financial reporting for revenues within a governmental entity is determined by the economic substance of the underlying transactions. Generally accepted accounting principles have established criteria for recognition based on the classification and characteristics of the transaction.

Within governmental entities, transactions may be classified as either exchange (or exchange-like) transactions or non-exchange transactions. Exchange transactions are those in which the parties involved give up and receive essentially equal values. Within a commercial enterprise, transactions between businesses and their customers meet this definition. Within a proprietary fund of a governmental entity, fees or charges made for goods or services represent exchange transactions.

Although similar to exchange transactions, exchange-like transactions represent situations in which the values exchanged may not be equal or the direct benefits may not be exclusively for the parties involved in the transaction. Examples include permits and professional or regulatory licensing fees. To clarify and expand existing guidance in the accounting and financial reporting of non-exchange transactions within governments, GASB issued Statement 33, Accounting and Financial Reporting for Non-exchange Transactions, and Statement 36, Recipient Reporting for Certain Shared Non-exchange Revenues.

These standards establish recognition criteria for non-exchange transactions reported on the accrual basis or the modified accrual basis of accounting.

Statement 33 describes four classifications of non-exchange transactions:

1. Derived tax revenues result from assessments imposed on exchange transactions, such as income taxes and sales taxes. Derived tax revenues and the related receivables normally should be recognized when the underlying transaction occurs with the criteria extended to include the availability criteria for revenues accounted for on the modified accrual basis.
2. Imposed non-exchange revenues result from assessments imposed on nongovernmental entities, other than assessments on exchange transactions. Property taxes, ad valorem taxes on personal property, and fines are common examples. A receivable is usually recognized at the time an enforceable legal claim arises. Imposed non-exchange revenues should be recognized in the first period in which the use of the revenues is permitted or required. For imposed non-exchange revenues accounted for on a modified accrual basis, recognition also depends on the availability of the resources.
3. Government-mandated non-exchange transactions occur when a government at one level provides resources to a government at another level and requires the recipient to use them for a specific purpose in accordance with the provider's enabling legislation. An example is the federal funds provided for food and nutrition programmes in school districts.
4. Voluntary non-exchange transactions result from legislative or contractual agreements, other than exchanges, entered into willingly by two or more parties. Certain grants and entitlements and most donations are examples of this type of transaction. Frequently, purpose restrictions and eligibility requirements are established by the provider.

For both government-mandated non-exchange transactions and voluntary non-exchange transactions, revenues and receivables should be recognized when all eligibility requirements have been met. For revenues accounted for on a modified accrual basis, the criteria are extended to include the availability of the resources.

GASB Codification Section 1600.106 states that revenues in governmental funds and other governmental fund financial resource increments are recognized using the modified accrual basis of accounting when they are susceptible to accrual, which means they must be both measurable and available. Revenues are measurable when the amount of the revenue is subject to reasonable estimation.

To be available, revenues must be subject to collection within the current period, or after the end of the period, but in time to pay liabilities outstanding at the end of the current period. Revenues in the proprietary funds are recognized using the accrual basis of accounting, (*i.e.,* in the period in which they are earned). They are classified either as operating or non-operating revenues. Operating revenues are generated by the primary activity of the fund. Conversely, non-operating revenues are not generated by the primary activity of the fund, but by other means, such as through grants or interest earnings.

Governmental entities account for a variety of revenues that generally may be presented in the financial statements of governmental funds in three broad categories.

- Local and intermediate sources are those revenues that are collected from the citizens of the district's service area and governmental and non governmental entities both within and outside the school district. Such revenues include property taxes, tuition, and interest income.
- State revenues are those revenues received from the state, excluding funds passed through the state from the federal government. Such revenues include state grants and state education foundation funding.
- Federal revenues are those revenues received from the federal government or its agencies either directly or through the state. Such revenues are primarily from federal programmes.

Proprietary fund revenues include charges for services, charges to other funds for services rendered, and grant revenues.

GOVERNMENT WIDE REPORTING

GASB Statement 34 introduces a number of new reporting concepts for revenues in the government wide statements. Essentially, revenues must be classified as either programme or general revenues on the Statement of Activities. The following sub-section outlines the basic reporting criteria established for revenues.

Programme Revenues

Programme revenues are revenues that are directly attributable to a specific functional activity. GAAP requires these revenues to be presented separately in the appropriate functional areas, providing a calculation of net expense for each activity. This net expense often represents the level of support required from the government's own resources. Programme revenues include fees collected from those who benefit from the programme, grants, and other contributions required by the resource provider to support a specific activity.

Programme revenues are reported on the Statement of Activities in the following three categories, if applicable:

1. Charges for services are revenues that arise from charges to customers or applicants who purchase, use, or directly benefit from the goods, services, or privileges provided. Examples are rental fees for school buses or facilities, athletic participant or spectator fees, summer school tuition, or library fines.
2. Programme-specific operating grants and contributions are revenues that occur from mandatory and voluntary non-exchange transactions with other governments, organizations, or individuals that are restricted for use in a particular programme. An example is a business grant to provide a scholarship for staff training.
3. Programme-specific capital grants and contributions are grants and contributions that consist of capital assets or resources that are restricted for capital purposes, such as purchasing, constructing, or renovating capital assets associated with a specific programme. These revenues should be reported separately from grants and contributions that may be used either for operating or capital expenses at the judgment of the reporting government. An example is a grant to purchase a school bus.

Programme revenues are reported at gross amounts. The Statement of Activities also reports programme expenses net of applicable programme revenues. GASB Statement 37 clarified that difference captions and additional categories for programme revenues may be used.

General Revenues

All revenues are general revenues unless they are required to be reported as programme revenues. General revenues are reported in the government wide statement of activities after programme revenues have been subtracted from functional expenses.

Classification of Revenues

P*rogrammes are financed from essentially four sources*:

1. *Type A*: Those who purchase, use, or directly benefit from the goods or services of the programme

2. *Type B*: Parties outside the reporting government's citizenry
3. *Type C*: Taxpayers
4. *Type D*: The governmental institution itself

FUND FINANCIAL STATEMENTS—REPORTING OF EXPENDITURES/EXPENSES

EXPENDITURES

GASB Codification defines expenditures as decreases in net financial resources. In governmental funds, the recognition of expenditures occurs in accordance with the modified accrual basis of accounting. Expenses incurred in proprietary funds are recognized using the accrual basis of accounting. Therefore, significant differences exist between the recognition of expenditures in governmental funds and the recognition of expenses by proprietary funds. In governmental funds, expenditures are usually recognized in the accounting period in which the goods or services are received and the liability for payment is incurred. However, in instances when current financial resources are not reduced as a result of the incurrence of a liability, an expenditure is not recorded.

A common example is the liability for compensated absences (*e.g.*, employee sick and vacation pay). Such liabilities result from current services received from employees; however, the payment of the liabilities usually does not occur until a future date. As a result, compensated absences relating to employees whose salaries are accounted for in governmental funds are not recorded as expenditures and liabilities of the fund until the due date for payment of the compensated absences.

GASB Interpretation No. 6 clarifies the guidance for recognizing certain liabilities and expenditures in governmental funds, including general long-term indebtedness such as compensated absences. The matured portion of long-term indebtedness, to the extent it is expected to be liquidated with expendable available financial resources, should be recorded as a fund liability and expenditure. The unmatured portion of the long-term indebtedness represents a general long-term liability to be presented in the government wide financial statements.

Types of Expenditures and Accounting Treatments

The major types of expenditures are operating, capital, debt service, and intergovernmental charges. Operating expenditures for governmental agencies include a wide range of expenditures. Often the largest portion relates to payroll and related employee benefits.

The modified accrual basis of accounting requires that proper accruals are made for the amount of unpaid salaries and related benefits earned by employees at year-end because these liabilities will be paid early in the next reporting period. The other types of operating expenditures should be accounted for in the same manner, with the recording of a liability when the goods or services are received and necessary accruals made at year-end.

- Capital expenditures relate to the acquisition of capital assets. Such expenditures may be recorded in the General Fund, Special Revenue Funds, or Capital Projects Funds, depending on the source of funding. Purchases of personal property, such as furniture and equipment, are usually recorded as expenditures in the General Fund if they are financed from operating budgets or in special revenue funds if they are financed from grants. Major projects, such as the construction of a school building financed by the proceeds of debt, should be accounted for in a Capital Projects Fund. Costs associated with acquiring capital assets in governmental funds are recorded as capital outlay expenditures when the liability is incurred, usually on receipt of the related asset.
- Debt service expenditures represent the payment of principal and interest needed to service debt. Such payments are usually recorded as expenditures in the Debt Service Fund on the due date. The General Fund may also be used if a Debt Service Fund is not required. The modified accrual basis of accounting provides that accruals for interest are not usually allowed. When funds have been transferred to the Debt Service Fund in anticipation of making debt service payments shortly after the end of the period (no more than 30 days), it is acceptable to accrue interest and maturing debt in the Debt Service Fund in the year the transfer is made. This option is available only if monies are legally required to be set aside in a Debt Service Fund and if used on a consistent basis.
- Intergovernmental charges relate to the transfer of resources from one school district to another, to or from other local governments, or to or from the state. Examples of such charges include contracted instructional services between public schools, other local governments, or state-operated schools and certain transfers of resources associated with state and local funding (*e.g.*, incremental costs associated with wealth redistribution). Such expenditures are accounted for in the General Fund using the modified accrual basis of accounting. In addition, payments between school districts and fiscal agents of cooperative services arrangements (*e.g.*, joint instructional or servicing agreements) are also considered intergovernmental charges.

In addition, transfers result in the reduction of a fund's expendable resources, but they are not classified as expenditures. A transfer is a legally authorized movement of monies between funds in which one fund is responsible for the receipt of funds and another fund is responsible for the actual disbursement.

In a transfer, the disbursing fund records the transaction as "Other Financing Uses" of resources and not as an operating expenditure, whereas the fund receiving the transfer does not record the receipts as revenue but rather as "Other Financing Sources" of funds.

EXPENSES

Expenses are defined as the outflows or expiration of assets or the incurrence of liabilities during a period from providing or producing goods, rendering services, or carrying out other activities that constitute the entity's primary operations.

Proprietary funds recognize expenses using the accrual basis of accounting (*i.e.,* when the related liability is incurred) without regard for the timing of the payment. This recognition criterion is consistent with the following guidelines discussed in Financial Accounting Standards Board (FASB) Concepts Statement No. 5. Although FASB Concepts Statements do not represent authoritative guidance for governments, the discussion is useful in classifying expense transactions within proprietary funds.

- *Associating cause and effect*: Some expenses (such as the cost of goods sold) are recognized on recognition of revenues that result directly and jointly from the same transactions or other events as the expenses.
- *Systematic and rational allocation*: Some expenses (such as depreciation and insurance) are allocated by systematic and rational procedures to the periods during which the related assets are expected to provide benefits.
- *Immediate recognition*: Many expenses (such as selling and administrative salaries) are recognized during the period in which cash is spent or liabilities are incurred for goods or services that are used up either simultaneously with acquisition or soon after.

As examples, the major types of governmental expenditures are accounted for differently in proprietary fund expenses as follows:

- *Capital*: Capital asset acquisition in proprietary funds is accounted for using the flow of economic resources method. Amounts disbursed for the acquisition of capital assets are not recorded as an expense. Instead, the appropriate property, plant, or equipment asset account is debited on the purchase. Depreciation expense is recorded to reflect the allocation of the cost of the assets to operations over the service life of the asset.
- *Debt service*: Principal payments on debt do not represent expenses for proprietary funds, but rather are recorded as a reduction of the obligation. Payments of interest represent expenses to be accounted for on the accrual basis of accounting. Accrual of interest at year-end is usually necessary to reflect the proper amount of expense for the period.

GOVERNMENT WIDE STATEMENTS —REPORTING OF EXPENSES

Governmental entities are required to present the government wide financial statements on the accrual basis of accounting. Thus, the Statement of Activities reflects the expenses of the entity for the reporting period. Entities are required to report all expenses by activities and programmes (by function), except certain indirect expenses. GASB has defined direct expenses as those that are specifically associated with a service, programme or department and thus are clearly identifiable to a particular function. Direct expenses include both operating and non-operating expenses, including depreciation and amortization of assets.

Functions, such as general administration or data processing services, may include indirect expenses of other functions. Governmental entities are not required to allocate indirect expenses to other functions, but may choose to do so. If indirect expenses are allocated, direct and indirect expenses should be presented in separate columns. A column totaling direct and indirect expenses may be presented, but is not required. Indirect expenses may be allocated to any of the primary government's functions. Although there are no standards for determining an allocation methodology, there should be a reasonable basis for expense allocations.

Depreciation expense should be included in the statement of activities as follows:

- Capital assets that can specifically be identified with a function. Depreciation should be included in the direct expenses of that function.
- *"Shared" capital assets*: Depreciation should be prorated as direct expenses of the appropriate functions on some reasonable allocation basis.
- Capital assets that essentially serve all functions. Depreciation is not required to be included in the direct expenses of the various functions but may be reflected as a separate line captioned "unallocated depreciation" in the Statement of Activities or as part of the general government function. If an entity chooses to use a separate line in the Statement of Activities to report unallocated depreciation expense, it should clearly indicate in the footnotes to the financial statements that this line item does not include direct depreciation expenses of the other functions. Because school buildings often serve multiple functions, many school districts are reporting the depreciation as "unallocated depreciation" for these assets.
- *General infrastructure assets*: Depreciation should not be allocated to the various functions, but should be reported as a direct expense of the function that the reporting government normally associates with capital outlays or as a separate line in the Statement of Activities.

- *SInterest expense*: Interest on general long-term liabilities, including interest on capital leases or other vendor financing arrangements, should be considered an indirect expense. Interest on long-term debt should be included in direct expenses only when borrowing is essential to the creation or continuing existence of a programme.

The difference between a "shared" capital asset and one that "essentially serves all functions" is the number of functions involved. As the number of functions increases, the ease, practicality, and usefulness of assigning depreciation to those functions decreases. Therefore, the depreciation of assets that serve many, or essentially all, functions is not required to be included in the direct expenses of those functions. A shared capital asset is generally used by only a few functions, and its use can be specifically identified to those functions.

FINANCIAL STATEMENTS

The new reporting model involves significant changes to the financial statements prepared and presented by governmental entities.

The next sub-section outlines the major elements of the financial statements and related disclosures as required by Statement 34:

- Basic Financial Statements
- Management's Discussion and Analyses (MD&A) and Other RSI
- Component Units

BASIC FINANCIAL STATEMENTS

Under the new financial reporting model, the basic financial statements are:

- Government-wide financial statements,
- Fund financial statements, and
- Note disclosures.

The basic financial statements replace the combined general-purpose financial statements (GPFS) required by the former reporting model.

Government–wide Financial Statements

The purpose of government-wide financial statements is to present the financial position and the operating results of the governmental entity as a whole.

The statements are expected to provide users with operational accountability information and to enable them to do the following:

- Understand the true financial position of the governmental entity, including capital and financial assets and long-term as well as short-term liabilities.
- Determine whether the entity is able to continue to provide current service levels and meet its obligations as they become due.
- Determine the operating results of the entity, including the economic

cost and the net cost of services, and assess the economy, efficiency, and effectiveness of operations.

GASB Statement 34 allows governments to elect to present budgetary comparison information as part of the basic financial statements, rather than as required supplemental information (RSI).

The government-wide financial statements are:

- Statement of Net Assets and
- Statement of Activities.

Statement of Net Assets

The Statement of Net Assets presents the financial position of the governmental entity and its discretely presented component units. This statement is required to present all financial and capital resources on the accrual basis of accounting. Statement 34 encourages the use of a net assets format, which subtracts liabilities from assets to reflect the net assets, rather than the standard balance sheet format, which presents a total for assets equal to a total of liabilities and net assets. However, either presentation is acceptable.

The Statement of Net Assets presents a columnar presentation of the assets, liabilities, and net assets of the reporting entity in two categories: governmental activities and business-type activities. Discretely presented component units are reflected in a separate column or columns on the face of the statement. Statement 34 does not alter the requirements for presenting component units as established by Statement 14, The Financial Reporting Entity. S

tatement 34 states that although internal service funds are reported as proprietary funds of the reporting entity, the activities accounted for in internal service funds are usually more governmental than business-type in nature. If enterprise funds are the predominant or only participants in an internal service fund, however, the entity should report the internal service fund's residual assets and liabilities within the business-type activities column in the Statement of Net Assets.

Other presentation requirements relative to the Statement of Net Assets follow:

- A total column is required for the primary government. A total column for the entity as a whole, including the discretely presented component units, may be presented but is not required.
- Comparative financial statements are not required but may be presented at the option of the governmental entity. If comparative financial statements are presented, all columns must be included for both years.
- Fiduciary funds and fiduciary component units are specifically excluded from the government-wide statements because fiduciary resources cannot be used to support the entity's programmes or other services.

- Statement 34 encourages the presentation of assets and liabilities that is based on their relative liquidity. A classified presentation, which distinguishes between current and long-term assets and liabilities, is also acceptable.

Statement of Activities

The operations of the governmental unit should be presented in a net (expense) revenues format in the Statement of Activities.

General revenues, contributions to term and permanent endowments, contributions to permanent fund principal, special and extraordinary items, and transfers should be reported separately after the total net expenses of the entity's functions to arrive at the "change in net assets" for the period.

The purpose of using this format is twofold:

1. To report the relative financial burden of each of the government's functions or programmes on its taxpayers
2. To identify the extent to which each function (programme) draws from the general revenues of the organization or is self-supporting through fees and intergovernmental aid

Revenues must be categorized just as to their purpose as either general or programme revenues in the statement of activities.

Fund Financial Statements

Fund Financial Statements are categorized into three fund types described as follows.

Governmental Fund Financial Statements

Governmental fund financial statements (including financial statements for the general, special revenue, capital projects, debt service, and permanent funds) should be prepared using the current financial resources measurement focus and the modified accrual basis of accounting.

Under this measurement focus and basis of accounting, revenues should be recognized in the accounting period in which they become available and measurable and expenditures should be recognized in the accounting period in which the fund liability is incurred, if measurable, except for unmatured interest on general long-term debt, which should be recognized when due.

Proprietary Fund Financial Statements

Proprietary fund financial statements (including financial data for enterprise and internal service funds) should be prepared using the economic resources measurement focus and the accrual basis of accounting. Revenues should be recognized in the accounting period in which they are earned and become measurable, and expenses should be recognized in the period incurred, if measurable.

Fiduciary Fund Financial Statements

Fiduciary fund financial statements (including financial data for fiduciary funds and similar component units) should be prepared using the economic resources measurement focus and the accrual basis of accounting.

Revenues should be recognized in the accounting period in which they are earned and become measurable, and expenses should be recognized in the period incurred, if measurable.

MANAGEMENT'S DISCUSSION AND ANALYSIS AND OTHER RSI

The management's discussion and analysis (MD&A) is part of the required supplementary information (RSI); however, it precedes the financial statements.

It should be based on currently known facts as of the date of the audit report and should:

- Provide a concise, unbiased, and easily readable description of the government's financial activities and
- Help users understand the relationship of the results reported in the governmental activities in the government wide financial statements and the results reported in the governmental funds financial statements (usually focused on the major funds).

The focus of the MD&A should be on the primary government. However, information on any discretely presented component units may be presented as well. GASB has stated that both the positive and negative aspects of the government's operations should be presented to inform the reader about whether the government is in better or worse financial condition than in the prior year. The focus should be on only significant or material items.

MD&A is restricted to the following topics, although there is no limit to the information that may be presented about these topics.

- Information and discussion on the basic financial statements presented, their relationship to one another, and the significant differences in the information they provide. The discussion should include the different methods of accounting used in the government wide and fund financial statements.
- Condensed financial information comparing the current year and the prior year. The analysis should include specific economic factors that contributed to the change. Charts and graphs may be used to supplement information in the condensed statements but should not be used in place of it.
- Objective analysis of the governmental entity's financial condition as a whole. Analysis of the government's overall financial position and results of operations should address both governmental and business-type activities separately.

- An analysis of balances and transactions on a fund basis, addressing the reasons for significant changes in fund balances or fund net assets. The analysis should also include information on whether restrictions, commitments, or other limitations significantly affect the availability of fund resources for future use.
- A discussion on significant variances among the entity's original budget, final budget, and actual expenditures for the General Fund or its equivalent and the impact of these variances on the entity's future liquidity.
- A description of activity relating to the government's capital assets and long-term debt activity during the year. This discussion should include commitments made for capital expenditures, changes in credit ratings, and debt limitations affecting the financing of planned facilities or services.
- A discussion of information about the modified approach used to report some or all of the infrastructure assets, if applicable.
- A description of currently known facts, decisions, or conditions expected to have an impact on financial position and results of operation. The term currently known is limited to events or decisions that have occurred, been enacted, adopted, agreed on, or contracted as of the date of the auditor's report. The discussion should address expected effects on both governmental and business-type activities.

Information that does not address the requirements above should not be included in the MD&A but instead may be reported as supplementary information or included in the letter of transmittal.

COMPONENT UNITS

It is essential that governmental financial statements provide an overview of the reporting entity that is based on financial accountability, yet allow users to distinguish between the primary government and its component units. GASB Statement 14, The Financial Reporting Entity, issued in June 1991, established criteria for evaluating potential component units and provided guidance in the statement presentation of those entities that met the criteria.

Component units are defined as legally separate organizations for which the primary government is financially accountable or for which the nature and significance of the relationship with the primary government are such that exclusion would cause the reporting entity's financial statements to be misleading or incomplete.

Financial accountability for a potential component unit is determined by either of the following:

- Appointment of the voting majority of the potential component unit governing board by the primary government and either
  - The ability to impose its will on the potential component unit or

  - A relationship of financial benefit or burden with the potential component unit.
- The potential component unit is fiscally dependent upon the primary government.

If a potential component unit does not meet either of the two tests above for financial accountability, an organization may still be included in the financial statements of the primary government based on the criterion that exclusion would result in a misleading or incomplete presentation of the financial reporting entity.

In May 2002, GASB issued Statement 39, Determining Whether Certain Organizations Are Component Units, which amended Statement 14 to establish the criteria for the inclusion of organizations on this basis.

A legally separate, tax-exempt organization should be reported as a component unit if all of the following criteria are met:

- The economic resources of the separate organization are received or held for the benefit of the primary government, its component units, or its constituents.
- The primary government, or its component units, may access or is entitled to a majority of the economic resources of the separate organization.
- The economic resources of an individual organization that the primary government, or its component units, is entitled to or may access are significant to the primary government.

This standard continues the requirement for inclusion of organizations based on the GASB Statement "misleading or incomplete" criterion but emphasizes that "financial integration" may also be a component of all of the aforementioned criteria. Additional guidance on evidence of financial integration is also provided in Statement 39.

Component units may be:

- Blended, as though they are part of the primary government, or
- Discretely presented.

GASB Statement 34 does not amend the definition of component units or the general reporting requirements.

Blended Component Units

Even though it is preferable to distinguish between the primary government and its component units, certain component units, despite being legally separate from the reporting entity, are so intertwined with the entity that they are, in effect, the same as the primary government. GASB has stated that these component units should be reported as part of the primary government. Thus, the component unit's balances and transactions should be reported in a manner similar to the way balances and transactions of the reporting government itself are reported. This method of inclusion is known as blending.

A component unit should be blended in either of these circumstances:

- The component unit's governing body is substantively the same as the governing body of the primary government.
- The component unit provides services entirely, or almost entirely, to the reporting entity or otherwise exclusively, or almost exclusively, benefits the entity even though it does not provide services directly to it.

Some component units account for their activities in a single fund; others use all or several fund types. If a component unit is blended, the types of funds of the component unit should be blended with those of the primary government by including them in the appropriate combining statements of the primary government. However, because the primary government's general fund is usually the main operating fund and often is a focal point for report users, a general fund should be presented only for the primary government. The general fund of a blended component unit should be reported as a special revenue fund.

Discretely Presented Component Units

Discrete presentation of component units refers to the method of reporting financial data of component units in a column(s) and row(s) separate from the financial data of the primary government. When component units are presented in the basic financial statements (*i.e.,* Statement of Net Assets and Statement of Activities), each statement should distinguish between the governmental and business-type activities of the government and between the total entity and its discretely presented component units, by reporting each in separate columns (and rows in the Statement of Activities).

Component units that are fiduciary in nature, however, should be included only in the fund financial statements with the entity's fiduciary funds. Statement 39 provides that a discrete presentation must be used for an organization that meets the requirements as a component unit under its new criteria.

3

Completing the Accounting Cycle

ACCRUAL ACCOUNTING

In 2011, two brothers sign a contract for a consulting project. The total contract price is $20,000. The brothers do most of the consulting work in 2011 and finish the job in 2012. They receive a $2,000 cash payment from the contract in 2011 and receive the remaining $18,000 cash in 2012. On December 31, 2011, the brothers prepare a 2011 income statement to use in applying for a bank loan. What amount of revenue should the brothers report for 2011? This simple example illustrates why accounting is much more than merely tabulating cash receipts and cash payments.

A proper measure of the brothers' economic performance in 2011 requires estimating the amount of the work completed in 2011. To report 2011 revenue as only the $2,000 cash received grossly understates the actual economic output produced during the year. In addition, the need for the year–end income statement means that the brothers can't wait until after the final contract payment is received before preparing a summary of their activities; the bank wants the income statement now. Accrual accounting is the process of recording expenses and revenues when incurred and earned, regardless of when cash is received, and of adjusting original transaction data into refined measures of a firm's past economic performance and current economic condition.

This accrual process is necessary because a business requires periodic, timely financial reports, and accrual information better measures a firm's performance than do cash flow data. The difficulty in using accrual accounting to generate a performance measure. Each horizontal bar represents a business deal like the production and sale of a car; the delivery of legal services for a specific lawsuit; or the development, delivery, and support of a piece of software. Some deals last less than a day from start to finish, like when a barber provides a haircut in exchange for cash. The obligations and responsibilities associated with other deals can stretch on for years. For example, when you buy a General Motors car, the deal is not done from your standpoint until four or five years later, after you have received all of the GM warranty services promised to you. And from GM's standpoint, the deal is not done until 40 or 50 years later, after GM has paid the assembly–line workers all of the pension benefits they earned through the labour hours spent assembling your car. Even though the economic loose ends of some business deals extend for years, financial statement users still require periodic reports about a company's operating performance.

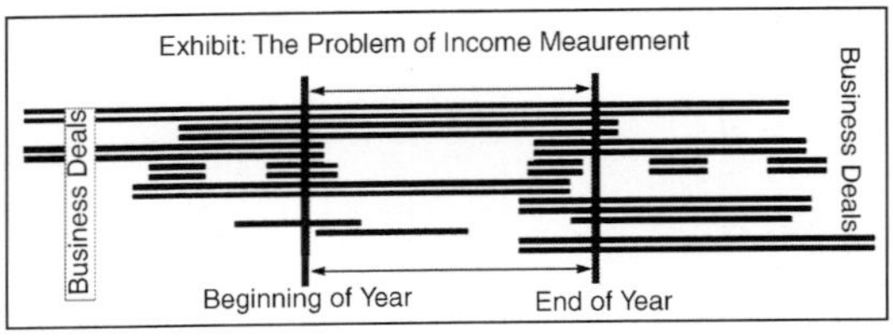

The beginning and the end of a year are arbitrary breaks in the life of an ongoing business. The job of accountants is to consider all business deals that were at least partially completed during a year and to measure the revenues, expenses, and profit associated with those deals. This profit is then reported as net income for the year. Accrual accounting is much more than mere "bean counting."

PERIODIC REPORTING

All businesses, large or small, periodically issue their financial statements so that users can make sound economic decisions. Current owners, prospective investors, bankers, and others need up–todate reports in order to compare and judge a company's financial position and operating results on a continuing, timely basis.

They need to know the following:

- The financial position of a company (from the balance sheet)
- The relative success or failure of current operations (from the income statement)
- The nature and extent of cash flows (from the statement of cash flows)

The financial picture of a company—its success or failure in meeting its economic objectives—cannot really be complete until the "life" of a business is over. However, managers, owners, and creditors cannot wait 10, 20, or 100 years to receive an exact accounting of a business. In order to provide timely accounting information, the time–period concept divides the life of an enterprise into distinct and relatively short (generally 12 months or less) accounting periods.

The 12-month accounting period is referred to as the fiscal year. When an entity closes its books on December 31, its reports are based on a calendar year. Most large corporations, and even many small companies, issue a report to stockholders as of a fiscal year–end. Most corporations prepare reports on a quarterly basis as well. This annual report includes the primary financial statements (balance sheet, income statement, and statement of cash flows) and other financial data, such as a management discussion and analysis of operations.

Although periodic reporting is vital to a firm's success, the frequency of reporting forces accountants to use some data that are based on judgments and estimates. Ideally, accounting judgments are made carefully and estimates are based on reliable evidence, but the limitations of accounting reports should be understood and kept in mind.

ACCRUAL– VERSUS CASH-BASIS ACCOUNTING

Closely related to the time–period concept is the concept of accrual–basis accounting. This important characteristic of the traditional accounting model simply means.

Revenue Recognition

How do we assign revenues to particular periods? First, we must determine when revenues have actually been earned.

The revenue recognition principle states that revenues are recorded when two main criteria have been met:

1. The earnings process is substantially complete (generally, a sale has been made or services have been performed).
2. Cash has been collected or collectibility is reasonably assured.

These two criteria ensure that both parties to the transaction have fulfilled their commitment or are formally obligated to do so. In simple terms, satisfying the first criterion demonstrates that the seller has done something; satisfying the second criterion demonstrates that the buyer has done something. The seller generally records sales revenue when goods are shipped or when services are performed.

When this occurs, the seller has completed his or her part of the transaction. The seller assumes, when shipment is made or services performed, that the buyer has given a valid promise to pay. The promise to pay, or the actual payment, would complete the buyer's part of the transaction. If, for example, General Motors sold and shipped $800 million of cars in 2012, but will not receive the cash proceeds until 2013, the $800 million would still be recognized as revenue in 2012, when it is earned and a promise of payment is received.

Both of the revenue recognition principle criteria have been met. On the other hand, if General Motors is paid in 2012 for cars to be shipped in 2013, it would not record those payments as revenues until the cars are actually shipped. Referring back to the two brothers, they would recognize as consulting revenue the amount associated with the proportion of the job that was completed in 2011. For example, if an objective estimate indicated that

80% of the consulting project was completed in 2011, then it would be appropriate for the brothers to recognize $16,000 ($20,000 × 0.8) as revenue in 2011—assuming that they felt they would be paid for the consulting work.

The Matching Principle

Once a company determines which revenues should be recognized during a period, how does it identify the expenses that have been incurred? The matching principle requires that all costs and expenses incurred to generate revenues must be recognized in the same accounting period as the related revenues.

The cost of the merchandise sold, for example, should be matched to the revenue derived from the sale of that merchandise during the period. Expenses that cannot be matched with revenues are assigned to the accounting period in which they are incurred.

For example, the exact amount of electricity used to make an automobile generally cannot be determined, but since the amount used for a month or a year is known, that amount can be matched to the revenues earned during the same period.

Exhibit: Determining Accrual Income

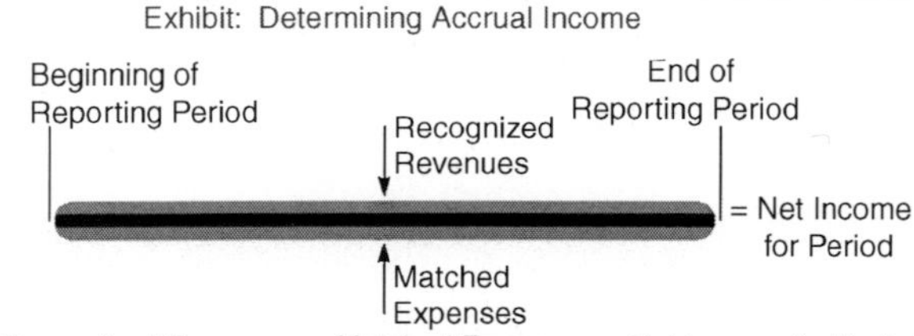

Recognized Revenues – Matched Expenses = Net Income for Period

This process of matching expenses with recognized revenues determines the amount of net income reported on the income statement. Net income is the most widely used indicator of how well a company has performed during a period.

To illustrate the difference between cash- and accrual-basis accounting, and to demonstrate why accrual-basis accounting provides a more meaningful measure of income, assume that during 2012, Karas Brothers billed clients $50,500 for consulting services performed in 2012. By December 31, Karas had received $22,000 in cash from customers, with the $28,500 balance expected in 2013.

During 2012, Karas paid $21,900 for various expenses that had been incurred. At December 31, 2012, Karas still owed $11,200 for additional expenses incurred. These expenses will be paid during January 2013. How much income should Karas Brothers report for 2012? The answer depends on whether cash- or accrual-basis accounting is used. As shown below, with cash-basis accounting, reported income would be $100. With accrual-basis accounting, reported income would be $17,400.

Karas Brothers: Reported Income for 2012

Cash–Basis Accounting		Accural–Basis Accounting	
Cash Receipts.................	$22,000	Revenues earned.................	$50,500
Cash Disbursements...........	21,900	Expenses incurred...............	33,100
Income................................	$ 100	Income................................	$ 17,400

How do we explain this $17,300 difference? Under cash-basis accounting, Karas Brothers would report only $22,000 in revenue, the total amount of cash received during 2012. Similarly, the company would report only $21,900 of expenses (the amount actually paid) during 2012.

The additional $11,200 of expenses incurred but not yet paid would not be reported. Using accrual–basis accounting, however, Karas earned $50,500 in revenues, which is the total increase in resources for the period (an increase of $22,000 in cash plus $28,500 in receivables).

Similarly, Karas incurred a total of $33,100 in expenses, which should be matched with revenues earned to produce a realistic income measurement. The combined result of increasing revenues by $28,500 while increasing expenses by only $11,200 creates the $17,300 difference in net income ($28,500–$11,200 = $17,300). As this example shows, accrual-basis accounting provides a more accurate picture of a company's profitability.

It matches earned revenues with the expenses incurred to generate those revenues. This helps investors, creditors, and others to better assess the operating results of a company and make more informed judgments concerning its profitability and earnings potential. Accrual-basis accounting is required by generally accepted accounting principles (GAAP).

ADJUSTING ENTRIES

Transactions generally are recorded in a journal in chronological order and then posted to the ledger accounts. The entries are based on the best information available at the time. Although the majority of accounts are up to date at the end of an accounting period and their balances can be included in the financial statements, some accounts require adjustment to reflect current circumstances.

In general, these accounts are not updated throughout the period because it is impractical or inconvenient to make such entries on a daily or weekly basis. At the end of each accounting period, in order to report all asset, liability, and owners' equity amounts properly and to recognize all revenues and expenses for the period on an accrual basis, accountants are required to make any necessary adjustments prior to preparing the financial statements.

The entries that reflect these adjustments are called adjusting entries. Adjusting entries are not made based on transactions; rather, they are the entries needed after careful analysis of revenues earned and expenses incurred. One difficulty with adjusting entries is that the need for an adjustment is not signaled by a specific event like the receipt of a bill or cash from a customer.

Rather, adjusting entries are recorded based on the circumstances at the close of each accounting period. It should be noted that these two steps are interrelated and may be reversed.

That is, revenue and expense adjustments may be considered first to fix the income statement, indicating which asset and liability accounts need adjustment to fix the balance sheet. *Each adjusting entry involves at least one income statement account and one balance sheet account.* T-accounts are helpful in analyseing adjusting entries and will be used in the illustrations that follow.

The areas most commonly requiring analysis to see whether adjusting entries are needed are:

- Unrecorded receivables
- Unrecorded liabilities
- Prepaid expenses
- Unearned revenues

UNRECORDED RECEIVABLES

In accordance with the revenue recognition principle of accrual accounting, revenues should be recorded when earned, regardless of when the cash is received. If revenue is earned but not yet collected in cash, a receivable exists. To ensure that all receivables are properly reported on the balance sheet, an analysis should be made at the end of each accounting period to see whether there are any revenues that have been earned but have not yet been collected or recorded.

These unrecorded receivables are earned and represent amounts that are receivable in the future; therefore, they should be recognized as assets. Where you mow lawns, plant shrubs, and perform other related services. You are able to provide these services year-round because you live in a region with a very mild climate.

Your company reports on a calendar-year basis and has determined the following on December 31, 2012:

- On November 1, you entered into a year-long contract with an apartment complex to provide general landscaping services each week and bill the customer every three months. The terms of the contract state that you will earn $400 per month.
- As of December 31, Lawn Care Revenue of $800 ($400 for November and $400 for December) has been earned but has not been recorded and will not be billed or received until the end of January 2013. No entry has been made since the end of October with respect to this contract.

As of year-end, no asset has been recorded, but an $800 receivable exists ($400 × 2), because two months' worth of revenue has been earned. To record this receivable, we must debit (increase) the asset Accounts Receivable for $800. With the debit, we have accomplished one step by fixing the balance sheet with regard to this transaction. The next step requires that we use the other half of the adjusting entry, the credit of $800, to fix the income statement. We know that the credit must be to either a revenue or an expense account, and the nature of the transaction suggests that we should credit Lawn Care Revenue for $800.

The adjusting entry is:

Dec. 31	Accounts Receivable..	800	
	Lawn Care Revenue...		800
	To record two months of earned revenue not yet received.		

Adjusting entries are recorded in the general journal and are posted to the accounts in the general ledger in the same manner as other journal entries. Again, note that each adjusting entry must involve at least one balance sheet account and at least one income statement account. After this adjusting entry has been journalized and posted, the receivable will appear as an asset on the balance sheet, and the lawn care revenue is reported on the income statement. Through the adjusting entry, the asset (receivable) accounts are properly stated and revenues are appropriately reported.

UNRECORDED LIABILITIES

Just as assets are created from revenues being earned before they are collected or recorded, liabilities can be created by expenses being incurred prior to being paid or recorded. These expenses, along with their corresponding liabilities, should be recorded when incurred, no matter when they are paid. Thus, adjusting entries are required at the end of an accounting period to recognize any unrecorded liabilities in the proper period and to record the corresponding expenses.

As the expense is recorded (increased by a debit), the offsetting liability is also recorded (increased by a credit), showing the entity's obligation to pay for the expense. If such adjustments are not made, the net income measurement for the period will not reflect all appropriate expenses and the corresponding liabilities will be understated on the balance sheet.

Assume that on December 31, 2012, your landscaping company has determined the following:

- Your brother has worked for the company since its inception. He is paid $700 every two weeks. The next payday is on January 7, 2013. Since December 31 falls halfway through the pay period, one-half of his wages should be allocated to 2012.
- You borrowed $2,000 from the bank with the promise that on the first of every month you would make a $178 payment—a portion of that payment being attributed to interest and a portion to principal. Your next payment is due on January 1, 2013, but the interest expense associated with that payment should be attributed to the period in

which the money was actually used—December 2012. Assume that interest of $20 must be recognized on December 31, 2012.

To represent its current financial position and earnings, your landscaping company must record the impact of these events in the accounts, even though cash transactions have not yet occurred.

The wages will not be paid until 2013. Under accrual–basis accounting, however, these costs are expenses of 2012 and should be recognized on this year's income statement, with the corresponding liability shown on the balance sheet as of the end of the year.

To fix the balance sheet, Wages Payable must be credited (increased) for $350. Recognition of this liability ensures that the balance sheet properly reports this liability, which was created during 2012 and exists as of the end of the year. The debit of this adjusting entry is to Wages Expense, resulting in the proper inclusion of this expense in the 2012 income statement. The adjusting journal entry is as follows:

Dec. 31	Wages Expense...	350	
	Wages Payable...	350	
	To Record obligation for Wages.		

The liability for the interest for the month of December is recorded by a credit (increase) to Interest Payable; this fixes the balance sheet. The debit of the adjusting entry is to Interest Expense, which properly includes this expense on the 2012 income statement.

The adjusting entry is:

Dec. 31	Interest Expense...	350	
	Interest Payable...	350	
	To Record Interest Incurred.		

The wages expense and interest expense would be reported on the income statement for the year ended December 31, and the liabilities (Wages Payable and Interest Payable) would be reported on the balance sheet as of December 31.

Because of these adjusting entries, the balance sheet will more accurately reflect the financial situation of your landscaping company.

PREPAID EXPENSES

- Payments that a company makes in advance for items normally charged to expense are known as prepaid expenses. An example would be the payment of an insurance premium for the next 18 months. Theoretically, every resource acquisition is an asset, at least temporarily. Thus, the entry to record an advance payment should be a debit to an asset account (Prepaid Expenses) and a credit to Cash, showing the exchange of cash for another asset. An expense is the using up of an asset. For example, when supplies are purchased, they are recorded as assets; when they are used, their cost is transferred to an expense account. The purpose of making adjusting entries for prepaid expenses is to show the complete or partial consumption of an asset. If the original entry is to an asset account, the adjusting entry reduces the asset to an amount that reflects its remaining future benefit and at the same time recognizes the actual expense incurred for the period. For the unrecorded assets and liabilities discussed earlier, there was no original entry; the adjusting entry was the first time these items were recorded in the accounting records. For prepaid expenses, this is not the case. Because cash has already been paid (in the case of prepaid expenses), an original entry has been made to record the cash transaction. Therefore, the amount of the adjusting entry is the difference between what the updated balance should be and the amount of the original entry already recorded. Assume the following about your landscaping company: On November 1, 2012, you purchased a six–month insurance policy on your old truck, paying a $600 premium. On December 15, 2012, you purchased several months' of supplies (fertilizer, weed killer, etc.) at a total cost of $350. At year-end, supplies costing $225 were still on hand.

For the prepaid insurance, record the payment of $600 on November 1 as follows:

Nov.1	Prepaid Insurance..	600	
	Cash..	600	
	Paid a Six–month Insurance Premium in Advance.		

This entry shows that one asset (Cash) has been exchanged for another asset (Prepaid Insurance). Over the next six months, you will use the auto insurance and the asset, Prepaid Insurance, will slowly be used up. As the asset is used, its cost is recorded as an expense.

At year-end, only those assets that still offer future benefits to the company should be reported on the balance sheet. Thus, an adjustment is required to reduce the prepaid insurance account to reflect the fact that only four months of prepaid insurance remain.

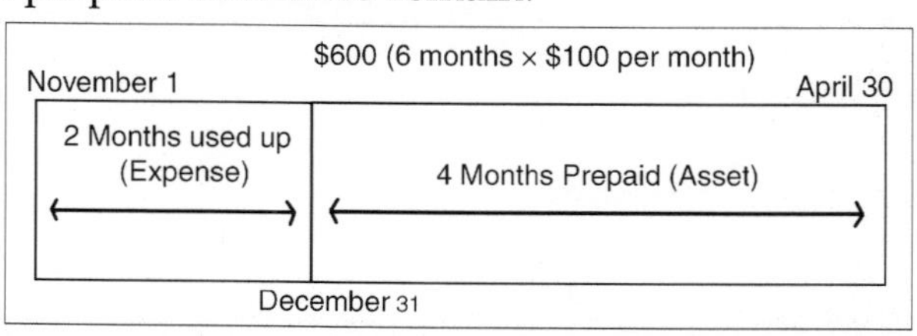

The adjusting journal entry to bring the original amounts to their updated balances at yearend is:

Dec.	Insurance Expense..	200	
	Prepaid Insurance..	200	
	To Record Insurance Expense for two Month: 2×$100=%200		

When the adjusting entry is journalized and posted, the proper amount of insurance expense ($200) will be shown as an expense on the income statement and the proper amount of prepaid insurance ($400) will be carried forward to the next period as an asset on the balance sheet. This is illustrated in the following T-accounts:

	Prepaid Insurance		Cash		Insurance Expense	
Original Entry (11/1/12)	600			600		
Adjusting Entry (12/31/12)		200			200	
Updated Balances (12/31/12)	400				200	
	To Balance Sheet				To Income Statement	

When supplies are consumed in the normal course of business, the asset account (Supplies on Hand) must be adjusted and the used-up portion charged as an operating expense (Supplies Expense) on the income statement. Thus, the adjustment for supplies is handled the same way as for any other prepaid asset. We initially recorded $350 of supplies as an asset:

Dec. 15	Supplies on Hand....................................	350	
	Cash...	350	
	Purched Supplies.		

At year-end, an adjustment must be made to recognize that only $225 of supplies remains. This also implies that $125 ($350–$225) of the supplies have been used and should be charged to expense. The entries are summarized in the following T–accounts:

	Prepaid Insurance		Cash		Supplied Expense	
Original Entry (12/15/12)	350			350		
Adjusting Entry (12/31/12)		125			125	
Updated Balances (12/31/12)					125	
	To Balance Sheet				To Income Statement	

Dec. 31	Supplies Expense..	125	
	Supplies on Hand..	125	
	To record the use of supplies.		

UNEARNED REVENUES

Amounts received before the actual earning of revenues are known as unearned revenues. They arise when customers pay in advance of the receipt of goods or services. Because the company has received cash but has not yet given the customer the purchased goods or services, the unearned revenues are in fact liabilities. That is, the company must provide something in return for the amounts received.

For example, a building contractor may require a deposit before proceeding on construction of a house. Upon receipt of the deposit, the contractor has unearned revenue, a liability. The contractor must construct the house to earn the revenue. If the house is not built, the contractor will be obligated to repay the deposit.

Assume the following about your landscaping company:

- On December 1, a client pays you $225 for three months of landscaping services to be provided for the period beginning December 1, 2012, and ending February 28, 2013. This client is going to Hawaii for an extended vacation and would like you to take care of the grounds in her absence.

Typically, the original entry to record unearned revenue involves a debit to Cash and a credit to a liability account.3 Here, since landscaping revenue is received three months in advance, the liability account would be Unearned Revenue, as shown below.

Dec. 1	Cash..	225	
	Unearned Revenue....................................		225
	Received three months' revenue in advance:		
	$75 × 3 = $225		

The credit to the liability account, Unearned Revenue, is logically correct; until you provide the landscaping service, the revenue received in advance is unearned and is thus an obligation (liability). The next step is to compute the updated balances at year-end.

As illustrated with the following time line, on December 31, two months' services (2 × $75 = $150) are still unearned and should be shown as a liability, Unearned Revenue, on the balance sheet. At the same time, $75, or one month's services, has been earned (1 × $75 = $75) and should be reported as Landscaping Revenue on the income statement.

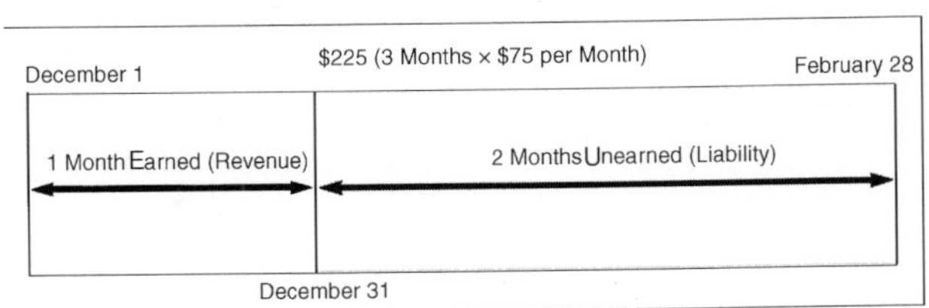

The first step of the adjusting entry is to fix the balance sheet. The reported liability of $225 is too much because some of the unearned revenue has been earned. The remaining obligation is $150 (2 × $75), so the liability must be reduced (debited) by $75 ($225–$150). The second half of the adjusting entry is used to correct the income statement. The $75 credit is made to Landscaping

Revenue, reflecting the fact that one month's revenue has now been earned. The appropriate adjusting entry is:

Dec. 31	Unearned Revenue...	75	
	Landscaping Revenue..	75	
	To record landscaping revenue for one months: $75 × 1 months = $75.		

	Unearned Revenue		Cash		Landscaping Revenue	
Original Entry (12/1/12)		225	225			
Adjusting Entry (12/31/12)	75					75
Updated Balances (12/31/12)		150				75
	To Balance Sheet				To Income Statement	

After the adjusting entry has been made on December 31, our accounts show $225 of cash received. Of this amount, $75 has been earned (1 month's service at $75) and would be reported as Landscaping Revenue on the income statement; $150 will not be earned until the next reporting period and would be shown as a liability on the balance sheet.

The 2008 financial statements for General Motors offer several illustrations of the potential impact of failing to make adjusting entries. GM reports that, as of December 31, 2008, it had unearned revenue totaling $3.253 billion. If GM had failed to make the adjustment necessary to record this unearned revenue, total revenue for 2008 would have been overstated by $3.253 billion, or 2.2%.

In addition, GM reported that its total warranty liability as of December 31, 2008, was $8.491 billion. This warranty liability falls in the category of unrecorded liabilities that are not reported in the financial statements unless an appropriate adjusting entry is made. Finally, GM also reported a $236 million asset related to future tax deductions; this asset would remain unrecorded unless a special adjusting entry were made at the end of the year to reflect the future tax benefits of events that had occurred in 2008 and preceding years.

CLOSING THE BOOKS

We have almost reached the end of the accounting cycle for a period. *Thus far, the accounting cycle has included the following:*

- Analyzing documents
- Journalizing transactions
- Posting to the ledger accounts
- Determining account balances
- Preparing a trial balance
- Making adjusting entries
- Preparing the financial statements

Just two additional steps are needed:

1. Journalizing and posting closing entries
2. Preparing a post-closing trial balance

REAL AND NOMINAL ACCOUNTS

To explain the closing process, we must first define two new terms. Certain accounts are referred to as real accounts. These accounts report the cumulative increases and decreases in certain account balances from the date the company was organized.

Real accounts (assets, liabilities, and owners' equity) appear on the balance sheet and are permanent; they are not closed to a zero balance at the end of each accounting period. Balances existing in real accounts at the end of a period are carried forward to the next period. Other accounts are known as nominal accounts. These accounts (revenues, expenses, and dividends) are temporary. They are really just subcategories of Retained Earnings and are reduced to a zero balance through the closing process at the end of each accounting period. Thus, nominal accounts begin with a zero balance at the start of each accounting cycle.

Transactions throughout the period (generally a year) are journalized and posted to the nominal accounts. These are used to accumulate and classify all revenue and expense items, and also dividends, for that period. At the end of the accounting period, adjustments are made, the income statement is prepared, and the balances in the temporary accounts are then closed to Retained Earnings, a permanent account.

Closing entries bring the income statement accounts back to a zero balance, which makes the accounts ready for a new accounting period. In addition, the closing entries transfer the net income or loss for the accounting period to Retained Earnings and reduce Retained Earnings for any dividends. Without closing entries, revenue and expense balances would extend from period to period, making it difficult to isolate the operating results of each accounting period.

CLOSING ENTRIES

Unlike adjusting entries, the actual mechanics of the closing process are not complicated. Revenue accounts normally have credit balances and are closed by being debited; expense accounts generally have debit balances and are closed by being credited. The difference between total revenues and total expenses represents the net income (or net loss) of the entity. For a corporation, net income is credited to Retained Earnings because income increases owners' equity.

A net loss would be debited to Retained Earnings because a loss decreases owners' equity. To illustrate the closing process, as suggested, again refer to Burger King's financial information. The closing journal entry is:

June 30	Net Sales and Revenues..	2,455
	Cost of Sales and Other Expenses........................	1,601
	Selling, General and Administrative expenses....	500
	Interest Expenses..	61
	Income Tax Expense...	103
	Retained Earnings..	190
	To close revenues and expenses to Retained Earnings.	

Closing entries must be posted to the appropriate ledger accounts. Once posted, all nominal accounts will have a zero balance; that is, they will be "closed." The dividends account is also a nominal (temporary) account that must be closed at the end of the accounting period. However, dividends are not expenses and will not be reported on an income statement; they are distributions to stockholders of part of a corporation's earnings. Thus, dividends reduce retained earnings. When dividends are declared by the board of directors of a corporation, the amount that will be paid is debited to Dividends and credited to a liability account, Dividends Payable, or to Cash if paid immediately. Because Dividends is a temporary account, it must be closed to Retained Earnings at the end of the accounting period. The dividends account is closed by crediting it and by debiting Retained Earnings, thereby reducing owners' equity.

Dec. 31	Retained Earning...	34
	Dividends...	34
	To close dividends to retained earnings.	

The books are now ready for a new accounting cycle. The closing process for the revenues, expenses, and dividends of a corporation is shown schematically in Exhibit.

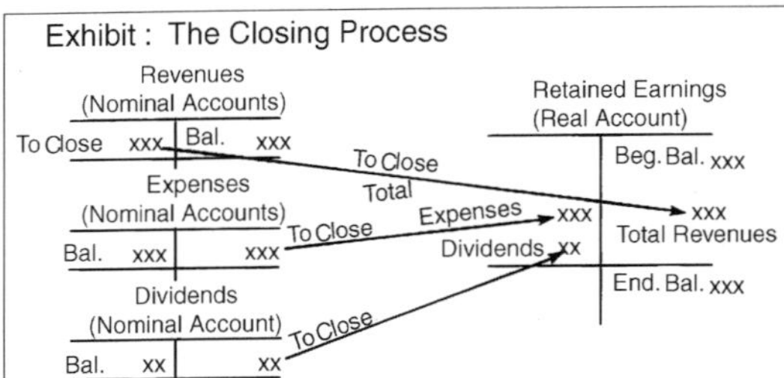

Exhibit : The Closing Process

PREPARING A POST–CLOSING TRIAL BALANCE

An optional last step in the accounting cycle is to balance the accounts and to prepare a post-closing trial balance. The accounts are to be balanced—debits and credits added and a balance determined—only after the closing entries have been recorded and posted in the general ledger. The information for the post–closing trial balance is then taken from the ledger. The nominal accounts will not be shown since they have been closed and thus have zero balances. Only the real accounts will have current balances. This step is for internal purposes only and is designed to provide some assurance that the previous steps in the cycle have been performed properly, prior to the start of a new accounting period. Exhibit illustrates a post–closing trial balance for Burger King.

Exhibit Post-closing Trial Balance

Burger King Holdings Inc.
Post-closing Trial Balance
June 30,2008
(in millions)

	Debits	Credits
Cash..	₹ 166	
Inventories...	16	
Receivables.......................................	139	
Property and Equipment................	961	
Intangible Assets...........................	1,082	
Other Assets.................................	323	
Accounts Payable...........................		₹ 130
Loans Payable................................		871
Capital Lease Liabilities..................		76
Deferred Income Tax Liabilities.......		86
Accrued Expenses and Other Liabilities.......		679
Capital Stock and Other...................		563
Accumulated Other Comprehensive Loss......	8	
Retained Earnings..................................		290
Totals...	₹ 2,695	₹ 2,695

4

Financial Statements

AN OVERVIEW

Financial statements are of many kinds: the ones we ha discussed here are annual financial statements. These are prepared once a year, on the basis of account books maintained by the organisation. There are three main statements that a non-profit normally prepares: Receipts and Payments Account, Income and Expenditure Account, and the Balance Sheet. These are then checked by the auditors, who issue a report.

This is called an audit report. The Receipts and Payments account is similar to a cash flow statement. Most NGOs follow cash basis of accounting. Therefore, in most of the cases, this is virtually the same as the Income and Expenditure Account. Both these statements show the activity during the year, and are, in a way, parallel to a narrative programme report.

The Balance Sheet, on the other hand, shows the financial status of the organisation on a particular day. Mostly, this day now is 31st March each year, when the Government of India closes its financial year. You are free to choose another date for closing the accounts—so long as you close them on 31st March also! The audit report is an important document. It can, and often does, give important information about the organisation's financial health.

Unfortunately, it is not written like a juicy news–story; most people, therefore, do not read it. The importance of audit report and the role of auditors is also discussed in this part. Going through this part will not make you a financial wizard or analyst. However, it will give a basic understanding of the annual financial statements, and how to use these in your work.

PURPOSE OF FINANCIAL STATEMENTS BY BUSINESS ENTITIES

"The objective of financial statements is to provide information about the financial position, performance and changes in financial position of an enterprise that is useful to a wide range of users in making economic decisions." Financial statements should be understandable, relevant, reliable and comparable. Reported assets, liabilities, equity, income and expenses are directly related to an organization's financial position. Financial statements are intended to be understandable by readers who have "a reasonable knowledge of business and economic activities and accounting and who are willing to study the information diligently."

Financial statements may be used by users for different purposes:

- Owners and managers require financial statements to make important business decisions that affect its continued operations. Financial analysis is then performed on these statements to provide management with a more detailed understanding of the figures. These statements are also used as part of management's annual report to the stockholders.
- Employees also need these reports in making collective bargaining agreements with the management, in the case of labour unions or for individuals in discussing their compensation, promotion and rankings.
- Prospective investors make use of financial statements to assess the viability of investing in a business. Financial analyses are often used by investors and are prepared by professionals, thus providing them with the basis for making investment decisions.
- Financial institutions use them to decide whether to grant a company with fresh working capital or extend debt securities to finance expansion and other significant expenditures.
- Government entities need financial statements to ascertain the propriety and accuracy of taxes and other duties declared and paid by a company.
- Vendors who extend credit to a business require financial statements to assess the creditworthiness of the business.
- Media and the general public are also interested in financial statements for a variety of reasons.

GOVERNMENT FINANCIAL STATEMENTS

The rules for the recording, measurement and presentation of government financial statements may be different from those required for business and even for non-profit organizations. They may use either of two accounting methods: accrual accounting, or cash accounting, or a combination of the two. A complete set of chart of accounts is also used that is substantially different from the chart of a profit–oriented business

FINANCIAL STATEMENTS OF NON–PROFIT ORGANIZATIONS

The financial statements that non-profit organizations such as charitable organizations and large voluntary associations publish, tend to be simpler than those of for-profit corporations. Often they consist of just a balance sheet and a "statement of activities" similar to the "Profit and Loss statement" of a for-profit. Charitable organizations in the United States are required to show their income and net assets in three categories: Unrestricted, Temporarily Restricted and Permanently Restricted.

PERSONAL FINANCIAL STATEMENTS

Personal financial statements may be required from persons applying for a personal loan or financial aid. Typically, a personal financial statement consists of a single form for reporting personally held assets and liabilities, or personal sources of income and expenses, or both. The form to be filled out is determined by the organization supplying the loan or aid.

AUDIT AND LEGAL IMPLICATIONS

Although laws differ from country to country, an audit of the financial statements of a public company is usually required for investment, financing, and tax purposes. These are usually performed by independent accountants or auditing firms.

Results of the audit are summarized in an audit report that either provide an unqualified opinion on the financial statements or qualifications as to its fairness and accuracy. The audit opinion on the financial statements is usually included in the annual report.

There has been much legal debate over who an auditor is liable to. Since audit reports tend to be addressed to the current shareholders, it is commonly thought that they owe a legal duty of care to them. But this may not be the case as determined by common law precedent. In Canada, auditors are liable only to investors using a prospectus to buy shares in the primary market. In the United Kingdom, they have been held liable to potential investors when the auditor was aware of the potential investor and how they would use the information in the financial statements.

Nowadays auditors tend to include in their report liability restricting language, discouraging anyone other than the addressees of their report from relying on it. Liability is an important issue: in the UK, for example, auditors have unlimited liability. In the United States, especially in the post-Enron era there has been substantial concern about the accuracy of financial statements. Corporate officers are personally liable for attesting that financial statements "do not contain any untrue statement of a material fact or omit to state a material fact necessary to make the statements made, in light of the circumstances under which such statements were made, not misleading with respect to the period covered by th[e] report."

Making or certifying misleading financial statements exposes the people involved to substantial civil and criminal liability. For example Bernie Ebbers was sentenced to 25 years in federal prison for allowing WorldCom's revenues to be overstated by billion over five years.

STANDARDS AND REGULATIONS

Different countries have developed their own accounting principles over time, making international comparisons of companies difficult. To ensure uniformity and comparability between financial statements prepared by different companies, a set of guidelines and rules are used. Commonly referred to as Generally Accepted Accounting Principles, these set of guidelines provide the basis in the preparation of financial statements.

Recently there has been a push towards standardizing accounting rules made by the International Accounting Standards Board. IASB develops International Financial Reporting Standards that have been adopted by Australia, Canada and the European Union are under consideration in South Africa and other countries. The United States Financial Accounting Standards Board has made a commitment to converge the U.S. GAAP and IFRS over time.

INCLUSION IN ANNUAL REPORTS

To entice new investors, most public companies assemble their financial statements on fine paper with pleasing graphics and photos in an annual report to shareholders, attempting to capture the excitement and culture of the organization in a "marketing brochure" of sorts. Usually the company's chief executive will write a letter to shareholders, describing management's performance and the company's financial highlights.

In the United States, prior to the advent of the internet, the annual report was considered the most effective way for corporations to communicate with individual shareholders. Blue chip companies went to great expense to produce and mail out attractive annual reports to every shareholder. The annual report was often prepared in the style of a coffee table book.

MOVING TO ELECTRONIC FINANCIAL STATEMENTS

Financial statements have been created on paper for hundreds of years. The growth of the Web has seen more and more financial statements created in an electronic form which is exchangeable over the Web. Common forms of electronic financial statements are PDF and HTML. These types of electronic financial statements have their drawbacks in that it still takes a human to read the information in order to reuse the information contained in a financial statement.

More recently a market driven global standard, XBRL which can be used for creating financial statements in a structured and computer readable format, has become more popular as a format for creating financial statements. Many regulators around the world such as the U.S. Securities and Exchange Commission have mandated XBRL for the submission of financial information. The UN/CEFACT created, with respect to Generally Accepted Accounting Principles, internal or external financial reporting XML messages to be used between enterprises and their partners, such as private interested parties and public collecting bodies. Many regulators use such messages to collect financial and economic information.

RECEIPTS AND PAYMENTS ACCOUNT

WHAT IS A RECEIPTS AND PAYMENTS ACCOUNT

NGOs are required each year to prepare a summary of their cashbook. This summary shows all the money that they received during the year. It also shows the payments that were made. This is called the Receipts and Payments Account.

UTILITY

Some people think that the Receipts and Payments Account is a leftover from the time of cash accounting. This is not quite correct. The Receipts and Payments Account has several advantages.

This is more so in the case of non-profit sector:

- Trustees and other laypersons find the Receipts and Payments Account easier to understand.
- This Account discloses all loan transactions, even those which have been squared-off during the year.
- Some accountants do not disclose revenue Grants in the Income and Expenditure Account. In such cases, the true Income of the Non-profit can be known only from the Receipts and Payments Account.
- Manipulation of financial statements has become very common these days. It is, however, not easy to manipulate the Receipts and Payments Account and the Income and Expenditure Account together.

RECEIPTS VS. INCOME

All receipts are not income. For example money received from sale of fixed assets, loans taken, advances from customers, etc. is not income. Similarly, all income may not be received during the year. This happens if the organisation follows accrual accounting. For example, money for credit sales may be received in the next year. Interest earned on fixed deposits.

PAYMENTS VS. EXPENDITURE

Using the same logic, all payments are not expenditure. For example, money paid for purchase of fixed assets, loans repaid or given to others, advances to contractors, etc. are not expenditure. In some cases, an expense may occur but may be paid later. For example, you may have organized a mela in Feb '02, but the bill of the tent house may be paid later in April '02. In this case, if you are following accrual accounting, then this will be shown as an expense in 2001–02, and as a payment in 2002–03.

COMMON ISSUES

Before discussing the methods of making a Receipts and Payments Account, let us deal with some commonly confused issues:

Loan Transactions

The Receipts and Payments Account should show all cash and bank transactions. This includes loans given or received. It even includes those loans that were given out and received back during the same year. Unfortunately, many accountants simply prepare the Receipts and Payments Account from the Balance Sheet and the Income and Expenditure Account. As a result, transactions settled during the year do not show up at all. This is not a good practice and should be avoided.

Advances for Expenses

During the year many staff members may be given advances for expenses. For example, people are given advance for traveling, for organising events, for purchasing stationery, etc. Should all these be shown in the Receipts and Payments Account? This is a difficult question. If we do not show these advances then some people may feel that we are suppressing information. But if we show these, then the Receipts and Payments Account will become hopelessly cluttered.

There are two ways to deal with this. One is to take a decision that all routine advances settled during the year will not be shown in the Receipts and Payments Account. This can also be disclosed in the Receipts and Payments Account by giving a note.

Second option would be to show all advances given on the payment side as one line item 'Advances for Expenses'. On the receipts side, a corresponding one line item can be shown as 'Settlement of Advances for Expenses'. This may look like below:

Table. FRCA Receipts and Payments Account (Partial)

Receipts	Amount	Payments	Amounts
Settlement of Advances for Expenses	40,224	Advances for Expenses	46,250

Why is there a difference of ₹6,026 between the two sides? This represents advances given to staff, for which bills have not been submitted by the end of the year.

Accrued Expenses/ Income

What happens to expenses or income, which have accrued during the year but not paid or received so far? These should not be shown in the Receipts and Payments Account of this year. These will be shown in the next year when the actual cash payments or receipts occur.

Cash or Bank?

For making the Receipts and Payments Account, cash and bank transactions are treated as being the same. Therefore, deposit or withdrawal of cash from bank account not shown as a receipt or payment. However, if you invest money in bank fixed deposits, this will be shown as payment item in the Receipts and Payments Account. Similarly, encashment of fixed deposits will be shown as a separate item of receipt.

Level of Detail

Receipts and Payments Account is a summary of the cash and bank book. This means that all items of one type can be added together and shown as a single line item. For example, salary is paid twelve times a year. However, we need not show 12 entries for salary. We can show just one entry 'Salary paid' in the Receipts and Payments Account.

However, can we add up all our expenses and show these as one item, say 'Rural Development'? No. This will give very little information. The basic purpose of preparing a Receipts and Payments Account will be defeated. We should therefore, try to give reasonable level of detail in the Receipts and Payments Account.

Using Trial Balance Figures

Most accountants use a shortcut to make the Receipts and Payments Account. They pick up most of the income/ expense figures from the trial balance. Then they derive other figures of receipts/ payments by using opening and closing balances of various accounts. This can work if the organisation is following cash basis of accounting. In case, the organisation follows accrual basis or mixed basis, then this shortcut can give wrong results.

Depreciation

Depreciation is not a cash payment. It is an estimated charge towards wear and tear of fixed assets. Therefore, depreciation never appears in the Receipts and Payments Account.

Computerised Accounts

What is the command for making a Receipts and Payments Account if your accounts are computerised? We do not know of any accounting software, which can generate a proper Receipts and Payments Account automatically. This may be because the software is unable to link up an advance with its settlement.

Local Contribution and FCRA

Does your FCRA funded project require local contribution also? Be careful how you account for it. Any local contribution, whether cash or in kind, can not be brought into FCRA account books. This should be accounted in the General or Indian cash book and posted to another sub-ledger maintained for concerned project. Please note that this sub-ledger is part of the Indian set of books and is different from the FCRA project ledger. Also do not include this local contribution in the FCRA Receipts and Payments Account when you file your FC-3. If you do, you may get a notice from FCRA 'for mixing up local and FCRA funds'.

HOW TO MAKE A RECEIPTS AND PAYMENTS ACCOUNT

Receipts and Payments Account should normally be consolidated, that is, it should show the picture of the entire organisation. This includes FCRA funds, government funds, other funds as well as own funds.

Table. Consolidated Receipts and Payments Account for the Year Ended 31st March'02

Receipts		Amount	Payments		Amount
Opening Balance:			Salaries: Programme Staff		9,24,300
– Cash	500		Salaries: Admn. Staff		2,75,200
– Bank	1,15,500	1,16,000	Watershed Development Works		24,27,356
Local Contribution		10,250	Rent		42,000
Grants from:			Stationary		24,350
– Indian Agencies		14,55,500	Loan to Staff		15,800
– Foreign Agencies		55,75,500	Revolving Fund Loans Given		4,85,760
– Govt. Dept.		8,75,000	Purchase of Land		1,00,000
Interest from:			Education Centers		11,85,320
– Bank		1,500	Health Programme		19,32,851
– FDs/ Investment		10,500	Traveling Expenses		2,53,057
– Rev.Fund Beneficiaries		12,500	Fuel and Maintenance		71,950
Loans taken		1,45,000	Leadership Programme		2,26,860
Sale of Motorcycle		5,000	Advances for Exp.		80,500
Advances for Exp. Settled		75,354	Loans Returned		1,06,000
Rev. Fund Loan Recoveries		1,10,200	Closing Balance:		
			– Cash	10,506	
			– Bank	2,30,494	2,41,000
Total		**83,92,304**	**Total**		**83,92,304**

However, in some cases, a limited Receipts and Payments Account is prepared. For example, a Receipts and Payments Account showing transactions for FCRA funds only is prepared and attached to the FC–3.

Similarly, some donor agencies ask for project based Receipts and Payments Account, showing transactions of projects supported by them. Following guidance applies mainly to the consolidated Receipts and Payments Account.

Opening Balance

Start with the opening balance of cash in hand, and cash in bank accounts. Remember to include the balance of all bank accounts and all cash books. Opening bank balances should be taken from the bank book and not from the bank pass book.

Receipts

Summarize all receipts appearing on the receipts side of the cash book and the bank book. These are added up separately for each head of account and shown on the receipts side of the Receipts and Payments Account.

Payments

Similarly, all payments appearing on the payments side of the cash book and the bank book are summarized. These also are added up separately for each head of account and shown on the payments side of the Receipts and Payments Account.

Closing Balance

The closing balance is once again taken from the cash book and bank book, as appearing at the end of the year.

Tallying the Two Sides

Now add up both the sides. The two totals should tally, if all the figures have been taken correctly. If the totals do not tally then you may have to go back to your account books and cross check the figures again.

INCOME AND EXPENDITURE

As the development sector grows, size and complexity of NGOs is also growing. To handle the large amount of funds, both the NGOs and the funding agencies need a better understanding of financial statements. This will help them raise and answer questions. The Balance Sheet shows how wealthy a person or organisation is. It is a status report and shows where the organisation has reached on a particular date. We deal with the Income and Expenditure Account. Income and Expenditure Account is like an activity report–it shows what you did in one year.

Mostly this account is prepared for a year though it can be prepared for a longer or shorter period also. It shows all the income for the year on one side and all the expenditure on the other side. The difference between the two sides is shown as 'surplus' or 'deficit'. If the right side is more, you get a surplus. If the left side is more, it means you spent more than you earned–the result is a 'deficit'.

HOW CAN I SPEND MORE THAN I EARNED

This is not difficult at all–see how easily the Government has been doing it for 50 years.

You do this mainly by:

- Borrowing money from others. The loans will not show up on the Income side–these are shown as liabilities.
- Spending stored surplus related to an earlier year. This adjustment will also show up in the Balance Sheet.

WHAT CAN THE INCOME AND EXPENDITURE ACCOUNT TELL US

For a good analyst, a decently prepared Income and Expenditure account is better than an annual narrative report.

It can tell you:

- How much the NGO received from different sources: grants, donations, interest, and other income.
- How did it spend the money: salaries, travel, and physical programme work.

And when you compare two or three accounts, you will know:

1. Whether the income of the NGO is rising or stagnating.
2. Whether it has been able to spend the money it receives.
3. Which types of expenses are growing at a higher rate than others.

With these figures, you can raise some relevant questions:

- Is it practical to raise such large amount of donations from villagers or from small towns?
- What are the expenses incurred against other income from consultancy, training, etc.?
- Why is the pattern of expenditure changing?
- Whether activities given in the narrative reports tie up with the Income and Expenditure Account?

IS IT DIFFERENT FROM THE RECEIPTS AND PAYMENTS ACCOUNT

The Receipts and Payments Account shows all receipts, including donations, grants, loans taken, sale of assets, and recovery of staff advances. In the Income and Expenditure Account, loans, sale of assets, recovery of staff advances, etc. are not shown.

Similarly, repayment of loans, purchase of fixed assets, etc. are shown in the Receipts and Payments Account, but not in the Income and Expenditure Account. Receipts and Payments Account is like a summary of the cash and bank book—it starts and ends with cash and bank balances. It can not tell you whether there is a surplus or deficit.

WHY IS THAT IMPORTANT

You may be spending more than you earn by borrowing money. In the long run, this will get you into serious financial problems.

The Receipts and Payments Account does not distinguish between 'income' and 'loans', etc. The Income and Expenditure Account can tell you whether you are breaking even each year or not. In any case, you need to know the figure of surplus or deficit to prepare your Balance Sheet.

WHAT HAPPENS TO THE SURPLUS

The surplus is transferred to the Balance Sheet and carried forward to the next year. In most cases, the surplus shows up due to wrong accounting policies. It represents unspent grants which will be spent next year. There are really very few NGOs who will have a genuine surplus. These NGOs may be doing public fund-raising or may be running some income generation activity, where they earn a profit.

IS 'PROFIT' DIFFERENT FROM 'SURPLUS'

The word 'Profit' is used for commercial organisations. 'Surplus' is used for non-profit bodies. Surplus is also sometimes called 'excess of income over expenditure'. The main difference between 'profit' and 'surplus' appears to be that you are not free to distribute the surplus among the members of the NGO.

Even the profit earned in income generation activities can not be given to the members of the NGO–it must be used for the organisation's objectives.

CAN WE TRANSFER SURPLUS TO GENERAL FUND

In most cases the surplus includes unspent grants. This part of the surplus can not be transferred to General Fund without the concerned Agency's permission. However, general donations from public or other similar income can be transferred to General Fund or some other specific fund.

WHAT ABOUT TRANSFERS TO CORPUS

The entire surplus can not be transferred to the Corpus. Some part of the surplus will represent amounts received for purchase of fixed assets. This can be transferred to 'Corpus' or 'Fixed Assets Fund' when the assets are purchased.

This provides a balancing effect on the liabilities side. If you receive a specific grant for your corpus, this can be transferred to the corpus. Donations from general public can be transferred to corpus, unless the donor has given some other instructions.

ARE GRANTS 'INCOME'

Some people say that grants are received for specific purposes and represent a liability. These should not be taken to Income and Expenditure Account but directly to the Liabilities side of the Balance Sheet. Unfortunately, this results in a distorted view. Even in case of NGOs receiving and spending crores as grants, the Income and Expenditure Account may show very little income or expenditure. Another view is to treat such grants as 'Conditional Income'.

This would mean that these become the organisation's income if these are spent properly. That is to say, these are spent according to the terms and conditions of the grant. In such case, the entire grant is shown as income and a provision is made for unspent grant at the end of the year. This presents a picture which is closer to reality.

WHAT IS A CONSOLIDATED INCOME AND EXPENDITURE ACCOUNT

NGOs often prepare separate Income and Expenditure Account for each funding agency. This reflects the transactions related to that particular project. However, they also need to prepare a Consolidated Income and Expenditure Account showing transactions r elated to all projects as also the General part. This is a compulsory requirement under Income Tax, Societies Act, as also Bombay Public Trust Act.

WHAT IS DEPRECIATION

When you build or purchase a fixed asset, it will last you for several years. A jeep may be useful for 5-10 years, a good building will last you for 90-100 years.

When you charge depreciation, you write off a proportionate amount each year. The jeep may be written off over 10 years by charging 10% depreciation each year; the building will be written off over 100 years by charging a lower rate.

Who Pays for Depreciation–the NGO or the Funding Agency

Neither the funding agency nor the NGO pays for depreciation in a direct sense. Indirectly, the funding agencies or donors pay for it in most of the cases. This happens when they give grants to purchase assets as new or replacement.

Should NGOs Charge Depreciation

It is very difficult to work out a proper rate of depreciation.

Commercial concerns charge depreciation because:

- It is required for calculating taxable profit;
- It is compulsory for companies if they want to declare dividend;

- It is recommended by most accounting bodies so that a reserve for replacement of the asset is created. The first two reasons are not relevant for NGOs.

They get a 100% tax write-off in the year they purchase an asset. They do not declare dividend either. Moreover, most assets are created out of grants.

When the asset becomes worn out, a fresh grant is sought for replacement. The ICAI has made AS - 6 on Depreciation Accounting compulsory from 1st April 1995. This applies to all NGOs which have any business or commercial type activities.

Depreciation Rates

The rates shown here are taken from the Companies Act and the Income Tax Act. In these Acts, many more rates are specified–for accurate information you should consult your auditors.

WDV or SLM

Asset	Companies Act		I.Tax
	SLM%	WDV%	WDV%
Office Building	1.63	5	10
Residential Building	1.63	5	5
General Equipment	5.15	15	25
Cars/Jeeps	7.07	20	20
Tractors	11.31	30	25
Bus/ Truck	11.31	30	25
Other Vehicles	7.07	20	25
Computers	16.21	40	25
Furniture	3.34	10	10
School Furniture	5.15	15	15

Note: SLM: Straight Line Method, WDV: Written Down Value.

These indicate the method of calculating depreciation: SLM means straight line method. Here the rate is applied to original cost of the asset each year. If an asset is worth ₹10,000 and the SLM rate is 10%, then the depreciation each year will be 10% of 10,000 or ₹1,000 each year. WDV means written down value method.

Here the rate is applied is applied to the net balance of an asset. If the asset is worth ₹30,000, and depreciation rate is 10%, then in the first year, depreciation will be ₹3,000. In the second year, it will be ₹2,700 [(₹30,000-₹3,000) x 10%]. In the third year, deprecation will be ₹2,430 [(₹30,000-3,000-2,700) x 10%].

FORMAT: GUJARAT AND MAHARASHTRA

A special format has been given under the Bombay Public Trust Act. This format gives minimum disclosure requirements. This has to be used by all NGOs registered under BPT Act.

HORIZONTAL OR VERTICAL

Horizontal Format

Most NGOs prepare the Income and Expenditure Account in horizontal format. Income is kept on the right hand side and expenditure on the left hand side. In this, it is similar to the Profit and Loss Account prepared by commercial organisations.

Using Schedules

But there the similarity ends. NGO tend to put all the line items on the main Income and Expenditure Account, instead of classifying these into schedules. This makes the accounts very difficult to understand. Use of schedules could solve this problem.

Classifying Account–Heads

Secondly, there is no standard basis of classifying account-heads–it follows the agency budgets. Similar expenditure may be classified differently under two different agency budgets. This causes confusion and makes comparisons difficult. In the present situation, there appears to be no real solution for this.

Vertical Format

When the Income and Expenditure Account is prepared vertically, Income items go on top. Below these the Expenditure items are shown. Total expenditure, when subtracted from Total Income gives you the surplus or deficit. There is no major advantage in the vertical Income and Expenditure Account except that it is easier to type and file, and shows total income and expenditure clearly.

BALANCE SHEET

A Balance Sheet is, to a true accountant, the crowning glory of a year's hard work. To an auditor, it is the beginning of an exciting hunt. What does a Balance Sheet mean to you–a piece of paper with meaningless figures? An annual ritual to keep the authorities and donors happy? If you say yes, you are probably right. Many Balance Sheets are the result of careless or 'creative' accounting. But not all. An honest Balance Sheet can give you invaluable insights into an organisation.

HOW TO READ A BALANCE SHEET

Quite simply, the Balance Sheet is a sheet of Balances to be carried forward to next year. However, accountants are rarely satisfied with simple things. They have divided the Balance sheet into two parts: Assets and Liabilities. To make things more complicated, they offer you two forms of Balance Sheet: the traditionally Horizontal and the trendy Vertical. But the Balance sheet is merely one part of the Final Accounts.

Final Accounts

Final Accounts are also called Financial Statements. Apart from the Balance Sheet, there are two other statements which form the Final Accounts: 'Income and Expenditure Account' and 'Receipts and Payments Account'. All three are prepared at the end of each financial year. In India, the financial year now is uniform and runs from 1st April to 31st March. In other countries, the financial year varies.

Audit Report

In addition to these three, there is an important statement called the 'Audit Report'. The audit report contains comments of the auditor regarding the truth and fairness of the first three statements. The Audit Report is prepared by an independent auditor.

Income and Expenditure Account

The Income and Expenditure Account is like an activity report. It tells you the income earned during one particular year. It also shows all the expenses for that year. For IGPs, this is called a Profit and Loss Account.

Receipts and Payments Account

The Receipts and Payments Account is also like an Income and Expenditure Account. But there are two important differences: one, it includes capital transactions during the year; and, two, it shows only those transactions where cash or cheque has been given or received during the year.

Balance Sheet

The Balance Sheet is like a status report. It will tell you what were the assets and liabilities of the NGO on, say, 31st March 1997. It will show all their assets. If the NGO has taken loans these will also be shown here. The Balance Sheet will also show you whether the NGO has a Corpus or Endowment Fund. Other things to look for:

Dynamic or Stable

You can often tell the age of an organisation by its Balance Sheet. As it grows older, its Balance Sheet grows heavier. Assets acquired for operations over the years get accumulated in the Balance Sheet. The organisation's need for a secure future leads to a larger corpus. But insecurity is often a spur to action. Once there is a feeling of stability, the organisation becomes less dynamic. This is reflected by the less active Income and Expenditure Account.

How much Cash

Cash in hand is important for day-to-day expenditure. But large amount of cash increases risk of theft and misuse. Normally a cash balance for three days' payments is sufficient. A larger balance may mean unusual circumstances, several field offices, lack of planned withdrawals or even a partially fictitious cash balance.

Bank Balance

Money lying in a savings account or current account is no good for anyone except the Bankers. Good financial management will show up in small bank balances with the rest of the money lying in short term bank deposits. Most funding agencies now accept this so long as the programme is not affected.

Ratio Analysis

While the word 'ratio' has links to the word 'rationality', some of the ratio analysis can be quite hilarious and irrational. Ratio analysis means analysing a relationship between two figures when there is a relationship. For example, there is a relationship between amount of work done and infrastructure needed.

So you can see the relationship between value of fixed assets and amount of programme expenditure. This can be done by dividing the total programme expenditure by the value of fixed assets. A ratio of '1' will raise eyebrows while a ratio of '5' may be quite acceptable.

Window Dressing

Very common in the corporate sector. Virtually unknown in the voluntary sector.

Notes to Accounts

Some of the figures in the Final Accounts often need additional explanation. These are given in the Notes to Accounts. Read these for better understanding of the Balance Sheet. Often important accounting Policies are also given here.

MORE TIPS ON READING A BALANCE SHEET

- If the Balance Sheet is not consolidated, it will carry some comment below the heading.
- It is also useful to compare this year's figures with last year. See if some of the amounts have remained unchanged.

- If creditors or debtors appear on the Balance Sheet, they are probably following Mercantile Basis of accounting.
- Revolving Fund loans are often treated as expenditure in accounts. In such a case, no such loans will appear on the assets side.
- Grants are sometimes not taken to Income and Expenditure Account—balance of amount received and spent is shown in the Balance Sheet.
- Fixed Assets are sometimes charged off to programme expenditure.
- Surplus shown in the Income and Expenditure is often due to expenditure on fixed assets—it is not a real saving of funds. Endowment Funds are often not properly set aside on the Liabilities side but merged with surplus for the year.

THE HORIZONTAL BALANCE SHEET

Most NGO Balance Sheets are prepared in the Horizontal form. This has two parts: right and left. Assets are shown on the right side; liabilities are shown in the left. There is an interesting history to this. Traditionally, left has been considered evil: at one point in Europe's history, left handed persons were thought to be witches and magicians and burnt at the stake. As we all know, all liabilities are also 'evil'–these are therefore shown on the left side of the Balance Sheet.

Table. Format of Horizontal Presentation of Balance Sheet

XYZ Company

Balance Sheet As at December 31st 2XXX

Assets	₹	**Liabilities and Stockholders'Equity**	₹	
Current Assets		Current Liabilities		
Cash	10,000	Accounts Payable	15,000	Accounts
Receivable	20,000	Salaries Payable	9,000	
Inventories	30,000	Total Current Liabilities	24,000	
Deposits,prepayments	5,000	Bonds Payable	20,000	
Total Current Assets	65,000	Mortgages	35,000	
		Total Liabilities	79,000	
		Stockholders'equity Property,	55,000	
Common Stock	50,000	Plant and equipment, net		
Intangible Assets	10,000	Retained Eamings	1,000	
Total Assets	130,000	**Total Liabilities and Stockholders**	130,000	

Assets

All the assets which you own are put on the Right Hand side. Secondly, these are put in a descending order of 'durability' or 'ease of realisation'. This means 'Land' comes right on top. 'Cash in Hand' comes right at the bottom. Buildings, equipment, furniture, debtors, recoverable advances, investments, bank balances come somewhere in between.

Fictitious Assets

The last line shows the total of all the assets. But watch out for the 'fictitious assets'. These should be deducted from the total of assets side, if you want to make any sense out of the Balance Sheet. Examples of fictitious assets are: 'accumulated deficit'; 'Miscellaneous expenditure remaining to be written off'. These are normally shown at the bottom, below 'cash in hand'.

Liabilities

On the left side, the most pressing liabilities are put at the bottom: these include bills payable, creditors, provision for expenses. These come short term 'unsecured loans' taken by you. Going upwards, you then put the 'secured loans' taken from people. Then come the Endowment Funds. Corpus comes right at the top: this is a notional figure and shows the net worth of the organisation.

THE VERTICAL BALANCE SHEET

Some people find this easier to prepare: you do not need a double–spread sheet for typing this. Most companies use this format–however, it is rarely seen in NGOs. The vertical form has given up its prejudice against left handed people–there are no left or right sides to this. It has two parts: 1. Sources of funds; and 2. Application of Funds

Balance Sheet

1– Apr– 2008 to 31– Mar– 2009 as at 31– Mar–2009

Sources of Funds:		
Capital Account		**55,00,000.00**
Balasubramanian's Share Capital A/c	7,13,000.00	
Kavitha's Share Capital A/c	2,76,500.00	
Mohan's Share Capital A/c	15,00,000.00	
Priya Ganesh's Share Capital A/c	5,65,500.00	
Sathish's Share Capital A/c	14,00,000.00	
Suresh's Share Capital A/c	4,75,500.00	
Loans (Liability)		**4,63,216.03**
Unsecured Loans	4,46,316.03	
HDFC Silver Credit Card	19,900.00	
Profit and Loss A/c		**62,38,991.92**
Opening Balance		
Current Period	62,38,991.92	
Unadjusted Forex Gain/Loss		**3.55**
Total		**1,22,02,211.50**

Application of Funds:			
Fixed Assets			**34,62,489.68**
Accumulated Depreciation on Fixed Assets			(–) 6,02622.20
Land $ Building		14,00,000.00	
Plant and Machinery		15,25,000.00	
Airconditioner		21,500.00	
Computers and Peripherals		90,460.00	
Furniture and Fixtures		1,22,420.00	
Motor Car–Hyundai GLX		9,05,731.88	
Investments			**5,00,000.00**
Investments		5,00,000.00	
Working Capital			**82,39,721.82**
Current Assets		1,36,79,562.33	
Closing Stock	13,58,831.73		
Loans and Advances (Asset)	15,99,000.00		
Sundry Debtors	65,16,336.68		
Cash– in– Hand	10,19,901.25		
Bank Accounts	29,35,492.67		
Advance Tax	2,50,000.00		
Less: Current Liabilities		54,39,840.51	
Duties and Taxes	65,206.54		
Provisions	91,618.38		
Sundry Creditors	50,76,720.00		
ESI Payable	210.00		
Interest on Car Loan A/c	1,56,275.59		
Salary Payable	49,810.00	Total	1,22,02,211.50

Application

The second part shows the assets of the organisation in descending order of durability. Fixed assets come first, Investments second and current assets come third. Current assets include debtors, advances, stocks, cash at banks, cash in hand. However, the current liabilities are deducted from the current assets to give a figure of net current assets. Only the net figure is shown in the total column. The fictitious assets are shown at the absolute bottom, below the current assets.

Sources

Going back to the first part, this shows the sources of these funds. At the bottom of this part, you have your unsecured loans, preceded by secured loans. This come the Endowment Funds. Right at top is the corpus, which is a difference between the total assets reduced by loans taken. In many ways, vertical form is easier to understand. The information is more organised and it is easier to work out ratios. Being typed on single sheets means less complications in xeroxing, filing and physical handling. Unfortunately, in several states, local regulations do not allow NGOs to use the vertical format.

5

Cash and Fund Flow Statement

CASH FLOW STATEMENT

In financial accounting, a cash flow statement, also known as *statement of cash flows* or *funds flow statement*, is a financial statement that shows how changes in balance sheet accounts and income affect cash and cash equivalents, and breaks the analysis down to operating, investing, and financing activities. Essentially, the cash flow statement is concerned with the flow of cash in and cash out of the business.

The statement captures both the current operating results and the accompanying changes in the balance sheet. As an analytical tool, the statement of cash flows is useful in determining the short–term viability of a company, particularly its ability to pay bills. International Accounting Standard 7, is the International Accounting Standard that deals with cash flow statements.

People and groups interested in cash flow statements include:

- Accounting personnel, who need to know whether the organization will be able to cover payroll and other immediate expenses
- Potential lenders or creditors, who want a clear picture of a company's ability to repay
- Potential investors, who need to judge whether the company is financially sound
- Potential employees or contractors, who need to know whether the company will be able to afford compensation
- Shareholders of the business.

PURPOSE

The cash flow statement was previously known as the flow of Cash statement. The cash flow statement reflects a firm's liquidity. The balance sheet is a snapshot of a firm's financial resources and obligations at a single point in time, and the income statement summarizes a firm's financial transactions over an interval of time. These two financial statements reflect the accrual basis accounting used by firms to match revenues with the expenses associated with generating those revenues.

Table. Statement of Cash Flow–Simple Example for the Period 01/01/2006 to 12/31/2006

Cash Flow from operations	₹ 4,000	
Cash Flow from Investing		₹ (1,000)
Cash Flow from Financing		₹ (2,000)
Net Cash Flow		₹ 1,000
Parentheses Indicate Negative Values		

The cash flow statement includes only inflows and outflows of cash and cash equivalents; it excludes transactions that do not directly affect cash receipts and payments. These non-cash transactions include depreciation or write-offs on bad debts or credit losses to name a few. The cash flow statement is a cash basis report on three types of financial activities: operating activities, investing activities, and financing activities. Non–cash activities are usually reported in footnotes.

The cash flow statement is intended to:

- Provide information on a firm's liquidity and solvency and its ability to change cash flows in future circumstances
- Provide additional information for evaluating changes in assets, liabilities and equity
- Improve the comparability of different firms' operating performance by eliminating the effects of different accounting methods
- Indicate the amount, timing and probability of future cash flows

The cash flow statement has been adopted as a standard financial statement because it eliminates allocations, which might be derived from different accounting methods, such as various timeframes for depreciating fixed assets.

HISTORY AND VARIATIONS

Cash basis financial statements were very common before accrual basis financial statements. The "flow of funds" statements of the past were cash flow statements. In 1863, the Dowlais Iron Company had recovered from a business slump, but had no cash to invest for a new blast furnace, despite having made a profit.

To explain why there were no funds to invest, the manager made a new financial statement that was called a *comparison balance sheet,* which showed that the company was holding too much inventory. This new financial statement was the genesis of Cash Flow Statement that is used today. In the United States in 1971, the Financial Accounting Standards Board defined rules that made it mandatory under Generally Accepted Accounting Principles to report sources and uses of funds, but the definition of "funds" was not clear."Net working capital" might be cash or might be the difference between current assets and current liabilities. From the late 1970 to the mid–1980s, the FASB discussed the usefulness of predicting future cash flows. In 1987, FASB Statement No. 95 mandated that firms provide cash flow statements. In 1992, the International Accounting Standards Board issued International Accounting Standard 7, *Cash Flow Statements*, which became effective in 1994, mandating that firms provide cash flow statements.

US GAAP and IAS 7 rules for cash flow statements are similar, but some of the differences are:

- IAS 7 requires that the cash flow statement include changes in both cash and cash equivalents. US GAAP permits using cash alone or cash and cash equivalents.
- IAS 7 permits bank borrowings in certain countries to be included in cash equivalents rather than being considered a part of financing activities.
- IAS 7 allows interest paid to be included in operating activities or financing activities. US GAAP requires that interest paid be included in operating activities.
- US GAAP requires that when the direct method is used to present the operating activities of the cash flow statement, a supplemental schedule must also present a cash flow statement using the indirect method. The IASC strongly recommends the direct method but allows either method. The IASC considers the indirect method less clear to users of financial statements. Cash flow statements are most commonly prepared using the indirect method, which is not especially useful in projecting future cash flows.

CASH FLOW ACTIVITIES

The cash flow statement is partitioned into three segments, namely:

1. Cash flow resulting from operating activities;
2. Cash flow resulting from investing activities;and
3. Cash flow resulting from financing activities. The money coming into the business is called cash inflow, and money going out from the business is called cash outflow.

Operating activities

Operating activities include the production, sales and delivery of the company's product as well as collecting payment from its customers. This could include purchasing raw materials, building inventory, advertising, and shipping the product.

Under IAS 7, operating cash flows include:

- Receipts from the sale of goods or services
- Receipts for the sale of loans, debt or equity instruments in a trading portfolio

- Interest received on loans
- Dividends received on equity securities
- Payments to suppliers for goods and services
- Payments to employees or on behalf of employees
- Interest payments

Items which are added back to the net income figure to arrive at cash flows from operations generally include:

- Depreciation
- Deferred tax
- Amortization
- Any gains or losses associated with the sale of a non–current asset, because associated cash flows do not belong in the operating part.

Investing Activities

Examples of Investing activities are:

- Purchase or Sale of an asset
- Loans made to suppliers or received from customers
- Payments related to mergers and acquisitions

Financing Activities

Financing activities include the inflow of cash from investors such as banks and shareholders, as well as the outflow of cash to shareholders as dividends as the company generates income. Other activities which impact the long–term liabilities and equity of the company are also listed in the financing activities part of the cash flow statement.

Under IAS 7:

- Proceeds from issuing short–term or long–term debt
- Payments of dividends
- Payments for repurchase of company shares
- Repayment of debt principal, including capital leases
- For non-profit organizations, receipts of donor–restricted cash that is limited to long–term purposes

Items under the financing activities part include:

- Dividends paid
- Sale or repurchase of the company's stock
- Net borrowings
- Payment of dividend tax

DISCLOSURE OF NON–CASH ACTIVITIES

Under IAS 7, non-cash investing and financing activities are disclosed in footnotes to the financial statements. Under US General Accepted Accounting Principles, non-cash activities may be disclosed in a footnote or within the cash flow statement itself.

Non-cash financing activities may include:
- Leasing to purchase an asset
- Converting debt to equity
- Exchanging non–cash assets or liabilities for other non-cash assets or liabilities
- Issuing shares in exchange for assets

PREPARATION METHODS

The direct method of preparing a cash flow statement results in a more easily understood report. The indirect method is almost universally used, because FAS 95 requires a supplementary report similar to the indirect method if a company chooses to use the direct method.

DIRECT METHOD

The direct method for creating a cash flow statement reports major classes of gross cash receipts and payments. Under IAS 7, dividends received may be reported under operating activities or under investing activities. If taxes paid are directly linked to operating activities, they are reported under operating activities; if the taxes are directly linked to investing activities or financing activities, they are reported under investing or financing activities.

Table. Sample Cash Flow Statement Using the Direct Method

Cash Flows from Operating Activities	
Cash receipts from customers	9,500
Cash paid to suppliers and employees	(2,000)
Cash generated from operations (sum)	7,500
Interest paid	(2,000)
Income taxes paid	(3,000)
Net cash flows from operating activities	2,500
Cash Flows from (used in) Investing Activities	
Proceeds from the sale of equipment	7,500
Dividends received	3,000
Net cash flows from investing activities	10,500
Cash flows from (used in) financing activities	
Dividends paid	(2,500)
Net cash flows used in financing activities	(2,500)
Net increase in cash and cash equivalents	10,500
Cash and cash equivalents, beginning of year	1,000
Cash and cash equivalents, end of year	$11,500

INDIRECT METHOD

The indirect method uses net-income as a starting point, makes adjustments for all transactions for non-cash items, then adjusts from all cash-based transactions. An increase in an asset account is subtracted from net income, and an increase in a liability account is added back to net income. This method converts accrual-basis net income into cash flow by using a series of additions and deductions.

Rules (Operating Activities)

The following rules can be followed to calculate Cash Flows from Operating Activities when given only a two year comparative balance sheet and the Net Income figure. Cash Flows from Operating Activities can be found by adjusting Net Income relative to the change in beginning and ending balances of Current Assets, Current Liabilities, and sometimes Long Term Assets.

When comparing the change in long term assets over a year, the accountant must be certain that these changes were caused entirely by their devaluation rather than purchases or sales or if they are nonoperating items.

- Decrease in non-cash current assets are added to net income
- Increase in non-cash current asset are subtracted from net income
- Increase in current liabilities are added to net income
- Decrease in current liabilities are subtracted from net income
- Expenses with no cash outflows are added back to net income
- Revenues with no cash inflows are subtracted from net income
- Non operating losses are added back to net income
- Non operating gains are subtracted from net income

The intricacies of this procedure might be seen as,

Net Cash Flows from Operating Activities = Net Income + Rule Items

For example, consider a company that has a net income of ₹100 this year, and its A/R increased by ₹25 since the beginning of the year. If the balances of all other current assets, long term assets and current liabilities did not change over the year, the cash flows could be determined by the rules above as ₹100—₹25 = Cash Flows from Operating Activities = ₹75. The logic is that, if the company made ₹100 that year and they are using the accrual accounting system then any income they generated that year which has not yet been paid for in cash should be subtracted from the net income figure in order to find cash flows from operating activities. And the increase in A/R meant that ₹25 of sales occurred on credit and have not yet been paid for in cash.

In the case of finding Cash Flows when there is a change in a fixed asset account, say the Buildings and Equipment account decreases, the change is subtracted from Net Income. The reasoning behind this is that because Net Income is calculated by, Net Income = Rev - Cogs - Depreciation Exp - Other Exp then the Net Income figure will be decreased by the building's depreciation that year. This depreciation is not associated with an exchange of cash, therefore the depreciation is added back into net income to remove the non-cash activity.

Rules (Financing Activities)

Finding the Cash Flows from Financing Activities is much more intuitive and needs little explanation.

Generally, the things to account for are financing activities:

- Include as outflows, reductions of long term notes payable
- Or as inflows, the issuance of new notes payable
- Include as outflows, all dividends paid by the entity to outside parties
- Or as inflows, dividend payments received from outside parties
- Include as outflows, the purchase of notes stocks or bonds
- Or as inflows, the receipt of payments on such financing vehicles.

In the case of more advanced accounting situations, such as when dealing with subsidiaries, the accountant must:

- Exclude intra-company dividend payments.
- Exclude intra-company bond interest.

A traditional equation for this might look something like,

Net Cash Flows from Financing Activities =[Divs Received from 3rd Parties]–[Divs Paid to 3rd Parties]– {Divs Paid to NCI but not Intracompany Div Payments}

Example: cash flow of XYZ:

XYZ co. Ltd. Cash Flow Statement (all numbers in millions of Rs.)			
Period Ending	03/31/2010	03/31/2009	03/31/2008
Net income	21,538	24,589	17,046
Operating activities, cash flows provided by or used in:			
Depreciation and amortization	2,790	2,592	2,747
Adjustments to net income	4,617	621	2,910
Decrease (increase) in accounts receivable	12,503	17,236	--
Increase (decrease) in liabilities (A/P, taxes payable)	131,622	19,822	37,856
Decrease (increase) in inventories	--	--	--
Increase (decrease) in other operating activities	(173,057)	(33,061)	(62,963)
Net cash flow from operating activities	13	31,799	(2,404)
Investing activities, cash flows provided by or used in:			
Capital expenditures	(4,035)	(3,724)	(3,011)
Investments	(201,777)	(71,710)	(75,649)
Other cash flows from investing activities	1,606	17,009	(571)
Net cash flows from investing activities	(204,206)	(58,425)	(79,231)
Financing activities, cash flows provided by or used in:			
Dividends paid	(9,826)	(9,188)	(8,375)
Sale (repurchase) of stock	(5,327)	(12,090)	133
Increase (decrease) in debt	101,122	26,651	21,204
Other cash flows from financing activities	120,461	27,910	70,349
Net cash flows from financing activities	206,430	33,283	83,311
Effect of exchange rate changes	645	(1,840)	731
Net increase (decrease) in cash and cash equivalents	2,882	4,817	2,407

FUND FLOW STATEMENT

A fund flow statement is a summary of a firm's inflow and outflow of funds. It tells us from where funds have come and where funds have gone. Fund flows statement can indicate whether sourcing of funds and their use match in ALM sense and also reveal the prudence or otherwise of a firm's financing and investment decisions.

A FIRM'S BALANCE SHEET

From a bank's perspective a borrower's balance sheet can be seen as:

1. Owner's fund and long term loans represent long term sources of funds
2. Current liabilities (including short term loans repayable within one year) represents short term sources of capital.
3. Thee whole of long term funds is not invested in long term assets but a portion of it is invested in short term or current assets as well. The extent by which current assets are financed by long term funds is known as net working capital or NWC.

If we convert balance sheets of two consecutive years into boxes and work out the change in amounts in the boxes, as suggested, get a fund flow statement.

Therefore, preparation of fund flow statement involves the followings steps:

- Take balance sheets as at two dates covering the period for which fund flows statement is intended to be prepared.
- Work out increase/decrease in each of items
- Classify change in each item under any of the four heads:
  - Long term sources
  - Long term uses
  - Short term sources
  - Short term uses.

The deficit or the surplus in the long term category will be equal to the surplus or deficit in the short term category.

PREPARING FUND FLOW STATEMENT

Generally changes in assets and liabilities lead to inflows or outflows of cash. Increase in assets or liabilities, however does not always lead to flow of funds, for instance, depreciation or any kind of revaluation.

Therefore, all increases/decreases in asset or liabilities will not form part of fund flow statement but only those that result in the flows of funds. The following table encapsulates the fund flow implications of changes in asset/ liabilities values.

Asset	Liability	Type of Fund Flow	Non–Fund Based Adjustments
Increase		Outflows	Upward revaluation
Decrease		Inflows	Depreciation
Increase	Inflows	Upward revaluation (as in the case foreign currency liabilities)	
	Decrease	Outflows	Depreciation (as in the case foreign currency liabilities)

When preparing fund flow statement we have to nullify the non-fund based adjustments in order to capture only those changes in the values of assets and liabilities that are accompanied by flows of fund. Increase in the item "reserves and surplus" indicate the amount of retained profits for the year. If we add profits distributed to this figure as suggested, get the amount of net profit for the year after taxes.

We need to adjust the net profit figure for all non-cash expenses and non-cash incomes. As a rule, we have to add all non-cash expenditure to and deduct all non-cash income from the figure of net profit. For depreciation in assets: Add depreciation to the change in reserve and surplus and correspondingly to the value of assets concerned.

The opposite holds for appreciation. For write offs: Add the amount of write offs to net profits. Income accrued but received and expenses incurred but not received reckoned in the profit and loss account should not be excluded from the profit figure for the purpose of Fund Flow Statement. The rationale for this rule is that so long as accrued incomes are expected to be received and outstanding expenses are expected to be paid in the normal course of business there is no harm in treating these as inflow or outflow of funds, albeit with a lag.

As regards changes in items of current assets and liabilities, we can either show the items separately or net them to arrive at the figure of "change in net working capital". It is however more informative to show the current items separately. The following example illustrates the preparation of fund flow statement.

Liabilities	**31–3–06**	**31–Mar–07**	**Assets**	**31–3–06**	**31–3–07**
	₹ lakh	₹ lakh		₹ lakh	₹ lakh
Capital	90	110	Fixed Assets	135	221
Res. and Sur	35	50	Inv. In Associates	30	86
Term Loan	110	150	Inventory	140	175
Cash Credit	75	90	Receivables	20	25
Trade Crs.	20	100	Cash and Bank	10	8
Bank Borr.	15	20	Other CA	10	5
Total	345	520	Total	345	520

The enterprise has made a profit of ₹ 95,00,000 during the year.A provision for tax of ₹ 30,00,000 has been made from the profit. An amount of ₹50,00,000 was withdrawn by the proprietor from the profits during the year. Besides, the following additional information in respect of the fixed asset items of the enterprise is also available.

₹ Lakh	**31–3–06**	**Addition**	**Disposal**	**31–3–07**
Gross FA	225	125	Nil	350
Total Depreciation	90		Nil	129
Net FA	135	125	Nil	221

The first step in working out fund flows is to compute the changes in assets and liabilities during 2006-07. This is shown in the following table.

Liabilities	**Change**	**Type**	**Assets**	**Change**	**Type**
Capital	+20	LTS	Fixed Assets	+86	LTU
Res. and Sur	+15	LTS	Inv. In Associates	+56	LTU
Term Loan	+40	LTS	Inventory	+35	STU
Cash Credit	+15	STS	Receivables	+5	STU
Trade Crs.	+80	STS	Cash and Bank	-2	STS
Other CL	+5	STS	Other CA	-5	STS
Total	175			175	

Note that increase in assets is use of funds while decrease in assets is source of funds and so forth as shown in Table. Further, depending on which 'box' the items belong the change can represent either a long term or short term source/use. Accordingly, the changes have been categorized as LTS, LTU, STS, STU in the table.

This is our skeleton fund flow statement. We now have to nullify the impact of non-fund based adjustments hidden in the above numbers. Also, certain adjustments are made just in order to make a more meaningful presentation. For example, we are told that the proprietor has withdrawn ₹50,00,000 from Capital A/c.

The withdrawal is fund-based adjustment not requiring any adjustment, strictly speaking. But according to our skeleton fund flow statement increase in reserve and surplus is ₹15,00,000. This figure is obviously after the withdrawal of ₹50,000.

The true profit is not therefore ₹15,00,000 but ₹65,000. Therefore, a better presentation would be to show profit from operations as ₹65,00,000 on the Source side and ₹15,00,000 as profits withdrawn on Uses side. This is arithmetically same as showing just ₹15,00,000 on the Source side. Therefore our adjustment is as under:

Profit from operations ₹lakh

Increase in reserves and surplus:15

Add: Profit withdrawn 50

Total 65

Provision for tax does not require any adjustment as even though a mere provision does entail fund flow as tax will have to be paid anyway; it is just a matter of timing. Finally, the increase in fixed assets shown as ₹86,000 in Table, does not represent the correct figure of fixed assets purchased as the fixed assets values include the effect of depreciation.

As suggested, have to nullify that:

- ₹ lakh
- Depreciation provision as on 31.3.2007–129
- Depreciation provision as on 31.3.2006–90
- Depreciation provided in 2006–07–39
- Profit before depreciation adjustment–65
- Add depreciation (non-cash expense)–39
- Correct cash profit (LT source of funds)–104
- Balance of fixed assets as at 31.3.20072–21
- *Add*: depreciation for 2006–07–39
- Balance of fixed asset as at 31.3.07 before depreciation–260
- *Less*: Balance of fixed asset as at 31.3.2006–135
- Fixed assets purchased during 06–07 (LT application of funds)–125

Table. Fund Flow Statement

Rs. Lakh			
Long Term Sources		**Long Term Uses**	
Increase in capital	20	Purchase of fixed assets	125
Profit from operations	104	Investment in associates	56
Increase in long term loan	40	Profit withdrawn	50
Long term deficit	67		
Total	231	Total	231
Short Term Sources		Short Term Uses	
Increase in CC	15	Incraese in inventory	35
Increase in Trade Creditors	80	Increase in receivables	5
Increase in Other Current Liabilities	5	Short term surplus	67
Decrease in cash	2		
Decrease in other current assets	5		
Total	107	Total	107

How do we interpret the above fund flow statement? Basically, it shows healthy cash flows from operations. However the problem is that the firm is using short term money to finance long term investments. This can lead to liquidity problems in future.

The onset of liquidity problems is visible as the firm has increased current assets by ₹33 lakhs as compared with increase in current liabilities by ₹100 lakh, which produces incremental current ratio of 0.33. Also, the promoter has withdrawn nearly half the profit, which is serious imprudence when he had plans to invest heavily in fixed assets.

From another angle, it can be argued that the promoter has withdrawn the more than the entire bank loan. Prima facie, this also appears to be a case of diversion of funds. In this manner a fund flow statement can be used to derive valuable information on the manner in which a firm raises and deploys its funds.

PREPARE A CASH FLOW STATEMENT

COMPONENTS OF A CASH FLOW STATEMENT

Operating Activities

The statement provides information about the cash generated from a company's daily operating activities. Operating activities are those which produce either revenue or are the direct cost of producing a product or service. Operating activities which generate cash inflows include customer collections from sales of their primary products or services, receipts of interest and dividends, and other operating cash receipts.

Operating activities which create cash outflows include payments to suppliers, payments to employees, interest payments, payment of income taxes and other operating cash payments.

Investing Activities

Investing activities include buying and selling noncurrent assets which will be used to generate revenues over a long period of time; or buying and selling securities not classified as cash equivalents. Cash inflows generated by investing activities include sales of noncurrent assets such as property, plant, and equipment. Investing activities can also include the purchase or sale of stock and securities. Lending money and receiving loan payments would also be considered investing activities.

Financing Activities

Financing activities include borrowing and repaying money, issuing stock (equity) and paying dividends. For example, if you borrow funds to purchase equipment or pay off a loan, the cash flow statement will enable you to determine how much cash was either generated or used as a result of those transactions.

Income Flows and Cash Flows

The income statement and balance sheet are based on accrual accounting which was developed based on the principle of matching. The matching principle states that revenues generated and the expenses incurred to generate those revenues should be reported in the same income statement. This emphasizes the cause Amortization and–effect association –between revenue and expense.

Many revenues and expenses result from accruals and allocations that do not affect cash. A company can operate at a profit and continually be short of cash. It can also generate huge inflows of cash from operations and still report a loss.

The statement of cash flows can explain how these situations might occur. Answers to these questions cannot be found in the other financial statements. There are two types of items that cause differences between income flows and outflows: noncash income or expense and nonoperating income or expense.

An example of a noncash item on the income statement would be depreciation or amortization. An example of a nonoperating item on the income statement would be a gain on the sale of an asset. These transactions must be reported on a cash flow statement in order to properly determine the true effect of conducting business on cash.

HOW TO PREPARE A CASH FLOW STATEMENT

Information used to prepare a cash flow statement is taken from the income statement for the current year and balance sheets for the past two years. Net income is adjusted for deferrals and accruals. The purpose of these adjustments is to convert the accrual basis income statement to a cash flow statement.

The cash flow statement follows an activity format and is divided into three parts: operating, investing and financing activities. Generally, the operating activities are reported first, followed by the investing and finally, the financing activities. Additionally, there are two methods of calculating and reporting the net cash flow from operating activities.

Both methods result in identical figures for net cash flow from operating activities because the underlying accounting concepts are the same:

- The direct method reports gross cash inflows and gross outflows from operating activities.
- The indirect method reconciles net income with net cash flow from operating activities by adjusting net income for deferrals, accruals, and items that effect investing and financing cash flows.

The first step in preparing the cash flow statement is to determine the net increase in cash and cash equivalents for the period. This amount will be a control figure and the cash flow statement will reconcile the inflows and outflows to this figure. The fictional company From the Roots Up will be used as the example throughout this booklet.

Table. Exhibit From the Roots up Income Statement

For the Year Ended December 31, 200Y (In Thousands)

Sales	**₹ 8,158**
Cost of Goods Sold	(4,895)
Gross Profit	**3,263**
General and Admin Expense	(367)
Depreciation and Amortization	(188)
Operating Expense	(1,468)
Personnel Expense	(816)
Bad Debt Expense	(33)
Operating Profit	**391**
Oher Income (Expense)	0
Interest Expense	(122)
Net Income	**₹ 269**

The current year income statement data is shown on Exhibitand the balance sheets from the prior two years have been combined on the cash flow worksheet. This is also referred to as the sources and uses statement. 200X

Table. From the Roots Up

Cash Flow Worksheet (In Thousands)

Comparative Balance Sheet	Prior Year 200X	Current Year 200Y	Balance Change	Cash Source (Cash Use)	Activity Type Assets
Cash	$169	$233	$54	Control	Cash
Net Accounts Receivable	705	884	(179)	Use	Operating
Bad Debt Reserve	(14)	(18)	(4)	Use	Operating
Inventories	983	1,160	(177)	Use	Operating
Other Notes Receivable	130	214	(84)	Use	Operating
Plant and Equipment	512	552	(40)	Use	Operating
Accumulated Depreciation	(102)	(110)	8	Source	Operating
Noncurrent Assets	72	68	4	Source	Operating
Total Assets	$2,455	$2,973			
Liabilities and Equity					
Accounts Payable	$353	$442	$89	Source	Operating
Salaries Payable	40	50	10	Source	Operating
Short–Term Loans Payable	28	50	22	Source	Operating
Other Current Liabilities	200	231	31	Source	Operating
Long–Term Debt–Bank	490	400	(90)	Use	Financing
Due to Shareholders	324	450	126	Source	Financing

Paid in Capital	500	698	198	Source	Financing
Retained Earnings	520	652	132	Source	Operating
Total Liabilities and Equity	$2,455	$2,973			

Begin with the balance sheet data by taking the cash balance of $223,000 from the most recent balance sheet and subtracting the cash balance of $169,000 from the prior year, which results in an increase in cash of $54,000. The cash flow statement must balance to this control number. Next, determine the change in each balance sheet account.

This is reflected in the Balance Change column of the worksheet. It is calculated by subtracting the prior year account balance from the current year balance. For example, accounts receivable in 200Y was $884,000 compared to $705,000 in 200X, which resulted in a $179,000 increase in accounts receivable. This process is continued for each of the balance sheet accounts. After calculating the account balance change, it is necessary to determine if the balance change is an inflow or an outflow of cash or a source or use of cash. To make this task simple use Table as a guide to determine the effect of each balance change.

Table. Cash Effects of Balance Sheet Account Changes

Cash Inflow	0-Cash Outflow
A Decrease in an Asset Account	An Increase in an Asset Account
An Increase in a Liability Account	A Decrease in a Liability Account
An Increase in an Equity Account	A Decrease in an Equity Account

The table shows a decrease in an asset balance and an increase in a liability or equity account are cash inflows. The opposite holds true for increases in an asset balance or a decrease in a liability or equity account, which results in a cash outflow. To complete the cash flow worksheet, determine if each account balance change is an operating, investing or financing activity.

Table. Cash Flows by Activities

The Operationg Activities Section of a Cash Flow Statement Reports the Information Listed Below.

Inflows of Cash		
Operating Activities	**Investing Activities**	**Financing Activities**
Collections form Customers	Collection on Loans	Issuance of Long–Term Debt
Interest Income	Sale of Debt Instruments	Issuance of Equity Securities
Dividends Receipts	Sale of Equity Instruments	
Other Operationg Cash Receipts	Sale of productive Assets	
Outflows of Cash		
Operating Activities	**Investing Activities**	**Financing Activities**
Payments to Suppliers	Purchase of Productive Assets	Payment of Dividends

Payments to Employees	Purchase of Debt Instruments	Acquisition of an Entity's
Interest Payments	Purchase of Equity	Own Equity Securities
Instruments		
Payment of Income Taxes	Making Loans	Repayment of Amounts
		Borrowed
Other Operation Cash		
Payments		

Using Table as your guide, beginning with the asset part of the cash flow worksheet, review each account. Remember, the change in cash and cash equivalents is the control number to which you reconcile your cash flow statement. Accounts receivable would be categorized as an operating activity, because it is related to collections from customers.

The change in inventory is classified as an operating activity, because it is a component of core operating activities. Plant and equipment transactions would be classified as investing, because the sale or purchase of productive assets which are expected to generate revenues in the future are defined as Investing Activities in Table.

CONSTRUCTING THE STATEMENT

Operating Activities

The Direct Method

The first method performed will be the direct method of calculating cash flow. This method combines information from both the Income Statement and the Cash Flow worksheet we created using the Balance Sheet. The result is an accurate indication of exactly what funds were collected in the form of cash, paid in the form of cash, and if the company actually generated cash. You can use Table as a guide for calculating the cash flow on a direct basis.

Table. Cash Flows from Operating Activities Using the Direct Method

Cash Collections from Sales	Sales—increase (+ decrease) in Accounts Receivable—Bad Debt
Expense	
Cash Payments to Suppliers	Cost of Goods Sold + increase (– decrease) in Inventory—increase (+ decrease) in Accounts Payable
Cash Payments for Expenses	Total Operating Expense Operating (excluding Bad Debt Exp)—other noncash expenses (depreciation/
amortization) + increase (-decrease) in Other Income/Expense	Other Accrued Liabilities +/– Other Income/Expense

Cash Paid for Interest	Interest Expense
Dividends/Withdrawals increase (–decrease) in Dividends	Dividends/Withdrawals Paid + Payable
Cash Paid for Taxes	Tax Expense—increase (+ decrease) in Accrued Taxes Payable—decrease (+ increase) in Prepaid Tax

The Indirect Method

The second method used to calculate the Cash Flows from Operating Activities is referred to as the Indirect Method. Using the Indirect Method, cash flows from Operating Activities are reported by adjusting net income for revenues, expenses, gains, and losses that appear on the income statement but do not have an effect on cash. Using Table as a guide, and Tables to determine if the change is an inflow or outflow, extract data from the Income Statement and Cash Flow Worksheet to prepare the Cash Flows from Operating Activities using the Indirect Method. Based on the formula provided in Table, reconcile From the Roots Up net income with net cash provided by its Operating Activities.

Table. Cash Flows from Operating Activities Using the Indirect Method

Adjustments to reconcile net income to net cash provided by operating activities.	
(+)	Depreciation
(–)	Amortization of Bond Premium
(+)	Amortization of Bond Discount
(–)	Gain on Sale of Equipment
(+)	Loss on Sale of Equipment
(+)	Decrease in Accounts Receivable
(–)	Increase in Accounts Receivable
(+)	Decrease in Inventory
(–)	Increase in Inventory
(–)	Decrease in Accounts Payable
(+)	Increase in Accounts Payable
(–)	Decrease in Accrued Expenses
(+)	Increase in Accrued Expenses
(+)	Decrease in Prepaid Expenses
(–)	Increase in Prepaid Expenses
(–)	Decrease in Taxes Payable
(+)	Increase in Taxes Payable

A comparison of the Direct Method with the Indirect Method indicates that either method will generate the same results. The Operating Activities of From the Roots Up generated \$142,000 in net cash during 200Y.

Investing Activities

Cash flow from investing activities is the second part of both types of cash flow statements. Investing activities are the changes to the cash position created by the buying or selling of non-current assets. This includes selling and replacing equipment that wears out or acquiring a new building or land to facilitate growth in a company. Investing activities can also include the purchase or sale of stocks, bonds and securities. Lending money and receiving loan payments are also considered investing activities. For a small business, the investing activities part of a cash flow statement usually reports the following information:

Cash Flows from Investing Activities:

+ Proceeds From Sale of Assets
– Purchases of Property and Equipment
= Total Net Cash Provided (Used) by Investing Activities.

For a given period, there may not be much in the way of investing activities. But over time, it is an important consideration for assessing how to choose to use the cash generated by your business.

Financing Activities

Financing activities on a cash flow statement reflect borrowing money and repaying money, issuing stock, and paying dividends. The financing activities part of the cash flow statement can be reduced to the following formula:

Cash Flows from Financing Activities:

+ Net Borrowing Under Line of Credit Agreement
+ Proceeds From New Borrowings
– Repayment of Loans
– Principal Payments Under Capital Lease Obligations
– Dividends/Distributions/Withdrawals Paid
+ Proceeds From Issuance of Stock
+ Partner/Owner Capital Contributions
= Total Net Cash Provided (Used) by Financing Activities.

This part of the cash flow statement is registering inflows of cash from loans received and loans repaid, and other cash inflows from outsiders and owners. If you have paid dividends or taken money from the business, it should be reported here.

HOW TO ANALYSE A CASH FLOW STATEMENT

Once you have constructed a cash flow statement, you will be much closer to understanding the financial position of your company. While a balance sheet and income statement are tools for management, without a cash flow statement they are limited barometers and may even be misleading.

Operating Activities

The cash flow statement will tell you where money came from and how it was used. When analyzing cash flow, the first place to look is the cash flow from operating activities. It tells you whether the firm generated cash or whether it needs a cash infusion. A few periods of negative cash from operating activities is not by itself a reason for alarm if it is based on plans for company growth or due to a planned increase in receivables or inventories. However, if a negative cash flow from operating activities is a surprise to managers and owners, it may be undesirable. Over time, if uncorrected, it can foretell business failure. Managers and owners should pay particular attention to increases in accounts receivable. The cash flow statement gives the true picture of the account. A large increase in accounts receivables may warrant new billing or collection procedures.

Investing Activities

The cash flow statement puts investing activities into perspective. At one glance, you can see whether or not a surplus in operations is being used to grow the company. A lack of investing activities, which is few purchases of new equipment or other assets, may indicate stagnant growth or a diversion of funds away from the company.

Financing Activities

The financing activities part of the cash flow statement will show repayments of debt, borrowing of funds, as well as injections of capital and the payment of dividends. As a company expands, this area of the cash flow statement will become increasingly important. It will tell outsiders how the company has grown and the financial strategies of management. Together, the three parts of the cash flow statement show the net change in cash during the period being examined. A comparison between past periods will give owners and managers a good idea of the trend of their business. Positive trends in cash flow may encourage owners to consider long-term financing as an aid to growth and increase their comfort level concerning the company's ability to generate cash for repayment. Strong cash flow will also make it easier to acquire financing and to negotiate with lenders from a position of strength. Preparation of a cash flow statement is the first step towards financial management for long-term success.

CHECKLIST

Operating Activities:

- When you prepared the operating activities portion of the cash flow statement by the direct method, did you also prepare it by the indirect method to reconcile net income to cash flow from operating activities?

- Has net income been adjusted for changes in accounts receivable, inventory, accounts payable, wages payable, and income taxes?

Investing Activities:

- Is every cash transaction to purchase equipment or other assets represented?
- If any loans were made by the company, are they reflected?

Financing Activities:

- Are all loan payments reported?
- Have all cash dividends been reported?
- Are there any unreported cash inflows from owners or investors?

Cash Flow Analysis:

- What is the trend in cash flow from operating activities for your company?
- Is there a reason for any large increase in accounts receivable?
- How do you expect the financing activities of your company to change in the next year and the next two years?

DIFFERENCE BETWEEN THE CASH FLOW AND FUNDS FLOW STATEMENTS

The cash flow statement, known formally as the Statement of Cash Flows, reports a company's *change in cash and cash equivalents* from one balance sheet date to another. The cash flow statement classifies the amount of the change according to operating, investing, and financing activities. The cash flow statement has been required by the Financial Accounting Standards Board since 1988, when it issued its Statement No. 95.

6

Income Statement

INTRODUCTION

The income statement summarizes the results of a firm's operations for a period of time. Four major types of items appear on income statements: revenues, expenses, gains, and losses. *Revenues* are inflows of assets (or reductions in liabilities) that result from providing goods and services to customers; they arise from a firm's ongoing operations. Sales of inventory to customers, for example, generate assets (cash or accounts receivable) and constitute revenues. *Expenses* arise from consuming resources in order to generate revenues. The cost of inventory sold to customers shows an expense.

Gains, as with revenues, increase assets or decrease liabilities, yet they arise from activities that are not central to a firm's major operations. For example, a gain would result from selling land for more than its carrying (book) value. *Losses* are similar to expenses in that they decrease assets or increase liabilities, but they are not central to a firm's major activities. The sale of land at an amount less than its carrying value would result in a loss.

AN ILLUSTRATED INCOME STATEMENT

The 1997 income statement for Altron Incorporated, a manufacturer of component parts used in advanced electronics equipment. The income statement is for the year ended January 3, 1998. Although most firms use a calendar year–end of December 31, Altron uses a 52-week year and prepares its financial statements as of the Saturday closest to December 31. A 52-week year enhances comparisons across quarterly reports because each quarter will have 13 weeks. Some firms use a natural year-end instead of a calendar year-end. That is, the financial statements are prepared shortly after the firm's busy season. Wal-Mart, for example, prepares its annual financial statements on January 31, which is a good fiscal year-end for them because December is their busiest time of year. By the end of January, Wal-Mart has completed its busy season; it has made any exchanges or refunds, and its inventory levels are probably rather low. This is a good time to tally results.

EXHIBIT Multiple Step Income Statement

Altron Incorporated
Income Statement
For the Year Ended January 3, 1998
(Dollars in thousands)

Net sales	₹172,428
Cost of sales	134,373
Gross profit	38,055
Selling, general and administrative expenses	14,844
Income from operations	23,211
Other income	1,503
Interest expense	31
Income before provision for income taxes	24,683
Provision for income taxes	10,016
Net income	₹14,667

Altron's income statement, similar to the income statements of many corporations, is highly condensed. It contains two revenue items, four expense items, and no gains or losses. However, Altron almost certainly did experience gains and losses, but their relative sizes were probably so small that they were combined with other items on the income statement. This is an application of the materiality principle, which states that separate disclosure is not required if an item is so small that knowledge of it would not affect the decision of a reasonable financial statement reader.

This principle can actually improve the usefulness of financial statements by eliminating the disclosure of inconsequential items, which helps analysts concentrate on items of importance. The major revenue line on Altron's income statement is labeled Net sales. Note that the terms sales and revenue are used interchangeably by many firms, while the term net implies that certain items have been deducted from the gross (or full) sales price. For example, most firms allow their customers to return merchandise within a specified period, and customers are usually offered a full refund upon returning the merchandise.

The original sales amount is included in gross sales. The refund amount is termed a sales return, and it is subtracted from gross sales in calculating net sales. Even if the term net is omitted, reported sales on the income statement are usually net sales. Cost of sales is often referred to as cost of goods sold. It reflects the cost to Altron of the goods sold to its customers. The difference between sales and cost of goods sold is called gross profit or gross margin.

Altron has elected to combine selling, general, and administrative expenses, although some companies report separate figures. Selling expenses include advertising costs, commissions to salespersons, depreciation of equipment used in the selling function, and a number of other items. General and administrative expenses consist of senior managers' salaries, accounting and auditing costs, insurance, depreciation of administrative offices, and so on. Operating income equals sales minus all costs and expenses incurred by normal operations. Operating income is a primary indicator of how well a firm has managed its operations and serves as a basis for comparing firms within the same industry.

Altron's income statement contains several other items. Other income can arise from a variety of sources, such as interest on investments. Interest expense reflects the firm's cost of borrowing money from creditors. Income taxes are imposed by the federal government, state and local governments, and foreign jurisdictions. Neither interest nor income taxes directly relate to a firm's operations. For example, interest expense is largely a function of how much the firm has borrowed to finance its operations. Differences in interest expense between firms are determined primarily by choices the firms have made in financing their businesses. Some firms elect to borrow heavily, which results in large interest charges.

Other firms rely on investments by owners; Interest charges are not paid on these funds and, because of this, interest expense is deducted after operating income is calculated. The bottom line of the income statement is called net income, earnings, or profit.

Although interest and income tax expenses do not affect operating income, they are appropriate deductions in the calculation of overall profitability. Because net income reflects the increase in net assets from all profit-oriented activities, it is the focus of much scrutiny by analysts, investors, and other financial statement readers. Keep in mind the difference between revenue and profit. Revenue refers to the total inflow of assets (or reduction in liabilities) from customers. Profit is the net increase in a firm's recorded wealth after deducting expenses from revenue. Altron's income statement presented is in the multiple-step format.

Multiple-step income statements calculate certain subtotals for the reader. Altron's statement contains subtotals for gross profit and operating income. In contrast, income statements using the single-step format summarize all revenues in one section and all expenses in another. A single-step income statement. Whereas the single-step approach is simpler, the multiple-step approach provides more information.

USES OF THE INCOME STATEMENT

A major purpose of the income statement is to show a firm's profitability, yet it also provides a number of additional performance measures. Revenue, for example, is a key measure of growth that reflects a firm's success in expanding its market. Additionally, comparisons of expense numbers from year to year indicate a firm's success in controlling costs. Operating income measures managers' performance in conducting a firm's operations. Income statement information provides the basis for a variety of decisions. Because earnings underlie a firm's ability to generate cash flows for dividends and growth, equity investors are interested in the income statement. Lenders are also interested in the income statement because a firm's ability to pay principal and interest in a timely manner ultimately depends on its profitability. A firm's management can use income statement information to make a variety of decisions.

For example, managers must constantly evaluate the prices they set for the firm's products and services. Pricing affects both profitability and growth. The income statement tells managers and investors how well the firm's pricing strategy has accomplished stated objectives. Corporations always strive to reduce the costs of their operations, and the income statement can also measure the success of cost-cutting initiatives. However, costcutting, such as employee layoffs, do not ensure increased profitability.

Apple Computer Inc. cut thousands of jobs in 1996 and 1997, yet continued to post losses. Continued competition from industry rivals and the loss of human talent are issues that must also be addressed.

EXHIBIT Single-Step Income Statement

Altron Incorporated
Income Statement
For the Year Ended January 3, 1998
(Dollars in thousands)

Revenues		
Net sales	₹172,428	
Other income	1,503	
		₹173,931
Expenses		
Cost of sales	134,373	
Selling, general and administrative expenses	14,844	
Interest expense	31	
Provision for income taxes	10,016	
		159,264
Net income		₹14,667

As a final illustration, managers often use the income statement when setting dividends. Net income is a primary measure of a firm's ability to pay dividends. In fact, some firms set a dividend target equal to a certain percentage of net income.

REVENUE RECOGNITION

A firm's earnings process often takes place over an extended period of time. A manufacturer's typical earnings process entails purchasing raw materials, manufacturing, storing and selling the finished product, and collecting cash from the customer. The manufacturer creates value through all these steps, but for accounting purposes, firms usually select a discrete point in time to recognize (record) revenue.

GENERAL RULE

The revenue recognition principle states that revenue should be recognized in the accounting records when:

- The earnings process is substantially complete, and
- The amount to be collected is reasonably determinable.

EXHIBIT Time Line of a Manufacturer's Earnings Process

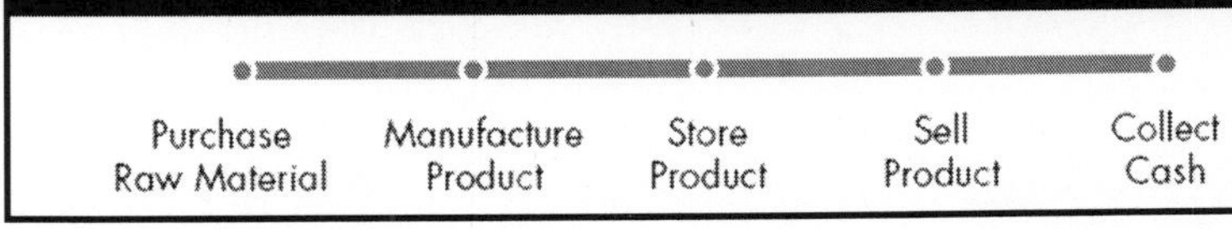

The first criterion prevents the recognition of revenue before a firm has fulfilled its obligation to the customer. The second criterion indicates that the sales price has been set and that the customer will probably pay the amount due. Both criteria ensure that revenue is not recognized prematurely.

If revenue is recognized too soon, the income statement will indicate that the firm has accomplished activities that it has not, which would mislead financial statement users. In most situations, these criteria are met at the point of sale, that is, when a product is delivered or a service is rendered to a customer.

Even if payment is not immediately received, a claim to cash (an account receivable) has been obtained, and revenue recognition is proper. Two additional comments need to be made about revenue recognition at the point of sale. First, many sellers guarantee their products' performance for a period of time. If a product malfunctions, the seller is obligated to incur the cost of correcting the problem. Does the existence of such a warranty indicate that the earnings process is not substantially complete at the time of sale? No, it does not. For most sellers, the warranty cost is relatively minor.

Thus, the earnings process is substantially complete at the time of sale. Second, when accounts receivable are obtained at the point of sale, can we be certain that cash will ultimately be collected? In most cases, absolute assurance cannot be obtained, but if the seller has done a good job of checking customers' credit histories, a reasonable estimate of worthless accounts receivable can be made. This estimate is used to adjust both the income statement and the balance sheet.

EXCEPTIONS

A number of exceptions exist to the general rule of thumb that revenue is recognized at the point of sale. One exception deals with the collectibility of receivables. If the seller is highly uncertain about the collectibility of a receivable, revenue recognition should be delayed beyond the point of sale to the point when cash is actually collected. This approach is sometimes used in the real estate industry. Another exception deals with long-term construction contracts (for bridges, highways, and so on). These projects can take several years to complete.

If revenue recognition is delayed until the earnings process is substantially complete, no revenue is recognized in any contract year except the final one, at which point all the revenue is recognized. Such an uneven pattern of revenue recognition would contrast with the actual earnings process, which takes place throughout the life of the contract.

Accordingly, if

- A binding contract exists between the buyer and the seller and
- The seller can reasonably estimate the costs to complete the project, then revenue, the related costs, and the resultant profit should be estimated and recognized each year by the percentage of completion method.

This method recognizes a portion of the revenue, cost, and profit each year just as to the percentage of the job completed. A similar situation exists with some service contracts. For example, consider a health club that sells one-year memberships for an immediate payment of ₹600. Revenue recognition at the point of sale is inappropriate because the earnings process has barely begun.

However, delaying revenue recognition until the twelfth month, when the earnings process is substantially complete, is also inadvisable. GAAP permits proportional revenue recognition each month over the contract's life. Most firms describe their revenue recognition policies in a note to the financial statements.

Because the earnings process has just begun at that point, the magazine records a liability instead of revenue. Recording a liability recognizes that Reader's Digest has an obligation to provide its customers something of value: either the magazine or a refund. Revenue is recognized as the magazines are mailed to the customers.

EXPENSE RECOGNITION

The matching principle governs expense recognition. It states that all costs that were incurred to generate the revenue appearing on a given period's income statement should appear as an expense on the same income statement. In other words, we should match expenses against revenues.

Revenues are first recognized and expenses are then matched with those revenues. By doing this, the income statement contains measures of both accomplishment (revenue) and effort (expenses), thereby enabling an assessment of firm performance. The matching principle is implemented in one of three ways.

ASSOCIATING CAUSE AND EFFECT

One method of implementing the matching principle is known as associating cause and effect. This implies that a clear and direct relationship exists between the expense and the associated revenue. Cost of goods sold is a good example. A retail store certainly cannot generate sales revenue without consuming inventory. Salespersons' commissions are another example. Because commissions are usually paid as a percentage of sales revenue, commission expense is tied directly to revenue.

SYSTEMATIC AND RATIONAL ALLOCATION

Another method used to implement the matching principle is systematic and rational allocation. Many costs cannot be directly linked to specific revenue transactions. They can, however, be tied to a span of years and allocated as an expense to each of those years. Sales equipment, as an example, is essential to generate revenue.

However, linking the cost of each display case, piece of furniture, and the like to specific sales transactions is difficult. Instead, the equipment's cost is systematically allocated as depreciation expense to the years during which the equipment helps generate revenue.

IMMEDIATE RECOGNITION

The final method of applying the matching principle is immediate recognition. Some expenditures have no discernible future benefit. In these cases, the expenditure is expensed immediately. Officers' salaries, utilities, and interest are treated in this manner.

A CLOSER LOOK AT THE INCOME STATEMENT

As indicated earlier, income statements summarize past transactions and events. Many users of income statements are interested in the past only to the extent that it can help predict the future. Financial statement users are concerned about earnings sustainability, which refers to the likelihood that earnings will persist in the future.

Historical income statements will be less useful for predicting the future if the results of ongoing operations are combined with the effects of events that are unusual or are not expected to recur in the future. Consequently, GAAP requires that income statements separately report certain items. This part describes these items and shows how they are displayed on the income statement.

DISCONTINUED OPERATIONS

If a firm ceases to operate (or plans to cease operating) a major segment of its business, separate income statement disclosure is required of its (1) continuing operations and (2) discontinued operations. The income statement of Hahn Automotive Warehouse, Inc., which sells replacement auto parts. Hahn traditionally had sold to both commercial concerns, such as automotive repair shops, and to retail customers (do-it-yourselfers) via its AUTOWORKS retail division, which Hahn decided to dispose of in 1997 because of poor profitability.

EXHIBIT Income Statement with Discontinued Operations

Hahn Automotive Warehouse, Inc.
Statement of Operations
For the Year Ended September 30, 1997
(Dollars in thousands)

Net sales	₹142,242
Cost of products sold	86,967
Gross profit	55,275
Selling, general and administrative expense	46,717
Depreciation and amortization	2,005
Income from operations	6,553
Interest expense	(4,670)
Other income	719
Income before provision for income taxes	2,602
Provision for income taxes	1,011
Income from continuing operations	1,591
Loss from discontinued operations:	
Write-down of investment, net of tax benefit	**(18,789)**
Loss from discontinued operations, net of tax benefit	**(3,937)**
Total loss from discontinued operations	**(22,726)**
Net loss	(₹21,135)

The first 11 lines of Hahn's income statement reflect the results of continuing operations. The discontinued operations part contains two line items; the first line reports the loss from the AUTOWORKS division, and the second line indicates the results of operating the segment. In making predictions about future earnings, most analysts would ignore the effects of these items by focusing on income from continuing operations. To qualify for separate reporting, the discontinued operation must represent an entire major line of business. Many divestitures do not qualify as an entire line of business and do not necessitate separate reporting. For example, a Wall Street Journal substance stated: "HCA-Hospital Corporation of America, bowing to weakness in the psychiatric hospital industry, said it will sell 22 hospitals and take an after-tax charge of as much as ₹300 million in the third quarter." The charge reflects operating losses and anticipated losses on the sale. Because HCA retained ownership of 26 psychiatric hospitals and 73 general hospitals, it did not dispose of an entire line of business. Treatment as a discontinued operation would be inappropriate.

The ₹300 million charge would be included in continuing operations. Thus, financial statement readers must be aware that continuing operations might contain revenues, expenses, gains, and losses that will not persist in the future. Some analysts would prefer to remove the ₹300 million charge from the current quarter's earnings when making projections about the future.

On the other hand, some analysts might view HCA's sale of hospitals as a normally recurring modification of the firm's strategy. Because these modifications are expected to occur periodically, these analysts would not remove the ₹300 million from reported earnings.

EXTRAORDINARY ITEMS

Extraordinary items are events and transactions that are unusual in nature and infrequent in occurrence. Unusual in nature implies that the event or transaction is, at most, incidentally related to a firm's typical operations. Infrequent in occurrence suggests that the item is not expected to recur in the foreseeable future. Extraordinary items usually include natural disasters and actions by foreign governments, such as expropriation of assets. Separate disclosure of extraordinary items enables analysts to make better projections of a firm's future operations.

A partial income statement for a California-based company, American Enterprises, Inc. (AE) and an accompanying note. It shows that AE lost a building in an earthquake, which meets the criterion of being unusual in nature. A question arises as to whether they are expected to recur in the foreseeable future. In California, earthquakes continue to occur with some regularity.

This is another accounting situation that requires judgment. Evidently, AE and its auditors feel that earthquakes in their area occur with sufficient irregularity that they are not expected to recur in the foreseeable future. Based on the footnote disclosures, analysts can exercise their own judgment about reported extraordinary items.

EXHIBIT **Partial Income Statement**

American Enterprises, Inc.
Partial Income Statement
For the Year Ended October 31, 2001
(Dollars in thousands)

Income before extraordinary gain	₹9,846
Extraordinary gain (net of income taxes of ₹1,047)	1,387
Net income	₹11,233

Note: The company's former headquarters building in San Francisco was severely damaged by an earthquake. After the sttlement with the insurers, the company retired the building and recognized an extraordinary gain of ₹1,387,000, net of income taxes of ₹1,047,000.

Note also that AE recognized a gain. A gain arose because the proceeds from the insurance settlement exceeded the carrying value of the building. Buildings are carried in the accounting records at depreciated historical cost, which does not reflect current market values. When making predictions about AE's future income levels, most analysts would remove the extraordinary gain from AE's reported net income:

Reported net income	₹ 11,233,000
Less extraordinary gain	1,387,000
Adjusted net income	₹ 9,846,000

INCOME TAXES

Given that many income statements have several major parts (continuing operations, discontinued operations, and extraordinary items), a decision must be made about where to report income tax expense. GAAP takes the reasonable position that taxes should be allocated to each major part. Consider again; one item listed is provision for income taxes. This is not Hahn's total income tax expense, however. It is the income tax associated with continuing operations.

The tax effects associated with discontinued operations are included in the calculation of those reported losses. This format shows discontinued operations net of tax. Note that discontinued operations generated a loss and that the tax effect is labeled a tax benefit. Losses yield tax benefits because they lower the taxes a firm must pay.

Consider a simple example. In 2001, Crimp Corporation earned, before taxes, a profit of ₹10,000 on continuing operations. It also incurred a ₹2,000 loss on discontinued operations. Assume a tax rate of 30%. Had the ₹2,000 loss not been incurred, Crimp's total tax expense would have been ₹3,000:

$$\text{Total tax expense} = ₹10{,}000 \times .3 = ₹3{,}000$$

However, given that Crimp did incur the ₹2,000 loss, its total tax expense is ₹2,400:

$$\text{Total tax expense} = (₹10{,}000 - ₹2{,}000) \times .3 = ₹24{,}00$$

Thus, the loss from discontinued operations reduced income tax expense by ₹600. The tax expense allocated to continuing operations is ₹3,000, and the tax benefit allocated to discontinued operations is ₹600. A partial income statement would appear as follows:

Crimp Corporation
Partial Income Statement
For the Year Ended December 31, 2001

Earnings before taxes	₹10,000
Income tax expense	3,000
Net earnings from continuing operations	7,000
Loss from discontinued operations (less income tax benefit of ₹600)	1,400
Net income	₹5,600

EARNINGS PER SHARE

Many financial numbers are stated on a per-share basis. Price per share and dividends per share are widely quoted in the financial press. Because a share of stock is the basic ownership unit in corporations, this mode of expression is quite useful. Consequently, GAAP requires that publicly held companies state net income on a per-share basis. In general terms, this requires dividing net income by the average number of shares of stock outstanding. The result is earnings per share (EPS):

$$\text{EPS} = \frac{\text{Net income}}{\text{Shares outstanding}}$$

Per-share amounts make it easier to relate the dividends, prices, and earnings of a given firm.

ANALYZING THE INCOME STATEMENT

As you've seen by now, the income statement contains a great deal of useful information about a firm. This part shows how to extract and interpret that information.

The income statements of OshKosh B'Gosh, Inc. (OB) for the years 1997 and 1996, which are summarized in serve as the basis for this part. One item on OB's income statement deserves special mention. In 1996, OB incurred a ₹32,900,000 special charge. The charge includes costs to close facilities, write down assets, and lay off employees.

Because OB did not discontinue an entire line of business, these changes do not qualify as a discontinued operation, yet this charge might not recur in the near future. Consequently, some analysts would delete this ₹32,900,000 loss in calculating ratios and evaluating trends.

VERTICAL ANALYSIS

Vertical analysis examines relationships within a given year. To do this with the income statement, divide each line by the first item, net sales. Net sales are a summary measure of a firm's total activities, so evaluating each income statement item relative to net sales makes sense.

The result yields common-size income statements in percentage terms. OB's common-size statements appear in. The first line of a common-size income statement is always 100% because the net sales figure is divided by itself. The second line of the common-size income statement, cost of products sold divided by net sales, is referred to as the cost of goods sold percentage. For a firm that is a merchandiser, one that simply buys and resells goods without changing their shape or form, this percentage reflects the relationship between the price the firm pays for the goods and the price it charges customers.

For a manufacturer, a firm that buys raw materials and component parts and reshapes them into a finished product, the cost of goods sold percentage can also indicate the efficiency of the manufacturing process.

EXHIBIT **Income Statements for 1997 and 1996**

OshKosh B'Gosh, Inc.
Income Statements
(Dollars in thousands)

	Year Ended December 31,	
	1997	1996
Net sales	₹395,196	₹444,766
Cost of products sold	250,815	300,495
Gross profit	144,381	144,271
Selling, general, and administrative expenses	115,439	122,055
Special charges and plant closings	—	32,900
Royalty income, net	(7,945)	(6,100)
Operating income (loss)	36,887	(4,584)
Interest expense	(305)	(1,088)
Other income	1,605	1,575
Income (loss) before taxes	38,187	(4,097)
Income taxes (benefit)	15,629	(5,216)
Net income	₹22,558	₹1,119

Note: During 1996, the company recorded special charges of ₹32,900,000 to close facilities, discontinue the company's Genuine kids retail store chain, and wind down th company's Europenan subsidiaries. Special charges (net of income tax benefit) reduced net income by ₹15,200,000 (₹1.23 per share) in 1996.

In assessing a firm's ability to generate cash flows, low costs and consequently low cost of goods sold percentages are desirable. This provides a larger profit per item sold. For every dollar of revenue in 1997, OB paid about ₹0.64 to manufacture the associated clothing.

The third line, gross profit (or gross margin) percentage, is calculated either by dividing gross profit by net sales or by subtracting the cost of goods sold percentage from 100%. It reflects the percentage of the sales price that exceeds the cost of goods sold.

It measures the percentage of revenue that is available to cover expenses other than cost of goods sold and to contribute towards profits. In 1997, about ₹0.36 of every OB sales dollar was available for these purposes. Given that a lower cost of goods sold percentage is desirable, a higher gross profit percentage is preferable.

Two basic strategies exist to increase the gross profit percentage (or, in other words, to decrease the cost of goods sold percentage).

- *First,* unit selling prices could be increased. This option is limited because of competition from other companies in the firm's industry.
- *Second,* efforts can be made to reduce the cost of goods sold. This can be done, for example, through more astute purchasing (such as buying in bulk to obtain a discount) or a more efficient manufacturing process. The fourth line of OB's common-size income statement reflects the relationship between selling, general, and administrative expenses and net sales.

Managers have substantial control over these costs, and percentages that increase over time are usually viewed with disfavour. Of the remaining items in The two most important are the operating income percentage and the net income percentage.

The operating income percentage is an indicator of management's success in operating the firm. The numerator, operating income (or loss), excludes both interest expense and taxes.

Because these expenses are not directly affected by operating (buying and selling) decisions, the operating income percentage is a better reflection of how management handles the day-to-day affairs of the firm.

The net income percentage reflects the firm's overall profitability, after interest and taxes, relative to its level of activity (net sales). Both ratios are indicators of a firm's financial success. Graphically depicts the information contained in Exhibit.

EXHIBIT **Common-Size Income Statements**

OshKosh B'Gosh
Common-Size Income Statements

	Year Ended December 31,	
	1997	1996
Net sales	100.0%	100.0%
Cost of products sold	63.5	67.6
Gross profit	36.5	32.4
Selling, general, and administrative expenses	29.2	27.4
Special charges and plant closings	—	7.4
Royalty income, net	(2.0)	(1.4)
Operating income (loss)	9.3	(1.0)
Interest expense	(.1)	(.2)
Other income	.5	.3
Income (loss) before taxes	9.7	(.9)
Income taxes (benefit)	4.0	(1.2)
Net income	5.7%	.3%

EXHIBIT **OshKosh B'Gosh Graphic Depiction of Common-Size Income Statements**

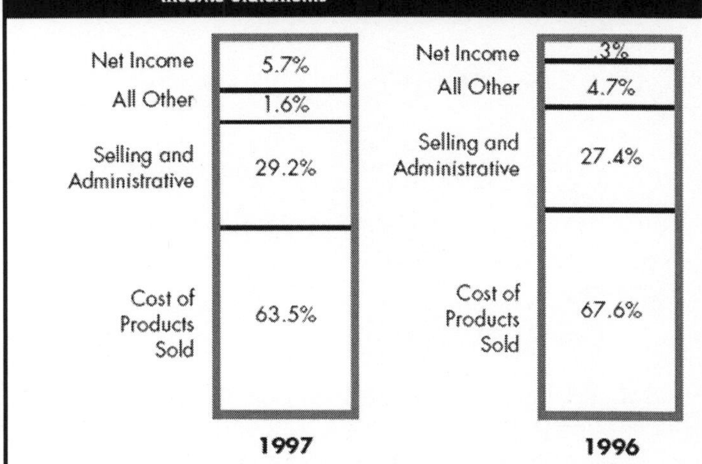

TREND ANALYSIS

Trend analysis involves comparing financial statement numbers over time. One way to implement this is to compare the common-size income statement items over time. The trends in OB's cost of goods sold percentage and its gross profit percentage are favourable. For example, the cost of goods sold percentage decreased from 67.6% in 1996 to 63.5% in 1997. This decrease could reflect decreases in the prices of raw materials, increased demand for its products (allowing an increase in selling prices) or efficiencies in the manufacturing process.

The trend in selling, general, and administrative expenses as a percentage of net sales is not favourable. They have increased from 27.4% of sales to 29.2% of sales. However, the total dollar amount of these costs has declined. Both operating income and net income show very desirable trends. However, if OB's special charge is not expected to recur, the operating income percentage and net income percentage should be adjusted for purposes of assessing performance and forecasting future results.

To adjust the 1996 operating income percentage, the special charge should be added to operating income because it has already been subtracted in arriving at that number.

$$\text{Adjusted operating income percentagae} = \frac{\text{Operating income} + \text{Special charge}}{\text{Net sales}}$$

$$= \frac{-₹4,584 + ₹32,900}{₹444,766} = 6.4\%$$

Because net income is an after-tax figure, the adjusted net income percentage must be modified on an after-tax basis.

The after-tax effect of the special charge was ₹15,200,000. The after-tax cost is smaller than the pre-tax cost of ₹32,900,000 because it reflects the benefit of a reduction in taxes due to the loss. The adjustment is accomplished by adding the ₹15,200,000 after-tax loss to net income.

$$\text{Adjusted net income percentage} = \frac{\text{Net income} + \text{After-tax special charge}}{\text{Net sales}}$$

$$= \frac{₹1,119 + ₹15,200}{₹444,766} = 3.7\%$$

Using these adjusted percentages for 1996 as a benchmark, OB's performance in 1997 has still improved, but not to the degree as the unadjusted percentages indicated.

HORIZONTAL ANALYSIS

Horizontal analysis is another form of trend analysis. It uses the figures from a prior year's income statement as the basis for calculating percentage increases and decreases over time. A horizontal analysis of OB's income statements. The figures in the exhibit are obtained by dividing the items in the 1997 income statement by their corresponding amounts in the 1996 income statement. The exhibit shows that net sales decreased 11.1% (100%–88.9%) between 1996 and 1997. A decrease in sales is often a cause of major concern. A sales decline could reflect a decrease in sales activity (number of units sold) or a decrease in unit selling prices. Either of these causes could have adverse effects on profitability.

Additional research regarding OB indicates that the sales decline was due primarily to two other factors. *First,* OB intentionally adopted the strategy of reducing its reliance on wholesalers, who are intermediaries that purchase the company's products and resell them to retail vendors, such as department stores.

OB concluded that its relationship with certain wholesalers was not sufficiently profitable to warrant continuation. The other major reason for the decline in sales was that OB discontinued its own European operations, which had a negative effect on sales. To replace these operations, however, OB granted a license to another organization that is more familiar with the European market. The license permits this organization to sell OB products in exchange for royalty payments.

Royalty income increased by 30%. Thus, OB's strategy was to trade the profit generated by its own European operations for the royalty income generated by its licensee. The strategies of OB that affected sales should also have impacted expenses. Cost of products sold is the largest single expense item. This item declined 16.5% (100%–83.5%) from 1996 to 1997. The decrease in cost of products sold is larger than the decrease in sales (11.1%).

This suggests that the actions taken by OB will have a positive effect on profitability. The decline in cost of products sold is also attributable to two other reasons; OB was able to find less expensive sources of raw materials, and OB improved the efficiency of its manufacturing operations. The latter was accomplished, in part, by plant closings, the costs of which were contained in the 1996 income statement. Also note that the decline in cost of products sold relative to sales is consistent with the results of the common-size income statements that showed that the cost of products sold had decreased as a percentage of sales.

The percentage change in operating income for 1997 is not available. This is due to the fact that an operating loss was generated in 1996 and operating income was generated in 1997. Although the 1997 figure can be calculated (36,887/–4,584–805%), care must be exercised when dealing with negative numbers. The negative denominator yields a negative percentage, yet the income in 1997 is much more positive than the 1996 loss. Even if absolute values are used, knowing that the 1997 operating income is eight times as large as the 1996 operating loss is not particularly insightful. Regardless of the difficulties with this calculation, the trend in operating income is extremely favourable.

EXHIBIT Horizontal Analysis of Income Statements

OshKosh B'Gosh
Income Statements—Horizontal Analysis

	Year Ended December 31,	
	1997	1996
Net sales	88.9%	100%
Cost of products sold	83.5	100
Gross profit	100.1	100
Selling, general, and administrative expenses	94.6	100
Special charges and plant closings	—	100
Royalty income, net	130.2	100
Operating income	NA	100
Interest expense	28.0	100
Other income	101.9	100
Income before taxes	NA	100
Income taxes	NA	100
Net income	2,015.9%	100%

NA = Not available

The trend in net income is also quite favourable. Net income in 1997 is 20 times greater than 1996 net income. This result underscores another pitfall in calculating ratios: the small denominator problem. The large percentage increase is not primarily due to 1997 being so superlative. Rather, the small net income generated in 1996 has the effect of inflating the calculated value. Although net income improved substantially in 1997, a percentage increase of 2,015.9% probably overstates the improvement.

OTHER RATIOS

Several ratios link the income statement and the balance sheet. Return on shareholders' equity (ROE) is of utmost importance to shareholders. To calculate ROE, divide net income by average shareholders' equity:

$$\text{ROE} = \frac{\text{Net income}}{\text{Average shareholder equity}}$$

ROE relates the earnings generated by a firm to the assets invested by its shareholders. It is obviously in the shareholders' best interest to have larger earnings generated on their investments. A potential investor, faced with competing investment choices, will use ROE to help identify the preferred investment. The denominator of ROE is average shareholders' equity. Because net income is earned over the course of a year, it makes sense to use the firm's average shareholders' equity during the year. As a practical matter, average shareholders' equity is usually calculated by averaging beginning and end-of-year shareholders' equity amounts, which are found on the balance sheet. OB's 1997 ROE is:

$$\text{ROE} = \frac{₹22,558}{(₹138,077 + ₹113,157)/2} = 18.0\%$$

A ROE of 18% is very close to OB's industry average. The 1997 ROE compares extremely favourably to the 1996 ROE of .8%.

EXHIBIT Summary of Selected Information

OshKosh B'Gosh
Selected Balance Sheet Information
(Dollars in thousands)

	1997	1996
Total shareholders' equity	₹113,157	₹138,077
Total assets	₹217,211	₹229,131

Another important ratio is return on assets (ROA). This ratio relates a firm's earnings to all the assets the firm has available to generate those earnings. ROA differs from ROE in that ROE utilizes only the assets that the shareholders supplied. ROE measures management's success in using the assets invested by shareholders, whereas ROA measures how successfully management utilized all the assets entrusted to it. To calculate ROA, divide net income, adjusted for interest expense, by average total assets:

$$\text{ROA} = \frac{\text{Net income} + \text{Interest expense}\left(1 - \text{tax rate}\right)}{\text{Average total assets}}$$

Why is interest expense added to net income in the numerator? A firm can acquire assets from two sources: owners and creditors. Interest expense is a cost incurred to acquire assets from creditors (*e.g.*, interest expense on bank borrowings). It arises from a financing decision (obtaining funds from creditors rather than owners), not an operating decision (utilizing assets). Because ROA is designed to measure managers' success in utilizing assets, interest expense is irrelevant. Its effect on net income should be eliminated when calculating ROA.

Interest expense has direct and indirect effects on net income, and both effects should be eliminated. Regarding the direct effect, because interest expense has already been subtracted in calculating net income, it is now added back. The indirect effect relates to taxes. Because interest expense is a deduction for tax purposes, tax expense is lower and net income is higher by an amount equal to interest expense multiplied by the tax rate.

Therefore, to adjust fully for the elimination of interest expense, net income must be increased by interest expense and decreased by interest expense multiplied by the tax rate. The difference between these two amounts is interest expense multiplied by 1 minus the tax rate):

$$\begin{array}{rl} + & \text{Interest expense} \\ - & \text{Interest expense} \times \text{tax rate} \\ \hline & \text{Interest expense} \times \left(1 - \text{tax rate}\right) \end{array}$$

Eliminating the effects of interest expense facilitates the comparison of asset utilization across firms that have different amounts of debt. Financial statements disclose, in the notes, firms' tax rates. OB's effective rate in 1997 was 40.9% and its ROA for 1997 was

$$\text{ROE} = \frac{₹22,558 + ₹305(1-.409)}{(₹196,033 + ₹174,788)/2} = 12.3\%$$

OB's 1997 ROA greatly exceeds its performance in 1996. The dramatic improvements in OB's ROE and ROA reflect the success of its operational changes. The final ratio discussed in this part is times interest earned. Because profits ultimately are a source of cash, and because cash is necessary for the payment of interest charges, creditors are concerned about the relationship between profits and interest expense. The times interest earned ratio shows how many times interest expense is covered by resources generated from operations, and creditors prefer higher times interest earned ratios. It is calculated by dividing earnings before interest and taxes by interest expense:

$$\text{Time interest earned} = \frac{\text{Earning before interest and taxes}}{\text{Interest expense}}$$

Earnings before interest and taxes, not net income, is used in the numerator. Because interest expense is already deducted in calculating net income, net income understates the resources available to cover interest expense.

Tax expense should not reduce the numerator because, in a worst case scenario, as income declines, taxes would be eliminated. OB's income statement does not contain a line item for income before interest and taxes. The easiest way to calculate this figure, given OB's income statement format, is to add interest expense to income before taxes.

In 1997, OB's income before interest and taxes would be determined as follows:

Income before taxes	₹38,187,000
Interest expense	305,000
Income before interest and taxes	₹38,492,000

OB's 1997 times interest earned ratio is 126.2:

$$\text{Times interest earned} = \frac{₹38,492}{₹305} = 126.2$$

This ratio indicates that interest expense is covered 126.2 times at present income levels. This is an outstanding ratio and reflects that OB has little outstanding debt. Given that potential creditors would look very favourably on a ratio this large, OB would likely have little problem securing additional financing, if it so desires.

LIMITATIONS OF ACCOUNTING INCOME

Although financial statement readers find reported accounting income very useful, it does have several limitations. Conceptually, we often think of income as an increase in wealth. If our bank account grows by ₹100 because of interest, we feel as though our income is ₹100. For many assets, however, accounting does not recognize an increase in value when it occurs. Instead, the value increase and the associated income are recognized at the time of the asset's disposal. Sometimes the difference between historical cost and current value can be quite large. Consider Hiroshi Fujishige, who owns a 58-acre farm across the street from Disneyland. The farm was purchased in 1953 for ₹2,500. Southern California real estate experts estimate its value to be ₹55,000,000.

In spite of this estimate, the Fujishige Farm balance sheet reflects the land at ₹2,500, and the increase in value has not appeared on any of Fujishige's income statements. In general, to recognize a value increase, accounting rules require the occurrence of a transaction for verification purposes. Financial statements do not reflect still other accomplishments of a firm. For example, the Wall Street Journal reported that the Food and Drug Administration planned to approve an anticlotting drug developed by COR Therapeutics, Inc. This was extremely good news for COR; in fact, its stock soared 79% on the news. However, this event was not included in its accounting records when the announcement was made. At that time, COR had not engaged in any transaction; no sales had been made. The financial statement effects of the drug sales will be recognized in the accounting records as they occur. Accounting's conservatism principle can also limit the extent to which accounting income reflects changes in wealth.

This principle states that when doubt exists about the accounting treatment for a given transaction, a conservative alternative should be selected. In other words, select the alternative that reports lower asset values and lower net income. For example, expenditures for research and development are immediately expensed, even when they result in valuable products or patents. Spending on employee training is expensed immediately, even though its objective is to create a more highly skilled workforce.

These examples suggest that the balance sheets of some companies may have undervalued or unrecorded assets; this, of course, implies that the net income figure on the income statement does not necessarily reflect changes in wealth. On the other hand, most accountants support the conservatism principle because it helps avoid overly optimistic financial statements.

In summary, to ensure that reliable and verifiable financial statements emerge from the accounting process, GAAP precludes the recognition of certain potential value changes. Because of this, accounting income does not strictly measure changes in wealth. However, it is a very useful performance measure on which the business community relies heavily.

ACCOUNTING INCOME AND ECONOMIC CONSEQUENCES

The managers of many publicly-held corporations receive bonuses that are based on reported accounting net income. These bonus plans typically include a floor and a ceiling. The floor requires that net income must reach a certain level before the bonus is activated, while the ceiling places a limit on the size of the bonus.

That is, the bonus is not increased as net income increases above the ceiling. Thus, managers prefer that net income falls at the high end of the range between the floor and the ceiling. Bonuses can motivate managers to undertake actions that will improve the operations of the firm, thereby increasing profits. Unfortunately, bonuses can also motivate managers to make accounting-related decisions that do not affect the underlying profitability of the firm, but that do affect reported accounting income.

For example, firms occasionally engage in big baths. These are accounting decisions that result in large losses in a single year. If reported earnings would otherwise have been below a bonus plan's floor, such losses have no effect on the current year's bonus. Moreover, by taking the losses all at one time, subsequent periods are relieved of those charges, and the chances of higher reported profits and bonuses in the future are maximized. The actions taken by Waste Management are within the bounds of allowable managerial discretion.

Other corporations, however, have been accused of much more questionable actions. For example, Miniscribe, a bankrupt disk-drive manufacturer, is alleged to have recognized revenue prematurely on shipments that customers had not ordered, improperly estimated uncollectible accounts receivable, and falsified inventory. The application of GAAP requires the exercise of judgment. At the same time, manager's self-interest is affected by reported accounting income. Accordingly, financial statement users should not be surprised that managers' self-interests influence their accounting policy judgments. As a result, financial statements may not be unbiased reflections about the underlying economic activities of firms.

7

The Balance Sheet

INTRODUCTION

This stage focuses solely on the balance sheet, which is often called the statement of financial position. Beginning with formal definitions of the basic elements of the balance sheet, the discussion describes the types of assets, liabilities, and owners' equity that are found on the balance sheets of most business firms. A variety of balance sheet ratios are presented to show how managers and investors use balance sheet information in making decisions.

ELEMENTS OF THE BALANCE SHEET

The previous two stages introduced you to the three basic financial statements. They showed how transactions and other events affecting business firms cause changes in the elements reported in the financial statements. This stage focuses solely on the balance sheet, which is often called the statement of financial position. At any given date, the balance sheet shows the sources from which the firm has obtained its resources and the ways in which those resources are currently employed. The basic accounting equation:

ASSETS = LIABILITIES + OWNERS' EQUITY

Another way to state this relationship is,

Uses of resources = Sources of resources

In other words, liabilities and owners' equity are the sources from which the firm has obtained its funds, and the listing of assets shows the way in which the firm's managers have put those funds to work. This relationship is showed as follows, based on the balance sheet for Sample Company at the end of 2000.

Uses of resources	=	Sources of resources
Assets	=	Liabilities + Owners' Equity
₹2,057,000	=	₹1,199,000 + ₹858,000
₹2,057,000	=	₹2,057,000

Viewed in this manner, there is no mystery to the fact that both sides of the balance sheet have the same total; they are merely two sides of a single coin, or two ways of describing the total wealth of the firm. The firm's wealth can be viewed in terms of sources of financing (from creditors and owners) and in terms of uses of resources (owning or controlling assets).

EXHIBIT A Balance Sheet

Sample Company Balance Sheet
at December 31,2000

Assets			Liabilities and Owners' Equity		
Current assets			Current liabilities		
Case	₹110,000		Accounts payable	₹260,000	
Accounts Receivable	466,000		Notes payable	225,000	
Inventories	812,000		Warranry obligations	112,000	
Prepaid expenses	32,000		Accrued expenses	75,000	
Total current assets		₹1,420,000	Taxes payable	27,000	
Noncurrent assets			Total current liabilities		₹ 699,000
Land	₹ 85,000		Noncurrent liabilities		
Buildings and equipment (net of accumulated depreciation of ₹313,000)	552,000		Bond payable	₹350,000	
			Martgage payable	150,000	
			Total noncurrent liabilities		500,000
			Total liabilities		₹1,199,000
Total noncurrent assets		637,000	Shareholders' equity		
			Paid-in capital	₹600,000	
			Retained earnings	258,000	
			Total shareholders' equity		858,000
Total assets		₹2,057,000	Total liabilities and Shareholders' equity		₹2,057,000

Another useful way to view the balance sheet is as the cumulative result of the firm's past activities. Liabilities represent the total amount the firm has borrowed during its existence, minus the amounts that have been repaid to date.

The owners' equity items show the total amount invested by owners, plus the total profits earned by the firm during previous periods, minus any amounts that have been distributed to owners. Similarly, the assets of the firm represent the total resources obtained by the firm from lenders and owners, minus those that have been consumed in the firm's operations, repaid to lenders, or distributed to owners.

DEFINITIONS OF ASSETS, LIABILITIES, AND OWNERS' EQUITY

The Financial Accounting Standards Board (FASB) has identified the essential characteristics of assets, liabilities, and owners' equity. The FASB definitions, "The Basic Concepts of Financial Accounting," and are summarized in Exhibit, provide a frame of reference that helps accountants identify the items to be included in the balance sheet.

For now, note that just as to the FASB's definitions, assets represent future benefits, liabilities represent future sacrifices, and owners' equity is the residual amount, or difference, between assets and liabilities. The following sides introduce you to the types of individual assets, liabilities, and owners' equity to be found on the balance sheets of most business firms. In studying these individual balance sheet items, keep in mind the FASB's definitions shown in Exhibit.

FASB DEFINITIONS OF ASSETS, LIABILITIES, AND OWNERS' EQUITY

Assets are probable future economic benefits obtained or controlled by a particaular entity as a result of past transaction or events. Liabilities are probable future sacrifices of economic benefits arising from present obligation of a particular entity or provide services to other entities in the future as a result of past transaction or events. Equity is the residual interest in the assets of an entity that remains after deducting liabities. In a business enterprise, the equity is the ownership interest.

Source: Statement of Financial Accounting Concepts No. 6, "Elements of Financial Statements" (Stamford, CT: FASB, 1980).

ASSETS

Assets represent "probable future economic benefits obtained or controlled by a particular entity as a result of past transactions or events." Future economic benefits come in many forms. For example, cash is an asset because it represents purchasing power; the firm can use cash to acquire goods and services, to repay debts, or to make distributions to owners. Inventories are assets because they are merchandise intended for sale to customers for cash and other assets.

The firm's buildings and equipment are assets because they enable the firm to perform its operations and to earn profits in the future. Assets typically represent tangible economic resources, such as cash, buildings, and trucks. On the other hand, some economic resources are intangible, such as patent rights and copyrights to a text or musical score. Assets may also be represented by promises of future payments from customers who bought goods or services on credit. Assets can be created by contract or acquisition of property rights, and yet they may not be visible to the human eye. All assets, however, have a common characteristic in that they represent probable future economic benefits to the firm.

Asset Classifications

Assets are classified into two overall categories: current assets and non–current assets. This distinction is based on the length of time before the asset is expected to be consumed or converted to cash. Current assets include cash and other assets that will typically become cash or be consumed in one year or one operating cycle, whichever is longer. Current assets are used quickly and repeatedly during a firm's normal operations.

This notion of using assets on a cyclical basis corresponds to a concept called turnover. Current assets turn over quickly, anywhere from daily to annually, and are usually generated in the normal course of business operations. The notion of turnover is used to differentiate current assets from other asset categories that are used (turn over) much more slowly over a number of years. To show, Sample Company's balance sheet shows that the firm's total assets of ₹2,057,000 are comprised of ₹1,420,000 in current assets and ₹637,000 in non-current assets. The balance sheet equation is easily expanded to show this additional detail:

Assets		=	Liabilities	+	Owners's Equity
Current	Non–current				
₹1,420,000 +	₹637,000	=	₹ 1,199,000	+	₹ 858,000
₹–2,057,000		=	₹2,057,000		

This classification of assets is useful to the analyst concerned with the liquidity of the firm. Liquidity reflects the ability of the firm to generate sufficient cash to meet its operating cash needs and to pay its obligations as they become due. This focus on liquidity will become clear as we discuss the ordering and valuation of individual current assets in the next part.

Current Assets

Current assets are listed in the order in which they are expected to be consumed or converted to cash. For example, Sample Company's current assets are listed in the following typical order of maturity or collectibility:

- Cash and cash equivalents,
- Accounts receivable,
- Inventories, and
- Prepaid expenses.

Cash and cash equivalents include currency, bank deposits, and various marketable securities that can be turned into cash on short notice merely by contacting a bank or broker. These amounts are presently available to meet the firm's cash payment requirements. Note that only securities that are purchased within 90 days of their maturity dates, or are scheduled to be converted to cash within the next 90 days, may be classified as cash equivalents.

Accounts receivable represent credit sales that have not been collected yet. They are converted into cash as soon as the customers or clients pay their bills (their accounts). Accounts receivable should turn over, or be collected, within the firm's normal collection period, which is usually 30 or 60 days. A slower accounts receivable turnover embodies more risk to the organization because the probability of nonpayment usually increases as turnover decreases.

Overdue accounts may imply that the customer is either unable to pay or is unwilling to pay because of disagreement over the amounts billed. Both cases imply that the amount of cash that will ultimately be collected is less than the amount originally billed to the customer. Managers are interested less in the total amount of accounts receivable than in the estimated cash to be generated from collections of the accounts. For this reason, accounts receivable are listed on the balance sheet at the amounts estimated to be actually collectible. This amount is termed the net realizable value of the receivables. For example, if management estimates that some portion of the amounts billed to customers will ultimately be uncollectible, then the estimated uncollectible portion will be deducted in valuing the accounts receivable on the balance sheet.

The uncollectible portion of the receivables is termed an allowance account, "Current Assets". Inventory represents items that have been purchased or manufactured for sale to customers. That is, inventory can either be created through the manufacturing and assembly efforts of the organization or be acquired from others and held for resale.

Inventory is the "stuff of commerce" dating back to merchants on camels and pirates raiding the high seas looking for bounty. Inventory can be as prosaic as black tea or salt, or it can be as glamorous as gold bullion or silver coins. Today, inventory is often "high tech," such as silicon wafers, memory chips, or disk drives. Should the company discover that some of its inventory is unsalable, or marketable only at a greatly reduced price, the reported value of the inventory should be reduced accordingly.

Prepaid expenses, the final category of current assets, represents unexpired assets such as insurance premiums. Insurance policies, for example, are frequently paid ahead on an annual basis. The unexpired portion, the portion of the policy paid for but not yet used, is shown as part of prepaid expenses, which are interpreted as current assets. Prepaids are usually minor elements of the balance sheet, and, in the usual course of events, prepaids will not be converted or turned into cash. Instead, the rights to future benefits will be used up in future periods.

The Operating Cycle and Liquidity

Manufacturing and merchandising firms' operating cycles include turning inventory into cash. Using three of the current assets discussed earlier, the operating cycle evolves from the purchase of inventory, to the exchange of inventory for a promised payment by a customer (an account receivable), and finally to the conversion of the receivable into cash.

Operating cycles may vary in length from just a few days (in the case of food retailers) to months (consumer appliance sellers) or even years (defence contractors). The operating cycle. The more quickly this cycle is completed, the more quickly the inventory is turned into cash, and liquidity is higher. When the operating cycle becomes longer, the firm's liquidity usually is lower.

Should the operating cycle become too long, the firm will be forced to incur debt in order to pay its suppliers of inventory. To some extent, the length of the operating cycle is outside management's control. The length of time permitted customers to pay their accounts, for example, may be governed by industry practice. To attract and retain customers, the firm may need to offer credit terms as liberal as those offered by its competitors.

EXHIBIT The Operating Cycle

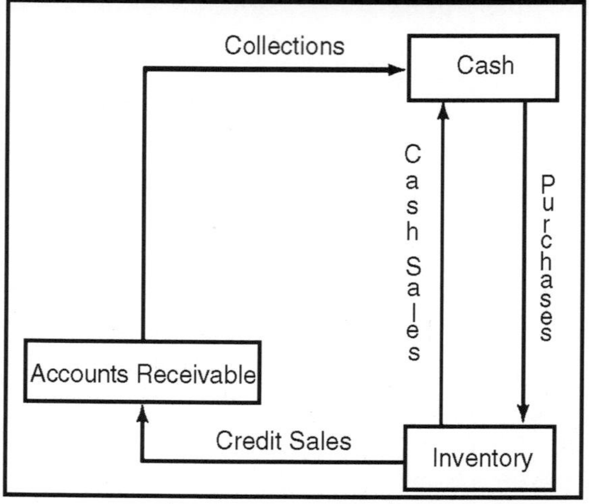

Likewise, the amount of inventory that the firm keeps on hand may be related to the length of its "production pipeline". Some products require a lengthy production process that entails a substantial investment in inventory at various stages of completion.

On the other hand, the turnover of accounts receivable and inventory may be influenced by management. For instance, managers may have considerable leeway in of fering credit terms to customers or in deciding how much inventory to keep on hand. The analyst, in attempting to assess the firm's liquidity, needs to understand these underlying factors that cause differences in the amounts of accounts receivable and inventories across firms and industries. The composition of current assets differs for two firms engaged in different industries.

Non–current Assets

Non-current assets are long-term assets that are used in the conduct of the business. Whereas current assets are liquid and turn over in relatively short time periods, non-current assets usually turn over very slowly, on the order of once in several years. In other words, while the operating cycle for current assets is usually less than a year, the replacement cycle for non-current assets is longer than a year.

In a high-tech organization, however, some non-current assets may be replaced more frequently. All non-current assets are recorded on the balance sheet at their historical acquisition costs. The disadvantage of this is that as time passes the historical costs of many non-current assets become out of date relative to their current market values. Consequently, they indicate little about the market value of the organization and about the future resources necessary to replace the assets. However, the historical costs listed on the balance sheet do represent the costs of these assets that will eventually be consumed by future operations.

Property, Plant, and Equipment

For most firms, non-current assets consist mainly of property, plant, and equipment. These assets are widely referred to as fixed assets. Property usually represents the land on which the firm's offices, factories, and other facilities are located. In most cases, property is a relatively minor portion of the total non-current assets, yet in some cases, such as firms engaged in mining, logging, or oil and gas exploration, property constitutes a major operating asset. Property is also valued on the balance sheet at its historical acquisition cost, and because property is usually one of the oldest assets held by an organization, its recorded historical cost is often the most out of date in terms of current market values.

Buildings and equipment represent the largest category of non-current assets. Buildings or plant may be office, retail, or factory buildings; warehouses or supply depots; or hospitals or health clinics. Equipment includes office desks and chairs, tools, drill presses, robots, computers, X-ray and other scanners, podiums, and so on. In other words, buildings and equipment are the primary productive assets of many organizations.

Whether widgets or rings are produced, whether knowledge or health is improved, buildings and equipment are necessary to produce most goods and services. Because buildings and equipment are long-lived assets, it would not make sense to treat their entire cost as expenses in the year they are acquired. On the other hand, because buildings and equipment gradually lose their economic value over time, it does not make sense to wait until the end of their service lives to recognize their declining usefulness to the firm. As a consequence, accountants gradually and systematically reduce the reported values of buildings and equipment on successive balance sheets in order to allocate expenses to individual years of asset use.

The reduction in the reported value of buildings and equipment during a period is called depreciation expense. On the balance sheet, the total amount of depreciation expense recognized to that date is called accumulated depreciation. It is subtracted from the initial cost of the asset. The resulting carrying value is referred to as the net book value of the asset. In The net book value of ₹552,000 for buildings and equipment is calculated by subtracting the ₹313,000 of accumulated depreciation from the original cost of ₹865,000:

Building and equipment	₹865,000
Less: Accumulated depreciation	–313,000
Net book value	₹552,000

In other words, of the original cost of ₹865,000, a total of ₹313,000 has been expensed, or written off, in previous periods. The net book value of these assets is unlikely to reflect their current resale value because of changes in technology, price inflation, and many other factors.

Accumulated depreciation is not an attempt to adjust carrying values to current resale values. It also does not represent any cash or other investments that the company has set aside for replacing the buildings and equipment. Rather, depreciating an asset is an attempt to apportion or allocate its original cost as an expense to the periods that benefit from the asset's use.

The net book value of buildings and equipment can be used to estimate the remaining productive capacity of the organization. For example, Sample Company's buildings and equipment are about 36% depreciated (₹313,000 accumulated depreciation divided by ₹865,000 initial cost). If Sample Company does not purchase additional buildings and equipment, then each successive balance sheet will show a lower net book value for these assets.

Such a declining net book value will signal to analysts that Sample Company is not replenishing its productive capacity on a regular basis. As a practical matter, most firms regularly invest in new plant and equipment and, as a result, the net book value of these assets usually increases over time. The percentage relationships between the initial cost and the accumulated depreciation of these assets may give analysts a rough gauge of the overall age of the firm's productive capacity. However, the analyst must usually refer to other disclosures in the financial statements to evaluate the firm's productive capacity.

Other Non-current Assets

In addition to property, plant, and equipment, many firms possess other non-current assets such as intangibles. Intangibles are non-current assets that lack physical substance and yet are important resources in the regular operations of a business. Intangibles often consist of legal rights, such as patents or copyrights. Such legal rights are vital to the operations of many firms and, in some cases, may be the most valuable resources owned by the organization. Consider, for example, the importance of copyrights to computer software developers or book publishers. The value of such firms depends almost entirely on the value of the copyrights that protect their legal rights to the products they have developed.

Accounting for intangible assets is similar to that of buildings and equipment because the initial costs are systematically recognized as expenses over the years that benefit from the use of the assets. Intangible assets are valued on the balance sheet at their historical costs, minus any amounts subsequently recognized as expenses. The term amortization is used in place of depreciation when referring to the consumption of intangible assets. Another important type of intangible asset is goodwill. Goodwill is a general label used by accountants to denote the economic value of an acquired firm in excess of the value of its identifiable net assets (assets minus liabilities). Goodwill reflects the adage that "the value of the whole differs from the sum of its parts." This economic value is largely due to factors such as customer loyalty, employee competence and morale, management expertise, and so on. In other words, the value of a successful business firm is usually much greater than the total values of its individual assets. The balance sheet recognition of good will depends on whether the firm's goodwill is internally generated or externally acquired. Internally generated goodwill evolves gradually as the firm develops a good reputation and customer base.

It also evolves as the firm cultivates successful relationships with its suppliers, trains and retains a skilled labour force, and conducts other value-enhancing activities. The costs incurred in generating this goodwill are generally not recorded as assets by the firm and instead are recognized as expenses when incurred.

The argument used to support the immediate expensing of these costs is the uncertainty and subjectivity involved in identifying future benefits. Externally acquired goodwill, on the other hand, usually arises when one business firm acquires another. In this case, the amount that the purchaser is paying for the goodwill of the seller can be more objectively determined by appraisers. "Reporting Issues for Affiliated and International Companies," which deals with various business combinations. The composition of non-current assets, and the relative amounts of current to non-current assets, varies across industries. Non-current assets differ between two firms in different industries.

Assets: Summary and Evaluation

Before leaving the asset side of the balance sheet, it is helpful to summarize the conventions used by accountants to define and value the firm's assets. We also identify here some of the limitations faced by analysts who must use asset values shown in the balance sheet to evaluate the firm's liquidity and productive capacity. As we have seen, accountants classify assets into two broad groups: current and non-current. In reporting current assets, the focus is on liquidity. For this reason, current assets are generally valued at the lower of their acquisition costs or present resale values. An exception to this rule is made for investments in the securities of other firms. These practices are useful to the analyst concerned with the ability of the firm to meet its short-term cash needs.

Non-current assets, on the other hand, are generally valued at their acquisition costs minus amounts that have been recognized as expenses in previous periods. These previously recognized expenses will have been shown as depreciation of buildings and equipment or as amortization of intangibles such as patents or good will. In reporting non-current assets, the focus is on the operating capacity of the firm; that is, the firm must focus on the structure of its long-lived assets, both tangible and intangible, which are necessary in order for the firm to produce goods or services.

The carrying values of these non-current assets represent the portion of their original acquisition costs that will be recognized as expenses in future periods. The carrying values of non-current assets rarely reflect their market values because inflation has usually caused asset replacement costs to increase beyond their reported values.

The experienced financial statement analyst is alert to two central issues in examining a firm's asset structure as reported on the balance sheet:

- Different valuation methods are used for various types of assets (cost, market values, lower of cost or market value).
- Many assets that are critical to the firm's successful operations are not shown on the balance sheet.

With respect to these "missing" assets, chief executive officers (CEOs) are fond of proclaiming:

- "Our employees are our most important resource."
- "Research today provides profits tomorrow."
- "Our reputation for quality ensures our success."

Regardless of these lofty statements, resources such as employee morale, productivity, research and development expertise, and a loyal and satisfied network of customers and suppliers are absent from the balance sheet. Accountants justify these omissions either because these valuable resources do not meet the conditions stated in the FASB's definition of assets or because there is no reliable method for measuring or valuing such resources.

LIABILITIES

Liabilities represent "probable future sacrifices of economic benefits" that are the result of past transactions or events. Many times they entail cash payments to other entities, such as repayment to lenders of amounts that have been previously borrowed. The concept of a liability is somewhat broader than this. Liabilities include any probable obligation that the firm has incurred as a consequence of its past activities. For example, many firms warranty their products and consequently are obliged to perform repairs or pay refunds when defects are later uncovered, so, as you can see, not all liabilities require that the firm repay specific dollar amounts on specified dates. Moreover, some liabilities require estimation and judgment in order to determine their amounts. All liabilities, however, have a common characteristic: They represent probable future economic sacrifices by the firm.

Liability Classifications

Just as with assets, liabilities are classified into two overall categories: current liabilities and non-current liabilities. The distinction is based on the length of time before the liability is expected to be repaid or otherwise satisfied by the firm and on whether payment will require the use of assets that are classified as current. Current liabilities are short-term obligations that are expected to utilize cash or other current assets within a year or an operating cycle, whichever is longer. Non-current liabilities represent obligations that generally require payment over periods longer than a year. To show, Sample Company's balance sheet shows that the firm's total liabilities of ₹1,199,000 are comprised of ₹699,000 in current liabilities and ₹500,000 in non-current liabilities. The following balance sheet equation shows this additional detail:

Assets		=	Liabilities		+	Owners' Equity
Current	Non–current		Current	Non–current		
₹1,420,000 +	₹637,000	=	₹699,000 +	₹500,000	+	₹858,000
₹2,057,000		=		₹2,057,000		

Current Liabilities

The current liabilities of Sample Company, consist of accounts payable, notes payable, warranty obligations, accrued expenses, and taxes payable. These liabilities represent various claims against the firm's economic resources. Accounts payable usually represents debts that the firm incurs in purchasing inventories and supplies for manufacturing or resale purposes. Accounts payable also includes amounts that the firm owes for other services used in its operations, such as rentals, insurance, utilities, and so on. Accounts payable are often called trade debt because they represent debt that occurs in the normal course of any trade or business.

Notes payable, the next current liability are more formal current liabilities than the accounts payable. A note may be signed on the borrowing of cash from a local bank. The note represents a legal document that a court can force the firm to satisfy. Warranty obligations represent the firm's estimated future costs to fulfill its obligations for repair or refund guarantees. These obligations refer to any products sold or services provided prior to the balance sheet date. Unlike accounts and notes payable, the exact amount of the firm's obligations for warranties cannot be determined by referring to purchase documents, formal contracts, or similar evidence.

Instead, the amount reported for the warranty obligation is based on management's judgment about future claims for repairs and refunds that may arise from past sales. The amount reported is an estimate, based in part on the past experience of the firm and its competitors. The FASB defines liabilities in terms of "probable future economic sacrifices". If Sample Company's products have required warranty repairs in the past, then it is probable that items sold recently will also require warranty repairs in the future. Because the sales have already occurred, the obligation exists at the balance sheet date, and these estimated amounts must be reported as liabilities. The next item listed among Sample Company's current liabilities is accrued expenses, which represent liabilities for services already consumed but not yet paid for or included elsewhere in liabilities. These accrued liabilities usually constitute only a minor part of current liabilities. Taxes payable comprise the final account listed among the current liabilities of Sample Company. Taxes payable represents unpaid taxes that are owed to the government and will be paid within a year.

Taxes payable may include employee withholding taxes, unemployment taxes, employer income taxes, or any number of other taxes that are incurred in the normal course of operations. Taxes payable are typically a relatively minor portion of current liabilities because governmental units require that taxes be paid on a timely basis.

The current liabilities of Sample Company are a representative sample of many short-term liabilities. Businesses engage in many credit-based transactions; most sales to businesses involve accounts receivable, and most purchases by businesses correspondingly involve accounts payable. As a result, the largest of the current liabilities usually consists of trade accounts payable. The other liability items, although less significant in dollar amount, also represent common business transactions and circumstances.

Non-current Liabilities

Non-current liabilities generally have longer maturities than the current liabilities discussed in the preceding part. Their maturity date is more than one year. Most non-current liabilities represent contracts to repay debts at specified future dates. In addition, these borrowing agreements often place some restrictions on the activities of the firm until the debt is fully repaid. We discuss a variety of different borrowing arrangements that are widely used. Sample Company has two types of non-current liabilities: bonds payable and mortgage payable. These liabilities are similar because they require Sample Company to make future payments of interest and principal. Yet they differ in terms of the collateral that Sample Company used to obtain the loan. Bonds payable are a major source of funds for larger business firms.

They represent liabilities that the firm incurs by selling a contract called a bond. A bond contains the firm's promise to pay interest periodically (usually every six months) and to repay the money originally borrowed (principal) when the bond matures. The amount of money that the firm receives from investors for its bonds depends on investors' views about the riskiness of the firm and the prevailing rate of interest. Investors rely on the ability of the firm to generate sufficient cash flows from its operations to meet the payments as they become due. Mortgage payable is similar to bonds payable because firms must also make principal and interest payments as they are due. Unlike most bonds, a mortgage represents a pledge of certain assets that will revert to the lender if the debt is not paid. The simplest example of a mortgage is that of a bank holding title to your house until your loan is fully paid. If the loan is not paid, the bank can sell the house and use the proceeds to pay off the debt. Mortgages on factories and hospitals are very similar. The problem in such cases is that there are often very few buyers of specialized assets such as factory buildings and equipment. In such cases, possible mortgage default represents more risk and higher costs to lenders.

It also indicates that most lenders will cooperate with borrowers to find alternative solutions to avoid defaults. From an analytical perspective, the analyst or manager must make sure that mortgage terms are being satisfied and that payments have been promptly remitted. For both bonds and mortgages, analysts will try to discern whether cash flows from operations are sufficient to pay the interest and principal.

Liabilities: Summary and Evaluation

Before leaving the liabilities or "borrowed resources" part of the balance sheet, it is useful to summarize various liabilities and to point out some limitations faced by analysts in assessing the firm's liabilities. Liabilities are classified as either current or non-current, based on their maturity dates. The current liabilities of the firm are closely related to its operations. As examples, trade accounts payable arise as a direct consequence of purchasing inventory; accrued expenses and taxes payable result from the firm's operating and tax expenses; and product warranty obligations occur because the firm has sold products covered by warranties.

For this reason, analysts often refer to these types of obligations as spontaneous or operating liabilities. In contrast, non-current liabilities consist mainly of long-term borrowing contracts that managers have negotiated with investors, banks, and other parties. This type of borrowing reflects a deliberate decision by managers to obtain funds from lenders, rather than to obtain additional investments from owners. The decision about how much of the firm's resources should be provided by long-term borrowing and how much should be invested by owners is a fundamental issue faced by all firms. Financial statement users are concerned with the firm's ability to pay both its short-term and long-term obligations as they mature.

We discuss some ratios that are useful for making these assessments. The analyst is aware of two important features of liability reporting. First, not all liabilities result from promises by the firm to repay specific amounts at determinable future dates. Instead, many liabilities require estimates of future events, such as the warranty obligations reported in Sample Company's balance sheet. Many other obligations reported by business firms entail similar liability estimates "Accounts Payable, Commitments, Contingencies, and Risks,". Second, the analyst is aware that some potential obligations of business firms either are not reported on the balance sheet or are reported at amounts that do not adequately reflect their potential future claims against the assets of the firm. Consider, for example, lawsuits against the firm.

At present, tobacco firms are disputing a lengthy list of ailments allegedly associated with cigarette smoking. Similarly, large chemical and nuclear industry firms are being sued over toxic wastes.

In these cases, the potential damages awarded to plaintiffs could result in awards of billions of dollars. Although these potentially ruinous lawsuits are based on business activities prior to the current balance sheet date, none of these firms reports significant contingent liabilities because the loss cannot be reliably estimated at this time.

OWNERS' EQUITY

This final element of the balance sheet represents the equity of the firm's owners. The FASB defines owners' equity simply as the "residual interest in the assets of an entity that remains after deducting liabilities."

This definition makes it clear that the balance sheet's valuation of owners' equity is determined by its valuations of assets and liabilities. This view of owners' equity as a residual amount is apparent when we rearrange the balance sheet equation in the following way:

Owners' Equity = Assets – Liabilities

Sample Company's balance sheet shows a firm that has been organized as a corporation, which is an entity that is owned by a group of shareholders. Although a corporation's owners' equity may be called shareholders' equity, in Sample Company, it comprises both paid-in capital, which represents direct investments by the owners of the firm, and retained earnings, which represents the earnings of the firm that have been reinvested in the business.

Sample Company's balance sheet shows that owners have paid ₹600,000 for shares of stock of the company. Sample Company has received this invested capital (probably in cash from investors) in exchange for its shares of stock. In addition, the firm has been profitable in the past, and Sample Company has reinvested ₹258,000 of those profits in the business. This ₹258,000 represents Sample's retained earnings.

If in the next year, Sample Company reports profits of ₹200,000 and pays dividends to shareholders of ₹75,000, then retained earnings will increase by ₹125,000 (₹200,000–₹75,000). Bear in mind, however, that retained earnings do not represent cash available for the payment of dividends. Rather, retained earnings reflect the amount of resources that a firm has obtained as a result of operations.

The firm has retained this increase for use in its operations, rather than returning it immediately to the investors as dividends. Those resources are presently invested as shown on the asset side of the balance sheet. For this reason, it is possible that a firm may have a large retained earnings balance, but have insufficient cash available for dividends. The reporting of shareholders' equity for two firms, one of which reports a negative (deficit) balance in retained earnings. This discussion of owners' equity completes our tour of Sample Company's balance sheet, and, at this point, you are aware of the typical components of the balance sheets of most business firms. As suggested, generally use the term shareholders' equity, rather than the more generic term owners' equity. The following part shows a variety of balance sheet relationships that are of interest to analysts.

BALANCE SHEET ANALYSIS

Various ratios are used to help interpret and understand financial statements. These ratios are guides to understanding changes in financial performance for one company from year to year and differences in financial performance between two or more companies. Ratios are most useful when comparisons are made, either between time periods or among different companies.

Ratios are useful shortcuts that permit the analyst to collapse the myriad details in financial statements into a few simple numbers. But remember that the ratio calculations are not the answers; they just show relationships. The analyst or manager must understand those relationships and make decisions on the basis of a host of information. Ratios are just one input to those decisions. In other words, ratios are one indicator of financial health and viability, but they do not tell the whole story.

Users of financial statements must be careful not to become too enamored of the ratios themselves and should not forget to look for other indicators that will permit better decision–making. Also, ratios are historical. Judgment is needed to use them for decision–making because future conditions may change. Bear in mind that ratios are only as good as the data that comprise them. The discussions will help you be aware of differences in accounting policies that can cause differences in ratios. Balance sheet ratios aid the analyst in assessing a firm's liquidity, asset management, and debt management policies, each of which is discussed in this part.

Vertical Analysis

Analysts usually begin with a review of the firm's assets, as well as its liabilities and owners' equity. This review begins with the preparation of a common-size balance sheet, which shows the percentage component of each major part to the grand totals on each side of the balance sheet. This analysis is called vertical analysis, or vertical percentage analysis, because it is based on the percentage relationship of each line in the balance sheet to the total. Exhibit has been revised as showing the vertical percentages for each account on the balance sheet.

These percentages are calculated by dividing each line by the total assets (₹2,057,000). Note that either total assets or total liabilities plus owners' equity can be used as the denominator for this calculation because the number is the same (₹2,057,000).

EXHIBIT Vertical Analysis

Sample Company Balance Sheet: Vertical Analysis at December 31, 2000

Assets			Liabilities and Owners' Equity		
Current assets			Current liabilities		
Cash	5.3%		Accounts payable	12.6%	
Accounts receivable	22.6		Notes payable	10.9	
Inventories	39.5		Warranty obligations	5.4	
Prepaid expenses	1.6		Accrued expenses	3.6	
Total current assets		69.0%	Taxes payable	1.3	
Noncurrent Assets			Total current liabilities		33.8%
Land	4.1%		Noncurrent liabilities		
Buildings and equipment (net of accumulated depreciation of ₹313,000)	26.9		Bonds payable	17.1%	
			Mortgage payable	7.3	
			Total noncurrent liabilities		24.4
			Total liabilities		58.2%
Total noncurrent assets		31.0	Shareholders' equity		
			Paid-in capital	29.3%	
			Retained earnings	12.5	
			Total shareholders' equity		41.8
Total assets		100.0%	Total liabilities and shareholders' equity		100.0%

Liquidity Ratios

Liquidity represents the ability of a company to convert its assets to cash, and liquidity ratios are often calculated from balance sheet data. Although there are many types of liquidity ratios, we focus here on a few of the more basic ones.

Current Ratio

The most popular liquidity ratio is the current ratio. The current ratio is calculated by dividing all current assets by all current liabilities:

$$\text{Current ratio} = \frac{\text{Current assets}}{\text{Current liabilities}}$$

For the data in Exhibit.

$$\text{Current ratio} = \frac{₹1{,}420{,}000}{₹699{,}000} = 2.03$$

Current ratios that represent good liquidity and financial health vary widely across firms and industries. Currently, many companies have a current ratio between 1.3 and 1.5. Many companies have short-term lines of credit and other borrowing capacities that permit them to operate with a nearly balanced amount of current assets and current liabilities. In any event, the analyst would be worried to find current liabilities substantially in excess of current assets (in other words, when the current ratio is considerably less than 1). Declining trends in the current ratio would also cause concern, especially in conjunction with declining trends in other ratios.

Quick Ratio

Another major liquidity ratio is the quick ratio, which is often called the acid test. In this context, "quick" means close to cash. To calculate this ratio, cash and receivables are added and then divided by all current liabilities. In computing the quick ratio, the net realizable value of the accounts receivable should be used.

The purpose of the quick ratio is to indicate the resources that may be available quickly, in the short term, for repaying the current liabilities. For this reason, inventory and prepaid expenses are left out. In other words, the quick ratio is a type of "disaster" ratio that is used to indicate a worst case scenario that might apply if no other resources are available to pay the current liabilities that are due within the next year.

$$\text{Quick ratio} = \frac{(\text{Cash} + \text{Receivables})}{\text{Current liabilities}}$$

$$\text{Quick ratio} = \frac{(₹110{,}000 + ₹466{,}000)}{₹699{,}000}$$

$$= .82$$

Values for the quick ratio are often less than 1.0, and a rule of thumb used by some analysts is that the quick ratio should not be less than .30. Again, declining trends should cause the most concern. When comparing two companies, a lower quick ratio and a lower current ratio do not, in and of themselves, indicate that the company with the lower values is in worse financial condition. Lower liquidity may be offset by a variety of other financial indicators, such that the company with lower liquidity ratios could still rank higher on its overall financial stability and financial health.

Asset Management Ratios

Asset management ratios focus on the composition of the firm's assets and on changes in the composition of assets over time (changes between successive balance sheets). A vertical analysis of the left side of the balance sheet allows the analyst to examine the percentages of the total assets devoted to each category. This examination gives some indication of the resources used for current assets relative to those used to provide operating capacity. In reviewing the percentage composition of a firm's assets, the analyst keeps several factors in mind.

First, to a large extent, the composition of assets depends on the industry in which the firm operates. In some cases, comparisons between industries may be meaningless. "Smokestack" industries, for example, such as metal fabrication, require large investments in factory buildings and heavy equipment, such that a major portion of these firms' assets are non-current. On the other hand, merchandising industries, such as department stores, require large amounts of accounts receivable and also substantial investments in inventories available for resale, but relatively minor investment in buildings and equipment.

Financial firms such as banks and insurance companies have relatively little in the way of inventories, factory buildings, and equipment. Instead, the assets of financial firms consist mainly of loans receivable and investments in securities (stocks and bonds) of other firms. A first step for the analyst in assessing a firm's asset composition is to be aware of any peculiar industry norms or special circumstances.

In addition to industry characteristics, the analyst knows that managers may have sound business reasons for structuring a firm's assets differently than those of its competitors. For example, some managers may extend liberal credit terms to customers as a way of improving sales and, as a result, may have a large accounts receivable balance. Other managers may carry large inventories for customer convenience or may stockpile inventories in anticipation of rising price or supply bottlenecks.

On the other hand, large amounts of accounts receivable may indicate that a firm has difficulty collecting its accounts. Similarly, large inventories may reflect obsolete items or declining product sales. In short, increases or decreases in specific components of a firm's total assets may be either good news or bad news. Any ratio computations are only the first step for the analyst. The creative art in ratio analysis is understanding the reasons for ratio differences among firms and over time.

DEBT MANAGEMENT RATIOS

The most inclusive and most useful debt management ratios are the composition ratios drawn from a vertical analysis of the right side of the balance sheet. Note the liability and equity composition ratios in the right-hand column of Exhibit. These percentage composition ratios indicate the relative proportions of various forms of debt and owners' equity used to finance the organization. The vertical analysis of Sample Company's sources of funds shows that 33.8% of all financing came from current liabilities. A smaller amount (24.4%) came from long-term liabilities, and the largest portion (41.8%) came from owners.

Of the 41.8% portion that came from owners, 29.3% was in the form of direct investment, and 12.5% was in the form of profits reinvested in the business. The ratio of total debt to total assets, also called the debt-to-assets ratio, is often used as a primary indicator of the firm's debt management. Exhibit shows that Sample Company's total liabilities are equal to 58.2% of total assets. As this key ratio increases or decreases, it indicates the firm's changing reliance on borrowed resources.

The lower the ratio, the lower the firm's risk because the organization will usually be better able to meet its obligations for interest and debt payments. A lower debt-to-assets ratio also suggests a lower risk of default. Default on a firm's liabilities is a costly event from both a lender's and a borrower's perspective and should be avoided if at all possible. The fact that

Sample Company's owners' equity provides 41.8% of the firm's resources suggests that the owners' equity of this firm offers substantial protection to lenders. Suppose, for example, Sample Company was unable to continue its operations and had to liquidate its assets, or, in other words, convert its assets to cash. In such a situation, Sample Company could incur losses of 41.8% of the assets' carrying value, and the cash received would still be sufficient to pay off all the firm's debts. Of course, nothing would then be left for the owners.

Limitations of Balance Sheet Analysis

Although the ratios reviewed in this part provide a useful starting point for assessing a firm's financial management policies, several limitations must be considered. First, ratio calculations are only the initial step in analyzing a firm's condition. They merely provide the analyst with a point of departure for asking further questions. Second, individual financial statements such as the balance sheet are seldom analysed separately from other statements. In fact, many of the most useful ratios used by analysts measure relationships among financial statements, rather than relationships within a single financial statement.

For this reason, as suggested, expand and enrich our study of ratio analysis after first describing the other primary financial statements. Third, information useful for analyzing and clarifying financial statements is contained in other parts of a company's financial reports. An important limitation in comparing financial ratios across firms is the fact that their accounting methods may differ. The varieties of different methods that firms may use in measuring assets, liabilities, shareholders' equity, revenues, and expenses. For now, be aware that financial ratios may be significantly affected by alternative accounting methods. The analyst attempts to adjust for differences caused by accounting methods in order to make valid ratio comparisons among different firms. The notes to the financial statements alert the analyst to the principal methods being used.

8

Statement of Cash Flows

AN OVERVIEW

This Accounting Standard is not mandatory for Small and Medium–Sized Companies, as defined in the Notification. Such companies are however encouraged to comply with the Standard.

OBJECTIVE

Information about the cash flows of an enterprise is useful in providing users of financial statements with a basis to assess the ability of the enterprise to generate cash and cash equivalents and the needs of the enterprise to utilise those cash flows. The economic decisions that are taken by users require an evaluation of the ability of an enterprise to generate cash and cash equivalents and the timing and certainty of their generation. The Standard deals with the provision of information about the historical changes in cash and cash equivalents of an enterprise by means of a cash flow statement which classifies cash flows during the period from operating, investing and financing activities.

SCOPE

An enterprise should prepare a cash flow statement and should present it for each period for which financial statements are presented. Users of an enterprise's financial statements are interested in how the enterprise generates and uses cash and cash equivalents. This is the case regardless of the nature of the enterprise's activities and irrespective of whether cash can be viewed as the product of the enterprise, as may be the case with a financial enterprise. Enterprises need cash for essentially the same reasons, however different their principal revenue-producing activities might be. They need cash to conduct their operations, to pay their obligations, and to provide returns to their investors.

BENEFITS OF CASH FLOW INFORMATION

A cash flow statement, when used in conjunction with the other financial statements, provides information that enables users to evaluate the changes in net assets of an enterprise, its financial structure (including its liquidity and solvency) and its ability to affect the amounts and timing of cash flows in order to adapt to changing circumstances and opportunities. Cash flow information is useful in assessing the ability of the enterprise to generate cash and cash equivalents and enables users to develop models to assess and compare the present value of the future cash flows of different enterprises. It also enhances the comparability of the reporting of operating performance by different enterprises because it eliminates the effects of using different accounting treatments for the same transactions and events.

Historical cash flow information is often used as an indicator of the amount, timing and certainty of future cash flows. It is also useful in checking the accuracy of past assessments of future cash flows and in examining the relationship between profitability and net cash flow and the impact of changing prices.

DEFINITIONS

The following terms are used in this Standard with the meanings specified:

- Cash comprises cash on hand and demand deposits with banks.
- Cash equivalents are short term, highly liquid investments that are readily convertible into known amounts of cash and which are subject to an insignificant risk of changes in value.
- Cash flows are inflows and outflows of cash and cash equivalents.
- Operating activities are the principal revenue-producing activities of the enterprise and other activities that are not investing or financing activities.
- Investing activities are the acquisition and disposal of long-term assets and other investments not included in cash equivalents.
- Financing activities are activities that result in changes in the size and composition of the owners' capital (including preference share capital in the case of a company) and borrowings of the enterprise.

CASH AND CASH EQUIVALENTS

Cash equivalents are held for the purpose of meeting short-term cash commitments rather than for investment or other purposes. For an investment to qualify as a cash equivalent, it must be readily convertible to a known amount of cash and be subject to an insignificant risk of changes in value. Therefore, an investment normally qualifies as a cash equivalent only when it has a short maturity of, say, three months or less from the date of acquisition.

Investments in shares are excluded from cash equivalents unless they are, in substance, cash equivalents; for example, preference shares of a company acquired shortly before their specified redemption date (provided there is only an insignificant risk of failure of the company to repay the amount at maturity). Cash flows exclude movements between items that constitute cash or cash equivalents because these components are part of the cash management of an enterprise rather than part of its operating, investing and financing activities. Cash management includes the investment of excess cash in cash equivalents.

PRESENTATION OF A CASH FLOW STATEMENT

The cash flow statement should report cash flows during the period classified by operating, investing and financing activities. An enterprise presents its cash flows from operating, investing and financing activities in a manner which is most appropriate to its business. Classification by activity provides information that allows users to assess the impact of those activities on the financial position of the enterprise and the amount of its cash and cash equivalents.

This information may also be used to evaluate the relationships among those activities. A single transaction may include cash flows that are classified differently. For example, when the installment paid in respect of a fixed asset acquired on deferred payment basis includes both interest and loan, the interest element is classified under financing activities and the loan element is classified under investing activities.

OPERATING ACTIVITIES

The amount of cash flows arising from operating activities is a key indicator of the extent to which the operations of the enterprise have generated sufficient cash flows to maintain the operating capability of the enterprise, pay dividends, repay loans and make new investments without recourse to external sources of financing.

Information about the specific components of historical operating cash flows is useful, in conjunction with other information, in forecasting future operating cash flows.

Cash flows from operating activities are primarily derived from the principal revenue-producing activities of the enterprise. Therefore, they generally result from the transactions and other events that enter into the determination of net profit or loss.

Examples of cash flows from operating activities are:

- Cash receipts from the sale of goods and the rendering of services;
- Cash receipts from royalties, fees, commissions and other revenue;
- Cash payments to suppliers for goods and services;
- Cash payments to and on behalf of employees;
- Cash receipts and cash payments of an insurance enterprise for premiums and claims, annuities and other policy benefits;
- Cash payments or refunds of income taxes unless they can be specifically identified with financing and investing activities; and
- Cash receipts and payments relating to futures contracts, forward contracts, option contracts and swap contracts when the contracts

are held for dealing or trading purposes.

Some transactions, such as the sale of an item of plant, may give rise to a gain or loss which is included in the determination of net profit or loss. However, the cash flows relating to such transactions are cash flows from investing activities.

An enterprise may hold securities and loans for dealing or trading purposes, in which case they are similar to inventory acquired specifically for resale. Therefore, cash flows arising from the purchase and sale of dealing or trading securities are classified as operating activities. Similarly, cash advances and loans made by financial enterprises are usually classified as operating activities since they relate to the main revenue-producing activity of that enterprise.

INVESTING ACTIVITIES

The separate disclosure of cash flows arising from investing activities is important because the cash flows represent the extent to which expenditures have been made for resources intended to generate future income and cash flows.

Examples of cash flows arising from investing activities are:

- Cash payments to acquire fixed assets (including intangibles). These payments include those relating to capitalised research and development costs and self-constructed fixed assets;
- Cash receipts from disposal of fixed assets (including intangibles);
- Cash payments to acquire shares, warrants or debt instruments of other enterprises and interests in joint ventures (other than payments for those instruments considered to be cash equivalents and those held for dealing or trading purposes);
- Cash receipts from disposal of shares, warrants or debt instruments of other enterprises and interests in joint ventures (other than receipts from those instruments considered to be cash equivalents and those held for dealing or trading purposes);
- Cash advances and loans made to third parties (other than advances and loans made by a financial enterprise);
- Cash receipts from the repayment of advances and loans made to third parties (other than advances and loans of a financial enterprise);
- Cash payments for futures contracts, forward contracts, option contracts and swap contracts except when the contracts are held for dealing or trading purposes, or the payments are classified as financing activities; and
- Cash receipts from futures contracts, forward contracts, option contracts and swap contracts except when the contracts are held for dealing or trading purposes, or the receipts are classified as financing activities.

When a contract is accounted for as a hedge of an identifiable position, the cash flows of the contract are classified in the same manner as the cash flows of the position being hedged.

FINANCING ACTIVITIES

The separate disclosure of cash flows arising from financing activities is important because it is useful in predicting claims on future cash flows by providers of funds (both capital and borrowings) to the enterprise.

Examples of cash flows arising from financing activities are:

- Cash proceeds from issuing shares or other similar instruments;
- Cash proceeds from issuing debentures, loans, notes, bonds, and other short or long-term borrowings; and
- Cash repayments of amounts borrowed.

REPORTING CASH FLOWS FROM OPERATING ACTIVITIES

An enterprise should report cash flows from operating activities using either:

- The direct method, whereby major classes of gross cash receipts and gross cash payments are disclosed; or
- The indirect method, whereby net profit or loss is adjusted for the effects of transactions of a non-cash nature, any deferrals or accruals of past or future operating cash receipts or payments, and items of income or expense associated with investing or financing cash flows.

The direct method provides information which may be useful in estimating future cash flows and which is not available under the indirect method and is, therefore, considered more appropriate than the indirect method. Under the direct method, information about major classes of gross cash receipts and gross cash payments may be obtained either:

- From the accounting records of the enterprise; or
- By adjusting sales, cost of sales (interest and similar income and interest expense and similar charges for a financial enterprise) and other items in the statement of profit and loss for:
  - Changes during the period in inventories and operating receivables and payables;
  - Other non-cash items; and
  - Other items for which the cash effects are investing or financing cash flows.

Under the indirect method, the net cash flow from operating activities is determined by adjusting net profit or loss for the effects of:

- Changes during the period in inventories and operating receivables and payables;
- Non-cash items such as depreciation, provisions, deferred taxes, and unrealised foreign exchange gains and losses; and

- All other items for which the cash effects are investing or financing cash flows.

Alternatively, the net cash flow from operating activities may be presented under the indirect method by showing the operating revenues and expenses excluding non-cash items disclosed in the statement of profit and loss and the changes during the period in inventories and operating receivables and payables.

REPORTING CASH FLOWS FROM INVESTING AND FINANCING ACTIVITIES

An enterprise should report separately major classes of gross cash receipts and gross cash payments arising from investing and financing activities, except to the extent that cash flows.

REPORTING CASH FLOWS ON A NET BASIS

Cash flows arising from the following operating, investing or financing activities may be reported on a net basis:

- Cash receipts and payments on behalf of customers when the cash flows reflect the activities of the customer rather than those of the enterprise; and
- Cash receipts and payments for items in which the turnover is quick, the amounts are large, and the maturities are short.

Examples of cash receipts and payments are:

- The acceptance and repayment of demand deposits by a bank;
- Funds held for customers by an investment enterprise; and
- Rents collected on behalf of, and paid over to, the owners of properties.

Examples of cash receipts and payments are advances made for, and the repayments of:

- Principal amounts relating to credit card customers;
- The purchase and sale of investments; and
- Other short-term borrowings, for example, those which have a maturity period of three months or less.

Cash flows arising from each of the following activities of a financial enterprise may be reported on a net basis:

- Cash receipts and payments for the acceptance and repayment of deposits with a fixed maturity date;
- The placement of deposits with and withdrawal of deposits from other financial enterprises; and
- Cash advances and loans made to customers and the repayment of those advances and loans.

FOREIGN CURRENCY CASH FLOWS

Cash flows arising from transactions in a foreign currency should be recorded in an enterprise's reporting currency by applying to the foreign currency amount the exchange rate between the reporting currency and the foreign currency at the date of the cash flow. A rate that approximates the actual rate may be used if the result is substantially the same as would arise if the rates at the dates of the cash flows were used. The effect of changes in exchange rates on cash and cash equivalents held in a foreign currency should be reported as a separate part of the reconciliation of the changes in cash and cash equivalents during the period. Cash flows denominated in foreign currency are reported in a manner consistent with Accounting Standard (AS) 11, The Effects of Changes in Foreign Exchange Rates. This permits the use of an exchange rate that approximates the actual rate. For example, a weighted average exchange rate for a period may be used for recording foreign currency transactions. Unrealised gains and losses arising from changes in foreign exchange rates are not cash flows.

However, the effect of exchange rate changes on cash and cash equivalents held or due in a foreign currency is reported in the cash flow statement in order to reconcile cash and cash equivalents at the beginning and the end of the period. This amount is presented separately from cash flows from operating, investing and financing activities and includes the differences, if any, had those cash flows been reported at the end-of period exchange rates.

EXTRAORDINARY ITEMS

The cash flows associated with extraordinary items should be classified as arising from operating, investing or financing activities as appropriate and separately disclosed. The cash flows associated with extraordinary items are disclosed separately as arising from operating, investing or financing activities in the cash flow statement, to enable users to understand their nature and effect on the present and future cash flows of the enterprise. These disclosures are in addition to the separate disclosures of the nature and amount of extraordinary items required by Accounting Standard (AS) 5, Net Profit or Loss for the Period, Prior Period Items and Changes in Accounting Policies.

INTEREST AND DIVIDENDS

Cash flows from interest and dividends received and paid should each be disclosed separately. Cash flows arising from interest paid and interest and dividends received in the case of a financial enterprise should be classified as cash flows arising from operating activities. In the case of other enterprises, cash flows arising from interest paid should be classified as cash flows from financing activities while interest and dividends received should be classified as cash flows from investing activities. Dividends paid should be classified as cash flows from financing activities. The total amount of interest paid during the period is disclosed in the cash flow statement whether it has been recognised as an expense in the statement of profit and loss or capitalised in accordance with Accounting Standard (AS) 10, Accounting for Fixed Assets.

Interest paid and interest and dividends received are usually classified as operating cash flows for a financial enterprise.

However, there is no consensus on the classification of these cash flows for other enterprises. Some argue that interest paid and interest and dividends received may be classified as operating cash flows because they enter into the determination of net profit or loss.

However, it is more appropriate that interest paid and interest and dividends received are classified as financing cash flows and investing cash flows respectively, because they are cost of obtaining financial resources or returns on investments. Some argue that dividends paid may be classified as a component of cash flows from operating activities in order to assist users to determine the ability of an enterprise to pay dividends out of operating cash flows. However, it is considered more appropriate that dividends paid should be classified as cash flows from financing activities because they are cost of obtaining financial resources.

TAXES ON INCOME

Cash flows arising from taxes on income should be separately disclosed and should be classified as cash flows from operating activities unless they can be specifically identified with financing and investing activities. Taxes on income arise on transactions that give rise to cash flows that are classified as operating, investing or financing activities in a cash flow statement. While tax expense may be readily identifiable with investing or financing activities, the related tax cash flows are often impracticable to identify and may arise in a different period from the cash flows of the underlying transactions. Therefore, taxes paid are usually classified as cash flows from operating activities.

However, when it is practicable to identify the tax cash flow with an individual transaction that gives rise to cash flows that are classified as investing or financing activities, the tax cash flow is classified as an investing or financing activity as appropriate. When tax cash flow are allocated over more than one class of activity, the total amount of taxes paid is disclosed.

INVESTMENTS IN SUBSIDIARIES, ASSOCIATES AND JOINT VENTURES

When accounting for an investment in an associate or a subsidiary or a joint venture, an investor restricts its reporting in the cash flow statement to the cash flows between itself and the investee/joint venture, for example, cash flows relating to dividends and advances.

ACQUISITIONS AND DISPOSALS OF SUBSIDIARIES AND OTHER BUSINESS UNITS

The aggregate cash flows arising from acquisitions and from disposals of subsidiaries or other business units should be presented separately and classified as investing activities. An enterprise should disclose, in aggregate, in respect of both acquisition and disposal of subsidiaries or other business units during the period each of the following:

- The total purchase or disposal consideration; and
- The portion of the purchase or disposal consideration discharged by means of cash and cash equivalents.

The separate presentation of the cash flow effects of acquisitions and disposals of subsidiaries and other business units as single line items helps to distinguish those cash flows from other cash flows. The cash flow effects of disposals are not deducted from those of acquisitions.

NON-CASH TRANSACTIONS

Investing and financing transactions that do not require the use of cash or cash equivalents should be excluded from a cash flow statement.

Such transactions should be disclosed elsewhere in the financial statements in a way that provides all the relevant information about these investing and financing activities.

Many investing and financing activities do not have a direct impact on current cash flows although they do affect the capital and asset structure of an enterprise.

The exclusion of non-cash transactions from the cash flow statement is consistent with the objective of a cash flow statement as these items do not involve cash flows in the current period.

Examples of non-cash transactions are:

- The acquisition of assets by assuming directly related liabilities;
- The acquisition of an enterprise by means of issue of shares; and
- The conversion of debt to equity.

COMPONENTS OF CASH AND CASH EQUIVALENTS

An enterprise should disclose the components of cash and cash equivalents and should present a reconciliation of the amounts in its cash flow statement with the equivalent items reported in the balance sheet. In view of the variety of cash management practices, an enterprise discloses the policy which it adopts in determining the composition of cash and cash equivalents. The effect of any change in the policy for determining components of cash and cash equivalents is reported in accordance with Accounting Standard (AS) 5, Net Profit or Loss for the Period, Prior Period Items and Changes in Accounting Policies.

OTHER DISCLOSURES

An enterprise should disclose, together with a commentary by management, the amount of significant cash and cash equivalent balances held by the enterprise that are not available for use by it. There are various circumstances in which cash and cash equivalent balances held by an enterprise are not available for use by it.

Examples include cash and cash equivalent balances held by a branch of the enterprise that operates in a country where exchange controls or other legal restrictions apply as a result of which the balances are not available for use by the enterprise. Additional information may be relevant to users in understanding the financial position and liquidity of an enterprise.

Disclosure of this information, together with a commentary by management, is encouraged and may include:

- The amount of undrawn borrowing facilities that may be available for future operating activities and to settle capital commitments, indicating any restrictions on the use of these facilities; and
- The aggregate amount of cash flows that represent increases in operating capacity separately from those cash flows that are required to maintain operating capacity.

The separate disclosure of cash flows that represent increases in operating capacity and cash flows that are required to maintain operating capacity is useful in enabling the user to determine whether the enterprise is investing adequately in the maintenance of its operating capacity. An enterprise that does not invest adequately in the maintenance of its operating capacity may be prejudicing future profitability for the sake of current liquidity and distributions to owners.

9

Current Assets

CASH AND CASH EQUIVALENTS

Cash is the most liquid asset a business can own. Most firms devote considerable effort to the management and control of cash. Because a firm's creditors expect payment in cash, a sufficient amount of cash must always be available to meet obligations as they become due. This necessitates careful scheduling of cash inflows and outflows. Although an adequate cash balance is essential, excessive holdings of cash should be avoided.

Cash deposited in checking accounts usually does not earn very much, if any, interest. Cash amounts over and above those needed to meet obligations due in the near future should be invested in assets earning higher returns. The liquidity of cash also makes it easily pilfered. Firms must institute internal control procedures so that cash is properly accounted for and safeguarded. Failure to do so may tempt employees to misappropriate the firm's cash and may also result in various accounting errors.

COMPOSITION OF CASH

Cash is composed of funds that are readily available. This includes cash on hand and cash on deposit in bank accounts that do not restrict the withdrawal of cash. Deposits in checking accounts would qualify because those balances can be withdrawn on demand. Because banks rarely enforce restrictions on withdrawals from savings accounts, they are usually classified as cash. Also classified as cash are money market funds permitting withdrawal by check, checks from customers awaiting deposit, and foreign currency. Items not classified as cash include certificates of deposit, stamps, and postdated checks. Large corporations may have hundreds of checking accounts. Multiple accounts are needed because firms have numerous physical locations and each location makes expenditures. Firms also find it convenient to use separate accounts for specific purposes.

Many firms use one or more checking accounts solely for payroll purposes, for example. All checking accounts are condensed into the one cash item on the balance sheet. Many firms keep petty cash funds on hand to pay for small, incidental expenditures, such as cab fare or delivery charges. These funds are included in the cash amount on the balance sheet. Many retailers also keep change funds. These funds enable cashiers to make change for their customers. Change funds are also included in the cash item on the balance sheet. As a part of borrowing agreements with banks, firms sometimes agree to maintain compensating balances. These are minimum amounts the firm agrees to keep on deposit at the lending bank in accounts that pay little or no interest. As a result, the bank is able to use these funds interest free. This provides the bank with additional compensation for lending funds to the firm.

Compensating balances are usually included in the balance sheet cash amount and are disclosed in the notes to the financial statements. Instead of showing a cash item on their balance sheets, some firms use the term cash and cash equivalents. Cash equivalents are short-term, highly liquid investments that will mature within three months. Examples include certificates of deposit, treasury bills, and commercial document (short-term obligations of corporations).Because cash equivalents can readily be converted into known amounts of cash, reporting a combined cash and cash equivalents figure is probably as informative as reporting each figure separately. OshKosh B'Gosh (OB) follows the practice of reporting a combined figure for cash and cash equivalents. Exhibit contains an excerpt from its financial statement note describing this policy.

CONTROL OF CASH

Cash is so liquid and so easily transported, special care must be exercised to ensure that it is properly recorded and safeguarded. Most corporations follow several sound management practices that enhance their control over cash. Employees who are permitted access to cash, for example, should not also have access to the accounting records for cash. Access to both cash and the accounting records might enable an employee to misappropriate cash and to conceal the theft by altering the records.

DISCLOSURE OF CASH REPORTING POLICY

OshKash B'Gosh, Inc. 1997 Annual Report Note 1 (Partial)

Cash equivalents consist of highly liquid dept instruments such as money market accounts and commercial paper with original maturities of three month or less. The company's policy is to invest cash in conservative instruments as part of its cash management programme and to evaluate the credit exposure of any investment. Cash and cash equivalents are stated at cost, whicch approximates market value.

As an illustration, retail clerks (who have ready access to cash) should not "read" the cash register. That is, they should not have the responsibility of ascertaining the daily sales total from the register's internal record and recording this amount in the accounting records. Clerks with such dual access could take some cash and hide the theft by reducing the firm's recorded cash collections. Checking accounts with banks provide firms with several cash control advantages.

First, cash receipts can be deposited daily. Limiting the amount of time that cash is on the firm's premises reduces the possibility that it will be misappropriated.

Second, checks provide a written record of a firm's disbursements. Such a record would not necessarily exist if disbursements were made in currency. Moreover, most firms require that checks be supported by underlying documentation such as purchase orders, invoices, and receiving reports. This helps ensure that only valid expenditures are made and provides the basis for an analysis of costs and expenses.

EXHIBIT Poor Control Over Cash

Third, by limiting the number of people authorized to sign checks, firms restrict access to cash and reduce the possibility that cash will be used for unintended purposes.

Finally, bank statements provide a monthly listing of deposits and withdrawals. So not only does the firm keep track of its cash flows, but so does the bank. Thus, the bank statement can be used to verify the firm's cash records. This verification process is accomplished via a bank reconciliation, which is a detailed comparison of the firm's records and the bank statement. Because the bank reconciliation may uncover errors related to cash, it should be prepared by an employee who has no other cash-related responsibilities.

ANALYSIS OF CASH

The most informative analysis of cash pertains to cash flows. "Statement of Cash Flows," examined the statement of cash flows, which summarized the inflows and outflows of cash. A firm's ability to generate cash enables it to pay obligations as they become due, replace and expand productive assets, and provide a return to investors. The balance sheet does not contain information about a firm's cash flows. It simply indicates the amount of cash a firm holds on a given date. Nevertheless, some useful information about cash can be obtained from the balance sheet. The amount of cash on hand

and the trend in the cash balance over time can be ascertained. Also, because most current liabilities are paid in cash, many analysts relate the cash balance to current liabilities. This is done via the cash to current liabilities ratio:

$$\text{Cash to Current Liabilities ratio} = \frac{\text{Cash}}{\text{Current liabilities}}$$

Exhibit contains cash-related information for OB. OB's cash position decreased substantially from 1996 to 1997. The cash balance declined from ₹31,201,000 to ₹13,779,000. The cash to current liabilities ratio also decreased significantly, from 70.4% in 1996 to 28.5% in 1997.

$$\text{Cash to Current liabilities ratio} = \overset{1997}{\frac{₹13{,}779}{₹48{,}286}} = 28.5\% \qquad \overset{1996}{\frac{₹31{,}201}{₹44{,}293}} = 70.4\%$$

EXHIBIT **Financial Statement Information**

OshKosh B'Gosh
Selected Cash-Related Information
(Dollars in thousands)

	1997	1996
Cash and cash equivalents	₹ 13,779	₹ 31,201
Current assets	₹131,048	₹148,934
Current liabilities	₹ 48,286	₹ 44,293

The decline in the cash balance and the cash to current liabilities ratio is potentially worrisome. What caused this decline? OB has attempted to operate more efficiently by utilizing a smaller cash balance. Although firms need to maintain a cash balance sufficient to meet their obligations, excessive cash balances are undesirable because idle cash earns, at best, a modest return. Given that OB has virtually no debt, has unused lines of credit available, and has strong cash flow from operations, the decline in the cash balance should not cause alarm. Note that the cash to current liabilities ratio is a severe test of liquidity. To see this, compare OB's 1997 cash to current liabilities ratio of 28.5% to its current ratio.

$$\text{Current ratio} = \frac{\text{Current assets}}{\text{Current liabilities}} = \frac{₹131{,}048}{₹48{,}286} = 2.71$$

Both ratios contain current liabilities in the denominator. However, because the cash to current liabilities ratio has a much smaller numerator, a lower ratio results.

IMPLICATIONS FOR MANAGERS

Financial statements provide managers and others with historical information about cash. Managers must ensure that sufficient cash is available on an ongoing basis to enable the firm to meet its commitments. As in many cases, managers must be proactive, not reactive, and the historical information can help with decision making. The management of cash begins with projecting the amount and timing of future cash flows. This enables firms to forecast their cash balances over the course of a specified time period. If positive net cash flows are expected, managers must identify profitable uses of that cash. Alternatively, if negative net cash flows are projected, managers must identify additional sources of cash. Possibilities include short-term debt, long-term debt, additional investments by owners, and the liquidation of assets. Other strategies might include attempting to speed up cash collections from customers and delaying payments to suppliers.

MARKETABLE SECURITIES

Many firms experience uneven cash flows during a year. Department stores, for example, make a large portion of their sales during November and December, resulting in significant cash inflows. In many instances, such large amounts of cash are not immediately needed to fund operations. Many firms elect to put excess cash balances into short-term investments. These investments, known as marketable securities, typically produce higher earnings than those available from bank accounts, thus enabling firms to increase their earnings.

TYPES OF INVESTMENTS

Firms can choose from two general types of securities. Equity securities represent ownership interests in other corporations. For example, General Motors (GM) can purchase shares of IBM stock, which would be reflected on GM's balance sheet as an asset. Firms can also invest in debt securities, which result from lending transactions. For example, if GM were to lend funds to IBM, IBM would probably issue a debt security as written evidence of the indebtedness.

The security might be commercial document (indicating short-term borrowing) or a bond (indicating long term borrowing). In either case, the security would appear on GM's balance sheet as an asset. This stage deals primarily with investments in equity securities that are classified as current assets. As you know, current assets are either consumed or converted into cash within one year. Thus, we cover only investments that will be held a relatively short period of time.

MARKETABILITY

This stage is also restricted to securities that are marketable. A security is marketable if it is traded on a securities exchange registered with the Securities and Exchange Commission (SEC) or if its price is available through the National Association of Securities Dealers Automated Quotations systems or the National Quotation Bureau.

Securities traded on foreign exchanges may also qualify. Securities that are not readily marketable are unlikely candidates for short-term investments of excess cash. Non-marketable securities cannot necessarily be liquidated when the investor desires to do so. Investments in non-marketable securities are usually classified as long-term investments.

BASIC ACCOUNTING

Accounting for Certain Investments in Debt and Equity Securities, governs the accounting for short-term investments in marketable securities. This standard requires that a firm classify such investments as either trading securities or available-for-sale securities. Trading securities are intended to be held for brief periods of time to generate profits from short-term differences in price. For example, investment banks will often buy an entire stock issue from a corporation with the intent of almost immediately selling the stock to the public.

The investment bank would classify the stock as a trading security. Marketable equity securities not classified as trading securities are classified as available-for-sale. Non-financial organizations classify most of their investments in marketable equity securities as available-for-sale. Proper classification is important because the accounting treatment differs for the two categories. Because most corporations classify their securities as available-for-sale, this stage emphasizes the accounting procedures for that classification.

Available-for-Sale Securities

Marketable equity securities classified as available-for sale should be accounted for at market value on the balance sheet date. The difference between a security's historical cost and its market value is an unrealised gain or loss. The term unrealised indicates that the gain or loss has not been confirmed by an actual sale. However, because the securities are highly marketable, the value change is virtually certain, and, accordingly, the gain or loss is a valid and useful measure of a change in wealth.

Unrealised gains and losses on available-for-sale securities do not, however, appear on the income statement. Instead, these gains and losses appear in a special part of shareholders' equity that is distinct from invested capital or retained earnings.

Also note that the marketable securities account continues to reflect the historical cost of the securities. The adjustment to market value is made to a valuation account, often labeled allowance for unrealised gain/loss. To show, assume that on December 1, 2000, Mega Company purchased marketable securities for ₹1,000. This analysis is straightforward.

	Assets		=	Liabilities	+	Shareholders' Equity
	Cash	Marketable securities				
Dec. 1	– ₹ 1,000	+ ₹ 1,000				

On December 31, the securities are still on hand and have a market value of ₹980. To record the value change, reduce marketable securities by ₹20 via the allowance for unrealised loss and reduce shareholders' equity by ₹20.

	Assets		= Liabilities	+ Shareholders' Equity
	Marketable securities	Allowance for unrealized loss		Unrealized loss on marketable securities
Bal.	₹1,000			
Dec. 31		– ₹20		– ₹20

In the asset part of the balance sheet, the ₹20 balance in allowance for unrealised loss is subtracted from marketable securities to show a net asset of ₹980. The account unrealised loss on marketable securities is a separate component of shareholders' equity. Keep in mind that it is not an income statement account.

Assume further that the securities are sold on January 10, 2001, for ₹990. Looking at the purchase and sale together, a ₹10 loss has been incurred. Because no loss was recognized on the income statement when the securities were revalued at the end of 2000, a ₹10 loss must now be reflected on the income statement. The analysis is most easily completed in two steps.

First, because the ₹20 loss is no longer unrealised, the entry to record that loss should be reversed.

Second, cash is increased by ₹990, marketable securities are reduced by ₹1,000, and a ₹10 loss is recognized. This loss is termed realised because it has been confirmed by a cash transaction. This loss appears on the 2001 income statement.

	Assets			= Liabilities +	Shareholders' Equity	
	Cash	Marketable securities	Allowance for unrealized loss		unrealized loss on marketable securities	Retained earnings
Bal.		₹1,000	–₹20		–₹20	–₹10
Jan. 10			+₹20		+₹20	(realized loss)
Jan.10	+₹990	–₹1,000				

Trading Securities

Trading securities are also accounted for at market value. One major difference exists between the accounting for trading securities and that for securities classified as available-for-sale. Unrealised gains and losses on trading securities are included in net income, as opposed to being reflected in a special part of shareholders' equity.

The FASB believes that, because trading securities are purchased to generate profits on short-term price changes, all unrealised gains and losses should be immediately reflected on the income statement.

Debt Securities

The accounting for debt securities is a bit more complex. If a firm intends to hold a debt security until its maturity date, the security is valued at historical cost. Debt securities not intended to be held until maturity appear on the balance sheet at market value. However, because debt securities classified as current assets will be liquidated within the next year, a large discrepancy between cost and market value is unlikely. Thus, in most cases, financial statement readers can view the marketable debt securities figure in the current asset part as a very close approximation to market value.

ANALYSIS OF MARKETABLE SECURITIES

Marketable securities are reflected on the balance sheet at market value. Because these securities can be readily converted into known amounts of cash, such a valuation rule seems quite reasonable. Analysts evaluate the liquidity of a firm, in part, by examining current assets.

The amount of cash a marketable security can be transformed into is likely to be much more relevant for liquidity assessment than is a security's historical cost. Your accounting common sense probably suggests that all unrealised gains and losses on marketable securities should appear on the income statement. SFAS No. 115 precludes this treatment for securities classified as available-for-sale. The FASB's justification for this position relates to liabilities.

The FASB tried but failed to agree on how to measure changes in the value of liabilities. Because net income might be distorted by including asset value changes in income while excluding similar changes for liabilities, the FASB decided to exclude changes in asset values from reported income. The FASB's required procedures can be challenged on at least three grounds.

First, some argue that two wrongs do not make a right. Changes in the value of marketable securities are valid gains and losses and should be included in net income, regardless of how liabilities are treated. Not doing so reduces the usefulness of net income as a measure of wealth changes and as an indicator of managerial performance.

Second, the FASB's procedures provide an opportunity for profit manipulation by management. By selecting to sell those securities that have either risen or fallen in value, managers can dictate whether gains or losses will be reported.

Third, the FASB created a new element of shareholders' equity (unrealised gain/loss on marketable securities) in order to exclude changes in the value of marketable securities from net income. This element is a new (and somewhat unusual) addition to the conventional financial accounting framework. Its existence compromises the basic notion that the change in shareholders' equity for a period equals net income plus the effects of direct contributions/ withdrawals by the shareholders.

ACCOUNTS RECEIVABLE

Revenue transactions are usually undertaken for cash or on credit. Firms obviously prefer to make sales for cash because funds are immediately available to meet obligations, invest in productive endeavors, pay dividends, and so on. Moreover, cash sales entail no uncertainty about collectibility.

CREDIT SALES

Many firms, however, make a significant portion of their sales on credit. They do so because customers prefer deferring their payments. Credit transactions enable purchasers to use their cash for a longer period of time before paying the seller.

Moreover, credit transactions permit the purchaser to inspect and actually use the goods prior to payment. Industry practices and competitive pressures force many firms to sell on credit, and credit sales to customers in the ordinary course of business give rise to accounts receivable (trade receivables). Before making a credit sale, the credit standing of the customer should be assessed. Credit-worthiness is an important consideration in making a credit sale because it bears directly on a potential customer's ability and willingness to ultimately make payment.

Various credit bureaus (such as Dun and Bradstreet and Equifax) provide credit ratings and other information for this purpose. Selling only to customers with high credit ratings, however, will not necessarily maximize profits. Although such a policy would minimize receivables that prove to be uncollectible, a number of potentially profitable sales might be eliminated and the profit on these sales may well overshadow the expense of uncollectible accounts.

Thus, a firm must decide how much credit to grant and to whom credit should be offered. Selecting a credit-rating cutoff in some middle range is probably optimal.

ACCOUNTING FOR CREDIT SALES

The analysis of credit sales is quite straight forward. The credit sale of merchandise for ₹100 would increase accounts receivable and shareholders' equity.

Assets	=	Liabilities	+	Shareholders' Equity
Accounts receivable +₹100				Retained earnings +₹100 (sales)

When the cash is ultimately collected, the balance in cash is increased, and the accounts receivable balance is decreased.

Assets		=	Liabilities	+	Shareholders' Equits
Cash +₹100	Accounts receivable –₹100				

Notice that revenue is recognized when the sale is made. The collection of cash does not result in the recognition of revenue. Rather, it merely transforms one asset (accounts receivable) into another (cash).

DISCOUNTS

When selling on credit, many firms offer discounts for early payment. Such discounts are offered primarily for two reasons. First, early payment by the customer enables the seller to have access to cash sooner. Second, the sooner an account is paid, the less opportunity there is for nonpayment. Typical discount terms are 2/10, net 30. This indicates that a 2% discount will be granted if payment is made within 10 days of sale; otherwise, full payment is due within 30 days of sale.

These particular terms offer a significant inducement for early payment. To see this, consider the 2% to be a finance charge assessed for extending credit from the 10th to the 30th day after sale. That is, the customer must pay 2% more than otherwise required if payment is delayed for those 20 days. Because there are about 18 20-day periods in a year (365/20), the quoted discount implies an approximate annual interest rate of 36% (2%–18), which is quite high relative to other sources of financing.

FACTORING ACCOUNTS RECEIVABLE

In some industries, sellers extend very generous credit terms to their customers. For example, furniture retailers sometimes do not require any payment until six months after sale. To obtain cash more quickly, these firms sell (factor) their receivables.

In most cases, the receivables are factored to a financial institution that charges a fee as compensation for the cost of collection, the delayed receipt of the cash, and potential uncollectible accounts. To show, assume that a furniture store has previously made a credit sale for ₹1,500. If the receivable is subsequently factored for ₹1,300, cash would increase by ₹1,300, accounts receivable would decrease by ₹1,500, and a ₹200 expense would be incurred.

Assets		=	Liabilities	+	Shareholders' Equity
Cash	Accounts receivable				Retained earnings
+ ₹1,300	– ₹1,500				– ₹200(financing expense)

UNCOLLECTIBLE ACCOUNTS

As noted earlier, revenue is recognized at the time a credit sale is made. Recognizing revenue increases a firm's assets and net income. However, given that some of the receivables may ultimately prove to be uncollectible, assets and net income might be overstated.

Year-End Adjustment

To avoid this possibility, firms make year-end adjustments to recognize that some of their accounts receivable will probably not be collected. Because firms are unlikely to know which particular accounts will prove to be uncollectible, the amount of the adjustment is an estimate.

To show, assume that on December 31, 2000, at the end of its first year of operation the Box Company estimates that ₹2,400 of its year-end accounts receivable balance of ₹100,000 will be uncollectible. Keep in mind that this is an overall estimate and that Box is currently unable to identify which particular customers will not fulfill their obligations. Accordingly, the adjustment does not directly reduce accounts receivable. Instead, a negative (contra) asset, allowance for uncollectible accounts, is used.

An expense is also recorded, which is consistent with the matching principle. One cost of generating sales is the receivables that will ultimately prove to be uncollectible. This cost (even though it must be estimated) should be deducted from the sales revenue that gave rise to those receivables. The analysis follows.

	Assets		=	Liabilities	+	Shareholders' Equity
	Accounts receivable	Allowance for uncollectible accounts (contra asset)				Retained earnings
Bal.	₹100,000					
Dec. 31		–₹2,400				– ₹2,400 (uncollectible accounts expense)

The net difference between the balances in accounts receivable and the allowance for uncollectible accounts is net accounts receivable, which is included in total assets on the balance sheet.

Accounts receivable, grass	₹100,000
Less allowance for uncollectible accounts	(2,400)
Accounts receivable, net	₹97,600

Exhibit contains OB's partial balance sheet. It shows the balance in the allowance account, as well as the net accounts receivable included in total assets.

EXHIBIT Partial Balance Sheet

OshKosh B'Gosh
Partial Balance Sheet
(Dollars in thousands)

	December 31, 1997	1996
Accounts receivable, less allowances of ₹4,225 in 1997 and ₹5,474 in 1996	₹23,278	₹20,504

From the information provided, gross accounts receivable on December 31, 1997, can be computed as ₹27,503,000:

Net receivable	=	Gross receivable	–	Allowance
₹23,278,000	=	Gross receivable	–	₹4,225,000
₹23,278,000	=	₹27,503,000	–	4,225,000

Write-Offs

When a firm subsequently ascertains that a particular customer will not pay, that customer's account is written off. This is done by reducing the balances in accounts receivable and in the allowance for uncollectible accounts. Continuing with the Box Company illustration, assume that on February 11, 2001, Box becomes aware that a customer who owes ₹450 has just gone out of business and that collection is extremely unlikely.

The balances in the accounts receivable and allowance accounts would each be reduced by ₹450.

	Assets		= Liabilities + Shareholders' Equity
	Accounts receivable	Allowance for uncollectible accounts	
Bal.	₹100,000	–₹2,400	
Feb. 11	– ₹450	+₹450	
	₹99,550	–₹1,950	

Because the balance in accounts receivable is reduced, as is the accompanying contra asset, the write-off has no effect on total assets or expenses. This is proper, because the asset reduction and expense were previously recorded. Box's net receivable is ₹97,600, both before and after the write-off.

	Before	After
Accounts receivable, gross	₹100,000	₹99,550
Less allowance	2,400	1,950
Accounts receivable, net	₹97,600	₹97,600

The effect of the write-off is depicted graphically in Exhibit.

Estimation Methods

Firms can estimate the year-end adjustment for uncollectible accounts in several ways. One approach is the aging method. In its simplest form, the aging method classifies the year-end accounts receivable balance into two categories: (1) current and (2) past due.

Suppose, for example, that a firm's sales terms are 2/10, net 30. This indicates that all accounts are due within 30 days of sale. On the balance sheet date, accounts that have been outstanding for 30 or fewer days are classified as current. The remainder are classified as past due. Based on a firm's past experience, industry norms, and current trends, the firm estimates the percentage of each category that will not be collected.

This is the step that requires the most judgment. Also, because older accounts are more likely not to be collected, the past-due category has a higher percentage of uncollectibles than the current category. These percentages are multiplied by each category's balance to estimate the allowance for uncollectible accounts.

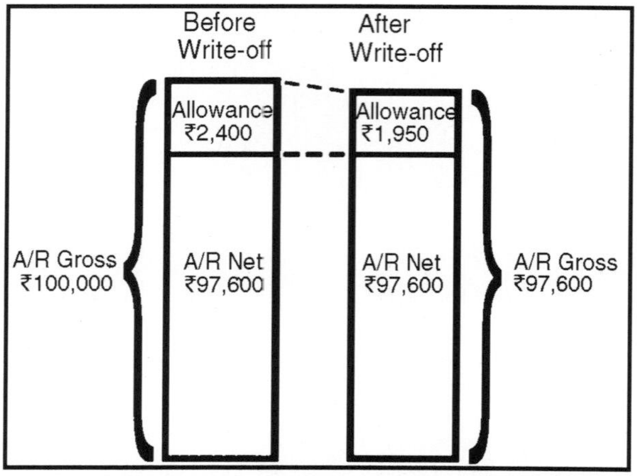

Box Company estimated its allowance to be ₹2,400 at the end of 2000. The aging analysis that resulted in this estimate is as follows:

Age Category	Balance	×	Percentage Estimated to Uncollectible	=	Estimated Amount Uncollectible
Current	₹90,000		2%		₹1,800
Past due	10,000		6%		600
Total	₹100,000				₹2,400

Although other estimation methods can yield different results on a year-to-year basis, over the long run their results will be quite similar.

ANALYSIS OF ACCOUNTS RECEIVABLE

The analysis of accounts receivable involves two issues: the relative size of accounts receivable and the adequacy of the allowance for uncollectible accounts. The financial statements of OB are used to show these issues. Exhibit contains some basic information about OB's receivables.

Size of Accounts Receivable

Because accounts receivable earn no return after the discount period has expired, firms should limit their investment in this asset.

The size of accounts receivable is usually assessed relative to the amount of credit sales. This seems appropriate because credit sales give rise to accounts receivable. Most firms do not separately disclose credit sales, so net sales are usually used.

A straightforward analysis divides gross accounts receivable by sales:

$$\text{Accounts receivable as a percentage of sales} = \frac{\text{Accounts receivable (gross)}}{\text{Sales}}$$

OB's trend is not favourable. Notice that although sales declined from 1996 to 1997, the balance in accounts receivable actually increased.

EXHIBIT **Financial Statement Information**

OshKosh B'Gosh
Selected Accounts Receivable-Related Information
(Dollars in thousands)

	1997	1996
Accounts receivable, gross	₹ 27,503	₹ 25,978
Allowance for doubtful accounts	₹4,225	₹5,474
Sales	₹395,196	₹444,766
Accounts receivable as a percentage of sales	7.0%	5.8%
Collection period	25 days	21 days
Allowance as a percentage of accounts receivable	15.4%	21.1%

Although the unfavourable trend might be due to less effective management of accounts receivable, it could also be due to a changing sales pattern. If, in 1997,OB made a relatively larger proportion of its sales near year-end, we would expect to see an increase in year-end accounts receivable. An alternative analysis involves calculating the average length of time it takes to collect a receivable. This is known as the collection period. It is calculated in two steps. *First*, calculate the average sales per day:

$$\text{Average sales per day} = \frac{\text{Sales}}{365}$$

Next, the collection period is calculated by dividing gross accounts receivable by average sales per day.

$$\text{Collection period} = \frac{\text{Accounts receivable (gross)}}{\text{Average sales per day}}$$

This ratio indicates the number of days sales in accounts receivable. OB's collection period increased from 21 to 25 days. This is consistent with the analysis of accounts receivable as a percentage of sales.

$$\begin{array}{lll} & 1997 & 1996 \\ \text{Average sales per day} = & \dfrac{₹395{,}196}{365} = ₹1{,}083 & \dfrac{₹444{,}766}{365} = ₹1{,}219 \\ \text{Collection period} = & \dfrac{₹27{,}503}{₹1{,}083} = 25\text{ days} & \dfrac{₹25{,}978}{₹1{,}219} = 21\text{ days} \end{array}$$

Exhibit contains a comparison of OB's ratios with Hartmarx Corporation, another apparel manufacturer, and, as a point of contrast, with Albertson's, a food store. OB's accounts receivable as a percentage of sales and its collection period are about one-third as large as those of Hartmarx.

At least four interpretations are possible:

1. OB is doing much better than Hartmarx in quickly collecting its receivables and minimizing its investment in this asset;
2. OB's sales pattern during the year differs markedly from that of Hartmarx (that is, OB makes substantially fewer sales at year-end than Hartmarx does);

3. OB is inducing its customers to pay quickly either through strong pressure or steep discounts;
4. OB factors more accounts receivable than does Hartmarx.

EXHIBIT Comparisons of Accounts Receivable Ratios

Accounts Receivable Ratios
Interfirm Comparisons
1997

	OB	Hartmarx Corp.	Albertsons
Accounts receivable as a percentage of sales	7.0%	20.4%	.8%
Collection period	25 days	75 days	3 days
Allowance as a percentage of accounts receivable	15.4%	6.7%	1.0%

Also note that food stores have a much shorter collection period than apparel manufacturers, which is due to the nature of food stores' credit sales. Most credit sales are made via customers' credit cards at major banks and food stores are able to collect these receivables from the banks very quickly. Some credit sales are made to businesses (such as restaurants and caterers), but these customers pay by check within a reasonable period of time.

Adequacy of Allowance for Uncollectible Accounts

The writing off a specific account as uncollectible has no effect on total assets or net income. Assets and income are affected by the year-end adjustment in which uncollectible accounts are estimated. A great deal of judgment and discretion is used by management in making this estimate. Accordingly, analysts must carefully assess the reasonableness of the allowance for uncollectible accounts. Few firms disclose their uncollectible accounts expense, yet most firms do disclose the year-end balance in the allowance for uncollectible accounts. The adequacy of this balance is usually assessed relative to the year-end accounts receivable balance. This is done by dividing the allowance by gross accounts receivable:

$$\begin{array}{l}\text{Allowance for uncollectible accounts as}\\ \text{a percentage of accounts receivable}\end{array} = \frac{\text{Allowance for uncollectible account}}{\text{Accounts receivable (gross)}}$$

OB's percentage decreased from 21.1% in 1996 to 15.4% in 1997.

$$\begin{array}{l}\text{Allowance for uncollectible accounts as}\\ \text{a percentage of accounts receivable}\end{array} = \overset{1997}{\frac{₹4,255}{₹27,503}} = 15.4\% \quad \overset{1996}{\frac{₹5,474}{₹25,978}} = 21.1\%$$

The reason for such a decrease is not entirely apparent. Perhaps OB made a conscious decision to decrease its sales to customers with dubious credit ratings. Such a change in the customer base would allow a decrease in the allowance for uncollectible accounts. "The Income Statement," that in 1997 OB ceased its European operations and terminated its relationship with certain domestic distributors. These changes altered the composition of OB's customer base and might justify the decline in the allowance for uncollectible accounts. Exhibit shows that OB's uncollectible accounts estimate is much more conservative than that of its competitor Hartmarx. Most analysts view conservative accounting practices with favour and feel that they result in earnings numbers of high quality.

Implications for Managers

As with any asset, managers should attempt to maximize the return on accounts receivable. One way to do this is to reduce the firm's investment in accounts receivable. Managers can employ several strategies to do this. Sales terms can be set so that the customer is obligated to make payment in a relatively short period of time. Managers should closely monitor accounts receivable collections to ensure that customers are paying within the agreed period. Discounts for early payment can also induce customers to pay quickly. However, discounts large enough to prompt early payment may prove to be quite expensive for the seller.

Also keep in mind that sales terms may be constrained by industry practices. That is, a firm must provide terms that are competitive with those offered by its rivals. In general, sales terms are just one product attribute in a firm's overall promotional strategy. Managers must also decide which customers will be granted credit. A trade-off exists between the amount of sales that can be generated and the level of uncollectible accounts expense incurred. Managers should set minimum credit ratings for its customers so that profitability is maximized.

INVENTORY

Inventory consists of products acquired for resale to customers. For many companies, inventory is a major asset and a significant source of revenue.

BASIC ACCOUNTING

Assume that several items of inventory are acquired for a total price of ₹100. This transaction results in an increase in inventory and a decrease in cash.

Assets		=	Liabilities	+	Shareholders' Equity
Cash	Inventory				
– ₹100	+ ₹100				

Now assume that half the inventory is sold for ₹75. This transaction is analysed in two steps. The revenue part increases cash and shareholders' equity by ₹75. The expense part decreases inventory and shareholders' equity by ₹50 (half of the ₹100 historical cost).

Assets		=	Liabilities	+	Shareholders' Equity
Cash	Inventory				Retained earnings
+₹75					+₹75 (sales)
	– ₹50				– ₹50 (cost of goods sold)

The difference between the sales price of ₹75 and the cost of goods sold (CGS) of ₹50 is the gross profit or gross margin.

COST FLOW ASSUMPTIONS

Most firms purchase inventory items on an ongoing basis. Usually, these purchases are not made at a uniform price. This poses an accounting problem when inventory is sold: What is the cost of the goods that were sold and what is the cost of the goods that remain on hand? Some firms find it advantageous to keep a record of the cost of individual inventory items.

These situations involve inventory units with a high dollar value and relatively few sales. Car dealerships are good illustrations. When negotiating with a customer over the selling price of a given car, for example, the cost of that particular car is important information for the dealer. Thus, these firms are motivated to keep a record of each car's cost. Moreover, a dealer's inventory consists of perhaps no more than 100 cars, and the dealer makes only a few sales per day.

Such activity levels do not present a significant record-keeping challenge. The specific identification method maintains accounting records showing the cost of each inventory item. For most businesses, however, the number of inventory units and the volume of purchases and sales are so large that the specific identification method would be very costly to implement. A grocery store, for example, may sell 1,000 cereal boxes in one day. This requires firms to use a cost flow assumption. Consider the following summary of inventory acquisitions:

	No of Units	×	Unit price	=	Total Cost
Beginnig inventory	30		₹4		₹120
Purchase on February 18	10		5		50
Purchase on June 8	20		6		120
Purchase on October 22	20		8		160
Total	80				₹450

Assume that 48 units were sold during the year and 32 units remain on hand at year-end. To prepare the financial statements, the cost of the ending inventory and the cost of goods sold must be determined.

Average Cost

The average-cost method calculates the weighted-average cost of an inventory item on hand during the period and applies this cost to the units sold and to the ending inventory. The average cost is calculated by dividing the cost of goods available for sale by the number of units available for sale. The cost of goods available for sale equals the cost of the beginning inventory plus the cost of all purchases during a period. It reflects the total cost of goods that were on hand at any time during the period and that were available for sale:

$$\text{Average cost} = \frac{\text{Cost of goods available for sale}}{\text{Number of units available for sale}}$$

$$\frac{₹450}{80} = ₹5.625$$

To calculate the cost of the 48 units that have been sold, multiply the average cost of ₹5.625 by 48:

Cost of goods sold = ₹5.625 × 48 = ₹270

To calculate the cost of the 32 units in ending inventory, multiply the average cost of ₹5.625 by 32:

Ending inventory = ₹5.625 × 32 = ₹180

Alternatively, once either cost of goods sold or ending inventory has been calculated, the following equation can be used to compute the other.

CGS = Beginnig inventory + Purchases – Ending inventory

Adding beginning inventory and purchases yields the cost of goods available for sale. Subtracting the cost of goods that have not been sold (the ending inventory) from the cost of all goods available for sale results in CGS (the cost of the goods that have been sold). If ending inventory is calculated first, the cost of goods sold can be computed as follows:

CGS	=	Beginning inventory	+	Purchase	–	Ending inventory
₹270	=	₹120	+	₹330	–	₹180

On the other hand, assuming that cost of goods sold is computed first, the equation can be rearranged and ending inventory can be calculated as follows.

Ending inventory	=	Beginning inventory	+	Purchase	–	CGS
₹180	=	₹120	+	₹330	–	₹270

This general equation can be used with all the inventory methods described in this part.

First-In First-Out

FIFO is an acronym for First In First Out, an abstraction in ways of organizing and manipulation of data relative to time and prioritization. This expression describes the principle of a queue processing technique or servicing conflicting demands by ordering process by first-come first-served (FCFS) behaviour: what comes in first is handled first, what comes in next waits until the first is finished, etc.

Thus it is analogous to the behaviour of persons standing in line, where the persons leave the queue in the order they arrive, or waiting one's turn at a traffic control signal. FCFS is also the shorthand name for the FIFO operating system scheduling algorithm, which gives every process CPU time in the order they come. In the broader sense, the abstraction LIFO, or Last-In-First-Out is the opposite of the abstraction FIFO organization, the difference perhaps is clearest with considering the less commonly used synonym of LIFO, FILO—meaning First-In-Last-Out. In essence, both are specific cases of a more generalized list (which could be accessed anywhere). The difference is not in the list (data), but in the rules for accessing the content. One sub-type adds to one end, and takes off from the other, its opposite takes and puts things only on one end. A priority queue is a variation on the queue which does not qualify for the name FIFO, because it is not accurately descriptive of that data structure's behaviour. Queueing theory encompasses the more general concept of queue, as well as interactions between strict-FIFO queues. In our illustration, the cost of goods sold under the FIFO method is based on the cost of the 48 units that were acquired first.

	No of Units	×	Unit Price	=	Total Cost
Beginnig inventory	30		₹4		₹120
February 18	10		5		50
June 8	8		6		48
CGS	48				₹218

Because the cost of goods sold under the FIFO method is based on the cost of the earliest acquisitions, ending inventory must consist of the costs from the most recent purchases (those made closest to the period's end). Based on the inventory and purchase data given in the last subsection, ending inventory consists of the costs associated with the 32 units acquired closest to the end of the year. This includes the 20 units purchased on October 22 and 12 of the units purchased on June 8. Only 12 of the 20 units purchased on June 8 are included because the ending inventory consists of 32 units.

	No of Units	×	Unit Price	=	Total Cost
June 8	12		₹6		₹72
October	20		8		160
Ending Inventory	32				₹232

Last-In First-Out

The Last-in First-out (LIFO) inventory method assumes that the costs associated with the purchases made closest to the period's end comprise the cost of goods sold. Therefore, the cost of goods sold is based on the cost of the 48 units acquired most recently.

	No of Units	×	Unit Price	=	Total Cost
October 22	20		₹8		₹160
June 8	20		6		120
February	8				40
CGS	48				₹320

Ending inventory, therefore, must be composed of the beginning inventory cost and the cost of the period's earliest acquisitions.

Based on the preceding illustration, ending inventory is calculated by identifying the cost of the 32 units acquired the earliest.

	No of Units	×	Unit Price	=	Total Cost
Beginning inventory	30		₹4		₹120
February 18	2		5		10
Ending inventory	32				₹130

The difference between FIFO and LIFO can be described by examining the cost of goods available for sale. The cost of goods available for sale equals the cost of beginning inventory plus the cost of the year's purchases. By year end, each inventory item either will have been sold or will remain on hand. FIFO assumes that the cost of goods sold consists of the costs of the beginning inventory and the earliest purchases, and that the ending inventory is comprised of the more recent costs. In contrast, LIFO assumes that the cost of goods sold consists of the most recent costs and that the costs of beginning inventory and the earliest purchases are included in ending inventory. These partitions of cost of goods available for sale are depicted in Exhibit.

EXHIBIT Partitioning Cost of Goods Available for Sale: FIFO Vs LIFO

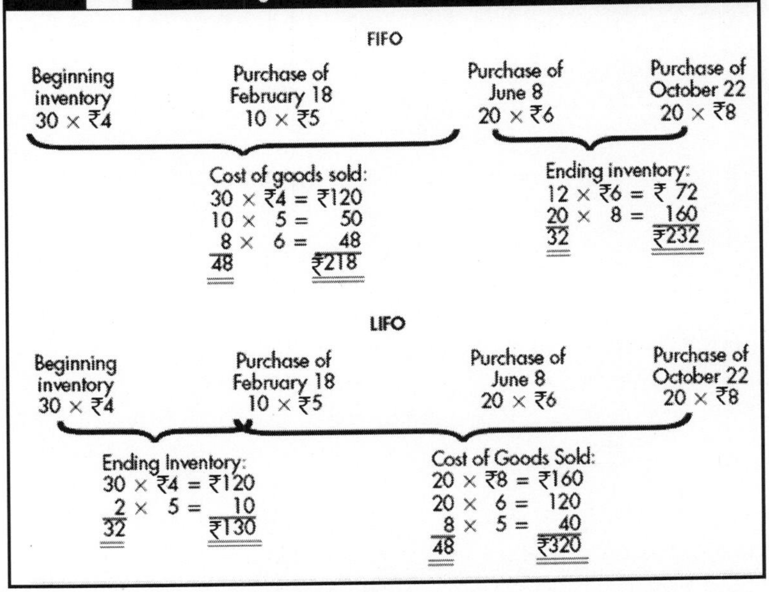

FINANCIAL STATEMENT EFFECTS OF INVENTORY METHOD

The choice of inventory method can have significant effects on financial statements. The effects of inventory method choice can be summarized as follows.

	FIFO	Average Cost	LIFO
Cost of goods sold	₹218	₹270	₹320
Ending inventory	₹232	₹180	₹130

Notice that the illustration reflects a period of rising inventory costs, which is the typical situation for many firms. The conclusions drawn in this part are dependent on rising prices. Opposite conclusions would be warranted in periods of price declines.

LIFO results in the highest cost of goods sold because:

- It assumes that the more recent costs are the first ones sold,
- These most recently acquired costs are the most expensive ones.

FIFO results in the lowest cost of goods sold, and the average cost method yields results between LIFO and FIFO. Because LIFO reports the highest cost of goods sold figure, it results in the lowest reported net income number. LIFO results in the lowest ending inventory value because it assumes that the earliest costs remain on hand at year-end, and these costs are the least expensive. FIFO yields the highest inventory value, and average cost falls between the two.

THE CHOICE OF INVENTORY METHOD

FIFO, LIFO, specific identification, and average cost are all acceptable inventory methods. Firms are free to choose one of these methods and consistently apply it across periods.

Interestingly, GAAP does not require that the assumed flow of costs corresponds to the actual flow of goods. Supermarkets, for example, put their older products on the front of shelves so that they will be sold before items acquired more recently; this helps preserve the general freshness of the merchandise available to customers. In this case, goods actually flow on a FIFO basis.

However, supermarkets are not required to use FIFO in the preparation of their financial statements. This raises a question about the factors that are considered by managers in selecting an inventory method. Because LIFO and FIFO yield the most dissimilar results, the following discussion focuses on them.

Taxes

The example we used to show the various inventory methods was characterized by a period of rising prices. Many industries have experienced decades of inflation in inventory costs. In such periods, LIFO assigns the higher, recently acquired inventory costs to cost of goods sold.

Of course, a higher cost of goods sold results in lower reported income. Thus, the selection of LIFO in inflationary periods reduces both reported pre-tax income and income taxes. Because a smaller check will be written to the IRS, the use of LIFO actually increases a firm's cash flow, even though reported net income is lower than under FIFO. In general, firms are not required to select the same accounting principle for financial reporting and for taxes. Because financial statements and tax returns serve different purposes, this makes sense.

LIFO, however, is an exception to this general rule. If LIFO is used for tax purposes, it must be used for financial reporting. Many firms prepare their tax return using LIFO to obtain the associated tax savings and are thus required to use it for their financial statements.

10

Budgeting

AN OVERVIEW

A major element of financial data activity rests in the act of budgeting. Budgeting is the process of allocating finite resources to the prioritized needs of an organization. In most cases, for a governmental entity, the budget represents the legal authority to spend money.

Adoption of a budget in the public sector implies that a set of decisions has been made by the governing board and administrators that culminates in matching a government's resources with the entity's needs. As such, the budget is a product of the planning process. The budget also provides an important tool for the control and evaluation of sources and the uses of resources.

Using the accounting system to enact the will of the governing body, administrators are able to execute and control activities that have been authorized by the budget and to evaluate financial performance on the basis of comparisons between budgeted and actual operations. Thus, the budget is implicitly linked to financial accountability and relates directly to the financial reporting objectives established by the GASB. The planning and control functions inherent to any organization, including schools, underscore the importance of sound budgeting practices for the following reasons:

- The type, quantity, and quality of goods and services provided by governments often are not subject to the market forces of supply and demand. Thus, enacting and adhering to the budget establishes restrictions in the absence of a competitive market.
- These goods and services provided by governments are generally considered critical to the public interest and welfare.
- The scope and diversity of operations in an organization make comprehensive financial planning essential for good decision-making.
- The financial planning process is critical to the expression of citizen preferences and is the avenue for reaching consensus among citizens,

members of the governing board, and staff on the future direction of the governmental unit's operations.

The link between financial planning and budget preparation gives the budget document a unique role in governmental organizations. Budgets in the public arena are often considered the definitive policy document because an adopted budget represents the financial plan used by a government to achieve its goals and objectives. When a unit of government legally adopts a financial plan, the budget has secured the approval of the majority of the governing board and reflects

- Public choices about which goods and services the unit of government will or will not provide,
- The prioritization of activities in which the unit of government will be involved,
- The relative influence of various participants and interest groups in the budget development process, and
- The governmental unit's plan for acquiring and using its resources.

In an educational environment, budgeting is an invaluable tool for both planning and evaluation. Budgeting provides a vehicle for translating educational goals and programmes into financial resource plans—that is, developing an instructional plan to meet student performance goals should be directly linked to determining budgetary allocations.

The link between instructional goals and financial planning is critical to effective budgeting and enhances the evaluation of budgetary and educational accountability.

OBJECTIVES OF BUDGETING

Performance evaluation allows citizens and taxpayers to hold policymakers and administrators in governmental organizations accountable for their actions.

Because accountability to citizens often is stated explicitly in state laws and state constitutions, it is a cornerstone of budgeting and financial reporting. GASB recognizes the importance of accountability with the following objectives in GASB Concepts Statement 1, *Objectives of Financial Reporting*:

- Financial reporting should provide information to determine whether current-year revenues were sufficient to pay for current-year services.
- Financial reporting should demonstrate whether resources were obtained and used in accordance with the entity's legally adopted budget. It should also demonstrate compliance with other finance-related legal or contractual requirements.
- Financial reporting should provide information to assist users in assessing the service efforts, costs, and accomplishments of the governmental entity.

Meeting these objectives requires budget preparation that is based on several concepts recognizing accountability. Accountability is often established by incorporating these objectives into legal mandates that require state and local public sector budgets to

- Be balanced so that current revenues are sufficient to pay for current services;
- Be prepared in accordance with all applicable federal, state, and local laws; and
- Provide a basis for the evaluation of a government's service efforts, costs, and accomplishments.

Although some form of a balanced budget requirement is generally necessary to ensure long-term fiscal health in any organization, variations such as the use of fund balance reserves to pay for current services may be appropriate over a short period.

Generally, however, all departures from this fundamental objective must be in accordance with applicable state and local laws and policies. Given the importance of demonstrating compliance with the approved budget, the financial reporting system must control the use of financial resources and ensure that budgetary appropriations and allocations are not exceeded.

To demonstrate compliance, accounting systems are usually operated on the same basis of accounting used to prepare the approved budget. Thus, the actual financial information captured by the accounting system is in a form comparable to the approved budget. Through budgetary integration, the financial accounting system becomes the primary tool to prove financial accountability.

Finally, the budget is evaluated for its effectiveness in attaining the organization's stated goals and objectives. Evaluation typically involves an examination of how funds were expended, the outcomes that resulted from the expenditure of funds, and the degree to which these outcomes achieved the stated objectives. This phase is fundamental in developing the subsequent year's budgetary allocations. In effect, budget preparation not only is an annual exercise to determine the allocation of funds, but also is part of a continuous cycle of planning and evaluation to achieve the stated goals and objectives of the organization.

BUDGETARY APPROACHES

Over the past 30 years, governmental entities in the United States have used a variety of budget approaches and formats. The development of more advanced budget philosophies reflects growth in both the scope and the complexity of governmental operations and the simultaneous need for systems that are capable of translating the variety of policy decisions into financial plans. Budgetary approaches, The National Advisory Council on State and Local Budgeting provides additional guidelines.

Various budgeting models continue to be commonly used and fall predominantly into categories of:

- line-item, or "traditional," budgeting;
- Performance budgeting;
- Programme and planning ("programming") budgeting (PPB);
- Zero-based budgeting (ZBB);
- Site-based budgeting.

In addition, many governments use a variety of hybridized versions to address the specific needs of the organization. Although these approaches are considered distinct in terms of the underlying preparation process, actual formats of the prepared budgets may be quite similar; for example, the format of a site-based budget may be quite similar to the format of a line-item budget. Each of the five basic approaches has relative advantages and limitations.

LINE-ITEM BUDGETING

Line-item budgeting is still the most widely used approach in many organizations, including schools, because of its simplicity and its control orientation. It is referred to as the "historical" approach because administrators and chief executives often base their expenditure requests on historical expenditure and revenue data. One important aspect of line-item budgeting is that it offers flexibility in the amount of control established over the use of resources, depending on the level of expenditure detail (*e.g.*, fund, function, object) incorporated into the document.

The line-item budget approach has several advantages that account for its wide use. It offers simplicity and ease of preparation. It is a familiar approach to those involved in the budget development process. This method budgets by organizational unit and object and is consistent with the lines of authority and responsibility in organizational units. As a result, this approach enhances organizational control and allows the accumulation of expenditure data at each functional level.

Finally, line-item budgeting allows the accumulation of expenditure data by organizational unit for use in trend or historical analysis. Although this approach offers substantial advantages, critics have identified several shortcomings that may make it inappropriate for certain organizational environments. The most severe criticism is that it presents little useful information to decision-makers on the functions and activities of organizational units. Since this budget presents proposed expenditure amounts only by category, the justifications for such expenditures are not explicit and are often unintuitive. In addition, it may invite micro-management by administrators and governing boards as they attempt to manage operations with little or no performance information. However, to overcome its limitations, the line-item budget can be augmented with supplemental programme and performance information.

PERFORMANCE BUDGETING

A different focus is seen in performance budgeting models. In a strict performance budgeting environment, budgeted expenditures are based on a standard cost of inputs multiplied by the number of units of an activity to be provided in that time period. The total budget for an organization is the sum of all the standard unit costs multiplied by the units expected to be provided. Although this strict approach may be useful for certain types of operations, many organizations require a more flexible performance approach. For example, expenditures may be based simply on the activities or levels of service to be provided and a comparison of budgeted and historical expenditure levels.

The performance approach is generally considered superior to the line-item approach because it provides more useful information for legislative consideration and for evaluation by administrators. Further, performance budgeting includes narrative descriptions of each programme or activity-that is, it organizes the budget into quantitative estimates of costs and accomplishments and focuses on measuring and evaluating outcomes.

Finally, the performance approach eases legislative budget revisions because programme activities and levels of service may be budgeted on the basis of standard cost inputs. However, performance budgeting has limitations owing to the lack of reliable standard cost information inherent in governmental organizations. Further, the performance approach does not necessarily evaluate the appropriateness of programme activities in relation to reaching an organization's goals or the quality of services or outputs produced.

Consequently, the performance approach has become most useful for activities that are routine in nature and discretely measurable (such as vehicle maintenance and accounts payable processing)-activities that make up only a relatively modest part of the total educational enterprise. But in sum, performance budgeting may offer considerable enhancement to the line-item budget when appropriately applied.

PROGRAMME AND PLANNING (PROGRAMMING) BUDGETING (PPB)

Programme budgeting refers to a variety of different budgeting systems that base expenditures primarily on programmes of work and secondarily on objects. It is considered a transitional form between traditional line-item and performance approaches, and it may be called modified programme budgeting. In contrast to other approaches, a full programme budget bases expenditures solely on programmes of work regardless of objects or organizational units. As these two variations attest, programme budgeting is flexible enough to be applied in a variety of ways, depending on organizational needs and administrative capabilities. Programme budgeting differs from approaches previously discussed because it is much less control- and evaluation-oriented. Budget requests and reports are summarized in terms of a few broad programmes rather than in the great detail of line-item expenditures or organizational units. PPB systems place a great deal of emphasis on identifying the fundamental objectives of a governmental entity and on relating all programme expenditures to these activities.

This conceptual framework includes the practices of explicitly projecting long-term costs of programmes and the evaluation of different programme alternatives that may be used to reach long-term goals and objectives. The focus on long-range planning is the major advantage of this approach, and advocates believe that organizations are more likely to reach their stated goals and objectives if this approach is used.

However, several limitations exist in the actual implementation of this approach, including changes in long-term goals, lack of consensus regarding the fundamental objectives of the organization, lack of adequate programme and cost data, and the difficulty of administering programmes that involve several organizational units. Yet despite its limitations, programme budgeting is often used as a planning device while budget allocations continue to be made in terms of objects and organizational units—a process that has been adopted in many schools throughout the nation. As with performance budgeting, PPB information may be used to supplement and support traditional budgets in order to increase their informational value.

ZERO-BASED BUDGETING

The basic tenet of zero-based budgeting (ZBB) is that programme activities and services must be justified annually during the budget development process. The budget is prepared by dividing all of a government's operations into decision units at relatively low levels of the organization. Individual decision units are then aggregated into decision packages on the basis of programme activities, programme goals, organizational units, and so forth. Costs of goods or services are attached to each decision package on the basis of the level of production or service to be provided to produce defined outputs or outcomes.

Decision units are then ranked by their importance in reaching organizational goals and objectives. Therefore, when the proposed budget is presented, it contains a series of budget decisions that are tied to the attainment of the entity's goals and objectives. The central thrust of ZBB is the elimination of outdated efforts and expenditures and the concentration of resources where they are most effective. This is achieved through an annual review of all programme activities and expenditures, which results in improved information for allocation decisions. However, proper development requires a great deal of staff time, planning, and paperwork. Experience with the implementation of this approach indicates that a comprehensive review of

ZBB decision packages for some programme activities may be necessary only periodically. Additionally, a minimum level of service for certain programmes may be legislated regardless of the results of the review process. As a result, ZBB has had only modest application in schools, although the review of programme activities makes ZBB particularly useful when overall spending must be reduced.

SITE-BASED BUDGETING

Site-based budgeting is widely considered the most practical for budgeting within the school district environment, by providing greater control and reporting of school-level data. This budgetary approach emphasizes the decentralization of budgetary decision-making. Site-based budgeting places local managers and other staff at the centre of the budget preparation process, making them responsible for both the preparation and the maintenance of the budget. Site-based budgeting is popular in many school settings. Within a school system, site-based budgeting generally involves granting increased budgetary authority to the school. Resources are allocated to the site, with budget authority for programmes and services granted to the school's principal and staff.

Campuses are normally allocated a certain level of resources that they have the authority to allocate to educational and support services. These budgetary allocations are meant to cover those areas over which campus decision-makers have control. For example, schools that have authority over staffing decisions may be allocated funds for staff costs using the site-based budgeting approach. In contrast, school districts that make staffing decisions centrally may not allocate funds to the individual school site for staff costs. The main advantage of site-based budgeting is that those who best understand the needs of a particular organization are empowered to make resource allocation decisions. This decentralization of budgetary authority may also increase local accountability. Another potential advantage of site-based budgeting is the increased level of participation of the public and staff in budget development. Many site-based budgeting systems create committees composed of staff and community members to determine budgetary allocations. These committees give members a voice from the inception of the budget process, rather than merely when the budget is presented for public review and approval.

Although site-based budgeting may provide substantial benefits, it also has limitations. First, organizations with limited resources may not be capable of granting a meaningful level of site-based budgetary authority. Even if an organization does have discretionary resources, it may be difficult to determine the areas of the budget for which local decision-makers should be held accountable. Finally, site-based budgeting may be burdensome to some local managers, may increase conflict between staff or departments, or may limit the organization's ability to ensure quality and sufficiency in the services it provides. These problems can be avoided somewhat through the careful design of site-based budgeting guidelines and through training for new budget stakeholders.

OUTCOME-FOCUSED BUDGETING

Consistent with the evaluation objective, government budgeting is becoming increasingly outcome-focused. Fiscal austerity, coupled with intense competition for governmental resources, has precipitated an effort to ensure more effective use of resources at all levels of government. Outcome-focused budgeting is the practice of linking the allocation of resources to the production of outcomes. The objective is to allocate government's resources to those service providers or programmes that use them most effectively. Outcome-focused budgeting is closely linked to the planning process in governments. For a government entity to focus on outcomes, goals and objectives must be identified and tied to budget allocations for the achievement of those objectives. This premise argues that mission-driven (synonymous with outcome-focused) governments are superior to those that are rule-driven because they are more efficient, are more effective in producing desired results, are more innovative, are more flexible, and have higher employee morale. In the context of increased governmental scrutiny of governmental costs, including schools, this model may receive more emphasis in the future.

OPERATING BUDGET RESPONSIBILITIES AND GUIDELINES

The development of annual budgets is part of a continuing planning process. The advent of site-based decision-making in some states has increased the integration of planning and budgeting at the school level; however, state laws generally allow considerable district autonomy in budget preparation. The organizational structure of a district, including the size and complexity of its administration and the degree of centralization, will affect the budgetary approach, the budget development process, and the final budget document. Beyond the requirements for federal and state programmes, the budget preparation process and related responsibilities will largely be determined by the local school board and superintendent.

The following stage contains information related to the significant aspects, phases, and outputs of the school district budgeting process. Although it is not meant to establish standards or requirements for districts, the stage may be useful in the development of sound budgeting procedures. Given the diversity of budgetary and financial reporting found in the individual states, the process described here may be customised to conform to particular local and state requirements. Additionally, the following discussion is typical of districts that use a site-based budgeting approach.

ROLES AND RESPONSIBILITIES

The local school board and the superintendent should establish a meticulous budget preparation process and guidelines. Thus, the delegation of budget responsibilities among administrators (districts wide) and schools (site-based) should be deliberately designed to require consensus at the highest levels of management. Because individuals may serve in a variety of roles in the budget development process, the division of duties may differ among districts. It is important, however, to clearly define the staff assignments and parameters if the budget development process is to operate efficiently. With the advent of site-based decision-making, individuals lacking previous budget experience need clear direction in order to provide effective input.

PREPARATION OF BUDGET GUIDELINES

Budget preparation guidelines typically are prepared by the assistant superintendent for business and finance or by an employee with similar responsibilities, such as a chief business official or a budget administrator, with direction from the school board, the superintendent, and other district and school administrators. A presentation with subsequent board approval of the budget process, guidelines, and calendar may be legally required or may be a locally imposed procedure.

However, as a minimum the guidelines should contain the following elements:

- A budget transmittal letter from the superintendent, which provides the overall context for budget development at the school level
- A budget overview, which explains the budgeting philosophy and approach, outlines the budget development process, and refers to major assumptions and changes in the budgetary process from the previous year
- Fiscal limitations to be observed, such as maintenance of service levels, specific percentage increases or decreases in resource allocations, and personnel hiring guidance
- A budget calendar of critical dates for budget completion, submission, and review
- Instructions concerning expenditure items to be budgeted at the school level and the detail required for submission
- A copy of standard budget preparation worksheets, submission forms, and diskettes
- A list of the account codes necessary for preparing the budget

Many of these elements may be combined into a budgetary overview included in the budgeting guidelines.

In addition to these elements, the preparation guidelines may also contain the following:

- Guidelines for estimating standard school resource allocations, which are determined by the budgetary approach used by the district and the availability of resources

- Guidelines for estimating the costs of specific expenditure categories, such as salaries and benefits, supplies, or fixed charges
- Instructions for submitting school budgets to the district office, including the number of copies, due dates, and personnel to contact for assistance

PREPARATION OF THE BUDGET CALENDAR

The budget calendar provides critical dates for the preparation, submission and review of school budgets. It is prepared during the planning process by the district budget office. A variety of simple techniques may be used to build the calendar, beginning with the previous year's calendar and modifying it for the current year. Problems that occurred in the prior year's budget cycle should be identified for changes to the current year's calendar. Additionally, changes in the budget development process should be incorporated into the current year's calendar. If the process has been substantially altered, creating an entirely new calendar may be necessary.

The following steps may be used to prepare a new budget calendar:

- Determine the necessary level of detail. If several calendars are used with varying levels of detail, they should be summarized in a master calendar to ensure that all activities and dates are consistent and compatible.
- Identify all activities that must be included in the calendar and arrange them chronologically.
- Assign completion dates to each activity. Although some districts may assign only completion dates, others may also assign suggested or mandatory start dates for certain activities to ensure their timely completion.

FINANCIAL FORECASTING AND PLANNING

Financial forecasting is the practice of projecting the quantitative impact of trends and changes in an operating environment on future operations. Therefore, it is an integral part of all ongoing planning efforts.

Financial forecasting is important for several reasons:

- Forecasting facilitates planning efforts by quantifying the future costs/benefits of strategic decisions. Thus, budgetary priorities may be evaluated on the basis of their long-term impacts.
- Forecasting clarifies trends, needs, and issues that must be addressed and evaluated in the preparation of budgets. For example, enrollment forecasting may reveal growing student populations and focus attention on the need for increased resource allocations for staff, facilities, or both.
- Forecasting enhances decision-making at all levels of administration. Forecasts provide valuable insight into future issues, which allows

administrators to be proactive. It creates the framework for anticipatory management.

Although financial forecasting should be a continuing process, it is most important as a component of budget development. Forecasts of projected enrollments, property tax base and revenues, costs associated with salary adjustments, and so on, are important elements in setting baseline budgetary guidelines and creating the basis for the assumptions used to prepare budgets. Additionally, forecasting provides fiscal impact analysis that may be integrated into the budget development process. Thus, current budgetary decisions may be evaluated for their long-term results.

When used before forecasts are prepared, several action steps may increase the reliability of the forecasts:

- *Clarify the intended purpose of the forecast.* The prospective audience may require a certain set of data and related assumptions.
- *Match the time frame with the purpose of the forecast.* Time frames for forecasts will vary just as to the purpose (*i.e.*, type) of forecast being prepared.
- *Ensure the accuracy of basic data.* Original source data should be used rather than extrapolated or summarized versions. Sources should be documented and verified if questions concerning data validity arise.
- *Specify the underlying assumptions.* Assumptions should be explicit in the forecasts with proper documentation based on actual data.
- *Be consistent in calculations.* Spreadsheet programmes are recommended for preparing forecasts to ensure the accuracy and consistency of calculations.
- *Examine data critically.* A scan of the data may reveal anomalies or errors that may adversely affect forecasts. Further, a comparison of initial values and forecasted values should be completed to ensure the reasonableness of forecasted values.
- *Recognize that forecasting requires insight and intuition.* Some variables or forecasting assumptions will always be a best guess. However, experience provides a basis for this type of estimation (Miller and McClure).

A variety of financial and related forecasts are necessary to the preparation of a comprehensive budget.

These include, but are not limited to:

- Student enrollment projections,
- Revenue and expenditure projections,
- Cash flow projections,
- Assessed property value projections, and
- Debt service cost projections.

CASH FORECASTS

Estimating and forecasting future conditions govern many critical business activities, such as inventory control, procurement of supplies, labour cost estimation, prediction of product demand, and prediction of cash requirement of a bank branch or ATM. Such predictions have been difficult, if not impossible. Incomplete understanding leads us to develop models that have uncertainties. In such cases, we resort to system identification models based on historical data. Input/Output data relevant to the application at hand must be collected over a period of time and analysed by automated model fitting procedures.

The key to all these forecasting applications is to capture and process the historical data such that it provides insight into the future. The ability to predict the future demand estimate of currency within a reasonable accuracy is called cash forecasting. Cash forecasting is integral to the effective operation of an ATM/branch network. The primary objective of cash forecasting is to ensure that cash is used efficiently and effectively throughout the branch network.

In this work, the problem of cash forecast has been studied in respect of a cash-balance branch and attempt has been made to:

- Adapt this forecasting model to the specific conditions in the various regions.
- Carry out short-term forecasts on the basis of alternative scenarios of the economic development.
- Include a comprehensive environmental impact analysis for forecast.
- Ensure implementation of forecasting tool.

Existing Approaches to Cash Forecasting

Techniques used for cash forecasting can be broadly classified into three groups:

1. Time-Series Method
2. Factor-Analysis Method
3. Expert-System approach

Time Series Method

This method predicts future cash requirement based on the past values of variable and/or past errors. The objective here is to discover the pattern in the historical data series and extrapolate that pattern into the future. The assumption in this method is that a cash requirement pattern is nothing more than a time series signal with known hourly, daily and seasonal periodicities. The difference between the prediction and the actual can be considered stochastic.

By the analysis of the random signals, a more accurate prediction can be obtained. Problems inherent with the time series approach include the inaccuracy of prediction and numerical instability. Generally, techniques in time series approach work well unless there is an abrupt change in the environment or sociological variables that are believed to affect the cash pattern.

Factor Analysis Method

This method is based on the determination of various factors that influence the cash requirement pattern, and calculating their correlation with cash. The purpose is to determine the functional form of this influence (independent variables) and to use this to forecast future values of the dependent variables.

The general approach consists of identifying the independent variables and then assuming a basic functional relationship between the dependent and independent variables, and finally determining the coefficients of the assumed functional relationship.

The main problem lies in the selection of the functional relationship, this usually has to be an iterative process, *i.e.* one assumes a certain form to the data, tests its validity, then assumes another form and tests its validity, and continues until a close fitting valid functional form is obtained. Estimating the functional form between the dependent and independent variables is more difficult when they have a non-linear relationship.

Expert Systems Approach

Expert systems are heuristic models which are usually able to take both quantitative and qualitative factors into account. Many models of this type have been proposed. A typical approach is to try to imitate the reasoning of a human operator.

The idea is then to reduce the analogical thinking behind the intuitive forecasting to formal steps of logic. Efforts to make expert systems general have run into a number of problems. As the complexity of the system increases, the system simply demands too much computing resources and becomes too slow. Expert systems have been found to be feasible only when narrowly confined.

Neural Networks Approach

Artificial neural networks offer a completely different approach to problem solving and they are sometimes called the sixth generation of computing. They try to provide a tool that programmes itself and learns on its own. Neural networks are structured to provide the capability to solve problems without the benefits of an expert and without the need of programming. They are capable of seeking patterns in data. Artificial neural networks (ANN) as they are often called refer to a class of models inspired by biological nervous systems. Neural networks forecasting has recently enjoyed considerable success in pattern recognition and prediction and as such has gained considerable research attention resulting in a plethora of substances on this subject. The concept is based on computing systems that are able to learn through experience by recognizing patterns existing within a data set. Neural systems require their implementer to meet a number of conditions.

These conditions include:

- A data set which includes the information which can characterize the problem.
- An adequately sized data set to both train and test the network.
- An understanding of the basic nature of the problem to be solved so that basic first-cut decision on creating the network can be made.
- These decisions include the activation and transfer functions, and the learning methods.
- An understanding of the development tools.
- Adequate processing power (some applications demand real-time processing that exceeds what is available in the standard, sequential processing hardware. The development of hardware is the key to the future of neural networks).

Once the necessary inputs (factors) are identified, it is relatively simple to train neural network to form a non-linear model of the underlying system and then use this model to generalize to new cases that are not part of the training data.

FUND BALANCE FORECASTS

Fund balance forecasting for governmental funds results from the budget development process. Periodic monitoring of balances is provided through budgetary integration with the accounting system and is necessary to ensure compliance with statutory and contractual fund balance requirements.

PLANNING FOR ANNUAL AND MULTIYEAR CONSTRUCTION AND GRANT PROGRAMMES

The following steps are basic to the planning process for both annual and multiyear construction and grant programmes.

- Review the stated goals and objectives to determine that they are the basis for the entity's activities and operations. Although normally developed during the strategic planning process, the goals and objectives should be periodically reviewed for appropriateness.
- Conduct formal or informal needs assessments or both. Most strategic plans include one or more needs assessments. The criteria used are normally developed locally; however, some granting agencies may require the use of certain criteria. A methodology that provides objective measurement of the needs of the unit under review is necessary and should include financial and other forecasts in order to properly identify those needs.

- Design programmes to attain the goals and objectives on the basis of the results of the needs assessment(s). The assessment process should identify and prioritize needs. From the results of this process, programme plans should be developed that meet the organization's needs. Programme planning should use an integrated approach to prevent the duplication of efforts, ensure the efficient use of resources, and ensure that all identified needs are addressed.
- Prepare programme budgets to support the implementation plans. With a programme plan in place, a budget can be developed. The traditional budgetary approach has been to appropriate only those monies necessary for the costs of the programme or project in its first fiscal year. At year-end, the appropriation expires and monies must be reallocated for each subsequent year of the programme or project. This approach is unnecessarily complex and may distract administrative and board focus from important budgetary issues. To avoid these problems, the development of multiyear programme budgets, whether for capital or special programmes, is recommended if state and local statutes permit multiyear budgeting.

BUDGETS FOR MULTIYEAR CONSTRUCTION PROJECTS

The development of multiyear construction budgets has two fundamental stages. The first stage involves extensive planning to identify facilities needs. A committee may be created specifically for capital planning or as part of a strategic planning effort. Identification of capital needs may also come from maintenance staff or from a contracted evaluation.

The evaluations should identify the costs for a particular programme, and from these inputs, a determination can be made regarding whether to pursue a construction project. Once this decision is made, the second stage involving budget development can begin. This process does not necessarily need to be incorporated into the annual budget process.

PREPARATION OF CONSTRUCTION PROJECT BUDGETS AND RELATED FINANCING

Following the decision to initiate a capital acquisition programme, funding mechanisms should be explored. This often involves some form of bonded indebtedness; however, building programmes may be funded with accumulated operating funds. Alternatively, capital leases and installment payments may be used.

In situations in which bond financing is used, the bond initiative must be reviewed and approved by the governing board before it is placed on the ballot. The size of the bond initiative for a particular programme may be determined by estimates of aggregate costs generated during the planning process and may not include detailed project budgets until funding has been secured. However, depending on the local political environment, bond initiatives may require detailed cost estimates that specifically identify the projects to be funded from the proceeds before the bond issue can be placed on the ballot. Financial advisers and bond attorneys may be consulted on the size, applicable tax regulations, marketing, and selling of bond issues. Other considerations include tax rate limitations or debt ceilings that may affect the amount of bonded debt that can be undertaken.

When funding has been secured, detailed project budgets should be developed. Individual budgets covering the life of each project are necessary for the proper monitoring of the related activity. Although cost estimates developed during the planning process may be used to determine the size of the bond initiative, actual project budgets must contain more detailed information. Architects, contractors, and staff should be involved in budget preparation, and it will be necessary to identify factors such as shifts in student populations, additional facility or site requirements, and so on, which may cause significant differences between the actual project budget and the cost estimates developed during the planning process. Construction project budgets using a multiyear format should be reviewed periodically by administrators with regular reports provided to the board on the progress of each project.

Bond attorneys and financial advisers also need to be informed periodically of the progress of projects using debt funds. In summary, the budgeting process is an integral part of the sound financial management of any organization. Adequately planning and managing the entity's resources play important roles as the movement for greater accountability expands in importance. Sound budgeting techniques, such as site-based budgeting, are being emphasized as school district administrators and funding agencies require a heightened level of justification for annual expenditures and decentralized decision-making. Site-based budgeting gains its popularity among administrators for its unique ability to effectively target funding because campus management largely makes the resource allocation decisions.

However, regardless of which budgeting technique is adopted, some benefits of preparing and managing a budget remain the same: greater control and accountability over financial resources as well as the demonstration that administrators are actively planning for future needs.

11

Governmental Accounting

AN OVERVIEW

Unlike most private sector organizations, governmental entities must be responsive to a number of different groups and organizations, including elected officials, other units of governments, investors, creditors, and citizens that are focused on monitoring their activities. All forms of monitoring include collecting and interpreting data, and this oversight function is often performed through information provided in governmental reports.

Among the most important types of communication is the annual financial report, which presents the financial position, operating results, and cash flows for a particular accounting period. All governments, including school districts, develop their annual financial reports in accordance with principles established by standard-setting authorities to provide consistency and comparability for users.

For governments to achieve the objective of accountability, financial information must be both relevant and reliable for reasonably informed users. Financial reports must satisfy numerous and diverse needs or objectives, including short-term financial position and liquidity, budgetary and legal compliance, and issues having a long-term focus such as capital budgeting and maintenance. Additionally, differences exist in the amount of detail that various users need.

Following a decade of research and analysis, the GASB recently concluded that to meet the varied needs of a wide range of users, governmental reports must provide information regarding the public entity as a whole in addition to the traditional fund financial statements. Accordingly, in June 1999 GASB introduced a new financial reporting model in Statement 34, Basic Financial Statements—and Management's Discussion and Analysis—for State and Local Governments. The new model integrates the traditional focus of governmental fund financial statements relating to fiscal accountability (and the modified accrual basis of accounting) with new forms of reporting (*e.g.*, government wide financial statements).

The two levels of financial reporting are intended to:

1. Provide more relevant information that will result in greater accountability by state and local governments and
2. Enhance the understandability and usefulness of the annual financial reports to users of these reports to enable them to make more informed economic, social, and political decisions.

This stage provides an overview of governmental accounting and financial reporting, including the new requirements, as well as a discussion of current approaches used in compiling financial reports.

In particular, the following elements are included:

- Governmental GAAP Hierarchy
- Measurement Focus and Basis of Accounting
- Fund Structure
- Internal Control Structure
- Other Issues Affecting Educational Entities

It is important for governments to provide effective financial information to constituencies in a consistent and clear format.

Specifically, the information provided by governments should contribute to accountability in the following areas:

- Financial position and results of operations
- Actual financial results compared with adopted budgets
- Compliance with finance-related laws, rules and regulations
- Efficiency and effectiveness of operations
- Maintenance of governmental assets

Consistency in financial reporting by governments is provided through accounting standards. GASB is the standard-setting authority of generally accepted accounting principles (GAAP) for state and local governments, including school districts. In cases for which no GASB pronouncement is applicable, other authoritative sources of guidance exist. The following stage presents a hierarchy of GAAP in descending order of authoritative literature for governments. The hierarchy was established in Statement of Auditing Standards (SAS) 69, The Meaning of Presents Fairly in Conformity with Generally Accepted Accounting Principles in the Independent Auditor's Report, effective March 15, 1992, and issued by the American Institute of Certified Public Accountants (AICPA).

GOVERNMENTAL GAAP HIERARCHY

- Consists of GASB Statements and Interpretations and AICPA and Financial Accounting Standards Board (FASB) pronouncements that have been specifically made applicable to state and local governmental entities by GASB Statements or Interpretations (periodically incorporated in the Codification of Governmental Accounting and Financial Reporting Standards).

- Consists of GASB Technical Bulletins and AICPA Industry Audit and Accounting Guides and Statements of Position that have been specifically made applicable to state and local governments by the AICPA and approved by the GASB.
- Consists of AICPA Accounting Standards Executive Committee (AcSEC) Practice Bulletins that have been specifically made applicable to state and local governments by the AICPA and approved by the GASB. Also included are consensus positions of groups of accountants organized by the GASB that attempt to reach consensus on accounting issues applicable to statement and local governmental entities.
- GASB Implementation Guides published by GASB staff. Additionally, practices that are widely recognized and prevalent in state and local government are included in this category.
- In the absence of a pronouncement covered by Rule 203 or another source of established accounting principles, other accounting literature, such as the following, may be considered, depending on its relevance to the circumstances:
  - GASB Concepts Statements
  - Pronouncements referred to in categories (a) through (d), SAS 69 of the hierarchy for nongovernmental entities when not specifically made applicable to state and local governments:
  - FASB Concepts Statements
  - AICPA Issues Documents
  - Statements of the International Accounting Standards Committee
  - Pronouncements of other professional associations or regulatory agencies
  - Technical Information Service Inquiries and Replies included in AICPA Technical Practice Aids
  - Accounting textbooks, handbooks, and articles

The appropriateness of other accounting literature depends on its relevance to particular circumstances, the specificity of the guidance, and the general recognition of the issuer or author as an authority.

MEASUREMENT FOCUS AND BASIS OF ACCOUNTING

Traditionally, the majority of governmental financial information has been maintained and reported in the fund financial statements on the modified accrual basis of accounting or the accrual basis for business-type activities. The recently enacted GASB Statement 34 establishes additional reporting (the government wide statements) that represents a major shift in the focus and content of governmental financial statements.

Collecting and reporting additional financial information required by the government wide statements add to the complexity of financial reporting activities and have significant implications for the traditional focus and basis of accounting used in governmental financial statements. The new government wide financial statements consist of a Statement of Net Assets and a Statement of Activities and are prepared using the economic resources measurement focus and the accrual basis of accounting.

Thus, revenues are recognized in the accounting period in which they are earned and become measurable without regard to availability, and expenses are recognized in the period incurred, if measurable.

Governmental fund financial statements continue to be prepared using the current financial resources measurement focus and the modified accrual basis of accounting. Revenues are recognized in the accounting period in which they become available and measurable, and expenditures are recognized in the period in which the fund liability is incurred, if measurable, except for unmatured interest on general long-term debt, which should be recognized when due.

Proprietary fund financial statements continue to be prepared using the economic resources measurement focus and the accrual basis of accounting. Like proprietary fund financial statements, fiduciary fund financial statements are prepared using the economic resources measurement focus and the accrual basis of accounting. Table summarizes the measurement focus and basis of accounting for each reporting element and type of fund.

Measurement Focus and Basis of Accounting for Financial Statements

Financial Statements	Measurement Focus Accounting	Basis of
Government-wide Financial Statements	Economic Resources	Accrual
Governmental Funds Financial Statements	Current Financial Resources	Modified Accrual
Proprietary Funds Financial Statements	Economic Resources	Accrual
Fiduciary Funds Financial Statements	Economic Resources	Accrual

GASB Statement 20, as amended by Statement 34, allows a government the option of applying FASB Statements and Interpretations issued after November 30, 1989, except for those that conflict with or contradict GASB pronouncements, to enterprise funds and government wide financial statements.

The election is made on a fund-by-fund basis; however, consistency in the application within a particular entity fund is encouraged.

FUND STRUCTURE

For governmental entities to ensure the proper segregation of resources and to maintain proper accountability, an entity's accounting system should be organized and operated on a fund basis. Each fund is a separate fiscal entity and is established to conduct specific activities and objectives in accordance with statutes, laws, regulations, and restrictions or for specific purposes.

A fund is defined in GASB Codification Section 1300 as a fiscal and accounting entity with a self-balancing set of accounts recording cash and other financial resources, together with all related liabilities and residual equities or balances, and changes therein, which are segregated for the purpose of carrying on specific activities or attaining certain objectives in accordance with special regulations, restrictions, or limitations. Statement 34 modified the structure of two categories of funds used by local governmental entities.

Specifically, the new reporting model introduces two new types of funds:

1. Permanent funds (in the governmental fund category). Permanent funds are required to be used to report resources that are legally restricted to the extent that only earnings (and not principal) may be used for purposes that support the reporting government programmes.
2. Private-purpose trust funds (in the fiduciary fund category). Private-purpose trust funds should be used to report all other trust arrangements under which principal and income benefit individuals, private organizations, or other governments.

The new model eliminates expendable and nonexpendable trust funds to focus fiduciary reporting on resources held for parties external to the reporting government: individuals, private organizations, and other governments. Fiduciary funds, therefore, cannot be used to support the government's own programmes.

With the incorporation of these changes, three categories of funds remain:

1. Governmental funds are those through which most governmental functions are accounted for. The acquisition, use, and balances of the government's expendable financial resources and the related current liabilities-except those accounted for in proprietary funds—are accounted for through governmental funds (general, special revenue, capital projects, debt service, and permanent funds).
2. Proprietary funds are used to account for a government's ongoing organizations and activities that are similar to those often found in the private sector. All assets, liabilities, net assets, revenues, expenses, and transfers relating to the government's business and quasi-business activities—in which changes in net assets or cost recovery are measured—are accounted for through proprietary funds (enterprise and internal service funds). Generally accepted accounting principles for proprietary funds are similar to those applicable to businesses in the private sector; the measurement focus is on determining operating income, financial position, and cash flows.

3. Fiduciary funds are used to account for assets held by a government in a trustee capacity or as an agent for individuals, private organizations, or other governmental units. The fiduciary fund category includes pension (and other employee benefit) trust funds, investment trust funds, private-purpose trust funds, and agency funds.

MAJOR FUNDS

The concept of major fund reporting is introduced and defined by GASB Statement 34 to simplify the presentation of fund information and to focus attention on the major activities of the entity. Rather than require each type of fund to be individually presented, Statement 34 requires the individual presentation of only major funds, with all other funds combined into a single column.

This reduces the number of funds presented on the face of the financial statements and directs the focus on the significant funds of the reporting entity. Major fund reporting is applied only to governmental (*i.e.*, general, special revenue, debt service, capital projects, and permanent funds) and enterprise funds. Internal service funds are excluded from the major fund reporting requirements. Fiduciary fund information is presented by type of fund rather than by major funds.

GASB defines major funds as those meeting the following criteria:

- Total assets, liabilities, revenues, or expenditures/expenses of the individual governmental or enterprise fund are at least 10 per cent of the corresponding total (assets, liabilities, and so forth) for all funds of that category (governmental funds) or type (enterprise funds).
- Total assets, liabilities, revenues, or expenditures/expenses of the individual governmental fund or enterprise fund are at least 5 per cent of the corresponding total for all governmental and enterprise funds combined.

Both criteria must be met in the same element (assets, liabilities, etc.) for both the 10 per cent and 5 per cent tests for a fund to be defined as major. However, Statement 34 permits a government to designate a particular fund that is of interest to users as a major fund and to individually present its information in the basic financial statements, even if it does not meet the criteria. However, a government does not have the option to NOT report a fund as major if it meets the criteria above.

It should be noted that in applying the major fund criteria to enterprise funds, the reporting entity should consider both operating and non-operating revenues and expenses, as well as gains, losses, capital contributions, additions to permanent endowments, and special items. When the major fund criteria are applied to governmental funds, revenues do not include other financing sources and expenditures do not include other financing uses. However, special items would be included.

INTERNAL CONTROL STRUCTURE

An integral part of proper accounting procedures rests in issues of controls and begins with internal accountability structures. The AICPA's Statement on Auditing Standards No. 78, Consideration of Internal Control in a Financial Statement Audit: An Amendment to Statement on Auditing Standards No. 55, (which incorporates the Committee of Sponsoring Organizations Report, Internal Control Framework) indicates that the elaborateness of the system of internal controls established within an organization is a matter of judgment on the part of management, with careful consideration for circumstances, such as the size of the organization and the number of personnel available, and the relationship between the costs and benefits of designing and implementing controls. In addition, the nature of internal control is such that even appropriate methods and systems will not guarantee that an entity's objectives will be achieved. Internal control is a process-affected by an entity's board of trustees, management, and other personnel-designed to provide reasonable assurance regarding the achievement of objectives in the following categories:

- Reliability of financial reporting
- Effectiveness and efficiency of operations
- Compliance with applicable laws and regulations

As a result, internal control consists of five interrelated components:

1. Control Environment
2. Risk Assessment
3. Control Activities
4. Information and Communication
5. Monitoring

CONTROL ENVIRONMENT

The control environment is established on the basis of the attitude of management towards internal control. It is the basis for all other elements of the system of internal control. AICPA Statement on Auditing Standards No. 78 states that the control environment "sets the tone of an organization, influencing the control consciousness of its people. It is the foundation for all other components of internal control, providing discipline and structure." As such, a management philosophy that is dedicated to establishing a sound business process and operating controls would tend to create a stronger internal control environment than a philosophy that is unaware of or unconcerned with internal controls.

The collective effort of various factors affects the control environment, including the following:

- Integrity and ethical values
- Commitment to competence
- Governing board or audit committee participation
- Management's philosophy and operating style

- Organizational structure
- Assignment of authority and responsibility
- Human resource policies and practices

The substance of internal controls is more important than the form because of the risk that controls may not be effectively implemented or maintained.

RISK ASSESSMENT

Risk assessment is the entity's identification and analysis of risks relevant to the achievement of its objectives and forms a basis for determining how the risks should be managed.

Risks can arise or change as a result of the following factors:

- Changes in operating environment
- New personnel
- New or revamped information systems
- Rapid growth
- New technology
- New grant programmes, building projects, or other activities
- Organizational restructuring
- Accounting pronouncements
- Federal regulations
- Finance-related statutes

Given the dynamic nature of governmental operating environments, the ability to anticipate and mitigate risks from these changes is a key factor in measuring the strength of internal controls. To the extent that the design of controls for new operations is an important aspect of planning efforts, an entity's level of internal control may be enhanced.

CONTROL ACTIVITIES

Control activities are the policies and procedures that help ensure that management directives are carried out.

Control activities can be divided into four categories:

- Performance reviews
- Information processing
- Physical controls
- Segregation of duties

The application of controls, such as the segregation of duties, is affected to some degree by the size of the organization. In small entities, procedures will be less formal than in large entities. Additionally, certain types of control activities may not be relevant in small entities.

INFORMATION AND COMMUNICATION

Information and communication represent the identification, capture, and exchange of information in a form and time frame that enable people to carry out their responsibilities.

Information systems encompass procedures and documents that do the following:

- Identify and record all valid transactions
- Describe, on a timely basis, transactions in sufficient detail to permit proper classification for financial reporting
- Measure the value of transactions in a manner that permits their proper recording in the financial statements
- Permit the recording of transactions in the proper accounting period
- Present properly the transactions and related disclosures in the financial statements

Senior management should deliver a clear message to employees about their responsibilities and role in the internal control system. Employees should also have a means for communicating the effectiveness and efficiency of these systems to upper levels of management.

MONITORING

Monitoring is a process that assesses the quality of internal control performance over time. Ongoing monitoring activities include regular management and supervisory activities and other actions taken during the normal performance of management's responsibilities. Further, periodic reviews of internal controls and related activities, performed with internal personnel or external resources, may be undertaken.

The nature and timing of these evaluations depend on the effectiveness of ongoing activities and the risk that internal controls are not performing as intended by management. Deficiencies in the system of internal controls should be reported to the appropriate level of management.

Management should clearly assign responsibility and delegate authority with sufficient care to ensure that:

- Persons who perform control procedures are held accountable for their performance by those who monitor these activities, and
- Persons who monitor the performance of control procedures are held accountable by senior management, the governing board, or the audit committee.

If accounting information is routinely used in making operating decisions, management is likely to establish effective controls and hold lower-level managers and employees accountable for performance. In addition, if management routinely uses accounting information in measuring progress and operating results, significant variances between planned and actual results are likely to be investigated. This review may detect the causes of the variances and affect the steps necessary to correct procedures that failed to prevent misstatements.

COMMON TYPES OF CONTROL PROCEDURES

Numerous control procedures and monitoring activities are performed by individuals in governmental entities to accomplish particular objectives. All these controls, however, can be classified within one of the basic categories of controls. Detailed control procedures or monitoring activities may be included in each of these categories, depending on the size of the entity and the sophistication of the particular control environment.

Access Controls

Certain controls prevent access to assets by unauthorized persons. Often these controls are physical in nature. For example, an organization might store inventories of supplies and commodities in locked storage areas, store currency in a vault or a locked drawer, and use alarm systems to restrict access by unauthorized individuals. If controls to prevent unauthorized access to assets are not effective, assets may be lost or stolen. If detective control procedures such as physical inventory counts are appropriately performed, shortages should be discovered in a timely manner.

In some cases, unauthorized access to assets may be gained through vulnerable accounting records-especially records maintained on computer systems. For example, if warehouse requisitions can be issued through a computer terminal, access to inventory may be gained through the system.

Controls over unauthorized access to assets through computer records may be physical (*e.g.*, terminals are kept in a locked room) or logical (*e.g.*, access to the computer programme or data files may be obtained only with the proper password or other user-identification method). Monitoring the control procedures that address unauthorized access includes observing physical control procedures, reviewing established access privileges with the manager of information systems, or reviewing reports of attempted computer access violations. Internal auditors often perform such activities.

Access controls, however, do not prevent individuals who have authorized access to assets from misappropriating them. Individuals who have authorized access to both assets and related accounting records may be in a position to conceal shortages of assets in the records. However, if duties are properly segregated, persons with access to assets will not have access to related accounting records, which may be altered to conceal shortages.

Controls over authorized access to assets are important to an organization, not only to prevent thefts, but also to ensure that assets are committed only after proper consideration by individuals who are knowledgeable and experienced. Authorization and approval are types of controls designed to prevent invalid or inappropriate transactions from occurring. An example is a procedure designed to ensure that disbursements are made only when authorized orders for goods and services have been received.

In many systems, access to computerized records (*e.g.*, shipping requests) can result in improper access to assets; therefore, procedures must be designed to limit access to computerized records.

Reconciliation and Comparison of Assets with Records

Reconciling and comparing assets with accounting records establish a system of independent verification, either through preparing an independent control document used to reconcile accounting records and assets or by directly comparing accounting records with related assets. Examples of these procedures include the reconciliation of physical inventory to accounting records and the preparation of a bank reconciliation.

Analytical Reviews

The purpose of analytical reviews is to evaluate summarized information by comparing it with expected results. Management personnel often perform analytical reviews to determine whether the entity is performing as planned. For example, a common analytical review procedure is the comparison of budgeted to actual performance, with investigation of any significant or material variances as determined by the analyst. Often, analytical reviews may be used to monitor other underlying control procedures.

Authorization and Approval

Authorization and approval procedures prevent invalid transactions from occurring. Thus, this type of control typically involves authorization or approval of transactions at specific dollar thresholds and manual (*e.g.*, requiring signatures of authorized individuals) or automated (*e.g.*, password protected) authorizations for computer transactions. The effectiveness of these procedures often depends on general computer controls over information security.

Reviews of Output

Reviews of output should be performed by district personnel who have the knowledge and experience to identify errors. Such reviews could be performed in both computer and manual systems. These reviews check the validity and accuracy of output by comparing it in detail with expected results. For example, a purchasing manager may compare recorded amounts or quantities purchased with separate records of purchase orders.

Transactional Reviews

Transactional reviews check the validity and accuracy of transaction processing by comparing it in detail with expected results. Reviews often use exception reports (usually computer-generated), which list items that failed to be processed because they did not meet specified criteria. For example, a computer-generated check may be rejected if it exceeds some dollar amount and requires a manual signature. Monitoring these types of control procedures involves reviews of results performed by management.

General Computer Controls

Computer systems frequently have common areas of control and related control procedures referred to as general computer controls. These controls directly or indirectly affect all systems that operate within a computer-processing environment.

General computer controls include the usual elements of effective internal control, that is, an individual or group responsible for control procedures and monitoring activities. Managers of the information systems function usually monitor the performance of general computer controls. Monitoring activities include observation, exception reporting, reviews of work performed, reviews of programme changes, oversight by information system steering committees, and the monitoring of user complaints. For example, the effectiveness of programmed control procedures such as edit checks and approvals depends on general computer controls that ensure that programme changes are not made improperly.

General computer controls include controls over computer operations; systems acquisition, development, and maintenance; information security; and information systems support:

- *Computer operations*: The computer operations staff is responsible for the day-to-day processing activities of the entity's system. It ensures that jobs are scheduled and processed as planned, data are properly stored on the system or tapes, and reports are distributed in a timely and accurate fashion.
- *Systems acquisition, development, and maintenance*: The systems acquisition, development, and maintenance staff is responsible for planning, acquiring or developing, testing, and implementing new application systems and changes to existing application systems. Such controls are usually important in larger processing environments where there is more development and maintenance activity. The systems are more complex and there is less reliance on purchased software.
- *Information security*: The information security function is responsible for administering and maintaining an entity's information security programme, including both physical and logical security. The primary goal of such a programme is to ensure that access to programme data, online transactions, and other computing resources is restricted to authorized users.
- *Information systems support*: Information systems support includes such functions as system software maintenance, database administration, comm-unications and network management, end-user computing, and other groups with technical and administrative support responsibilities.

Certain governmental entities may use external service organizations for executing and recording certain transactions, such as payroll processing. In such situations, the entity needs to ensure that the service organization has adequate controls over processing the transactions.

In the final analysis, maintaining the internal control environment and related control procedures is an integral part of management's responsibilities. In the context of governmental accounting and reporting, the control environment has a direct impact on an entity's ability to collect and present accurate financial information. Thus, the internal control environment and related procedures are key areas of concern to an entity's external auditor.

OTHER ISSUES AFFECTING EDUCATIONAL ENTITIES

School districts are the most common special governmental units. In some states, school districts operate as a fiscally dependent part of another local governmental entity such as a city or county; in other states, school districts are legislatively independent with authority to levy taxes and set budgets. School districts may or may not have common boundaries with another political subdivision.

Regardless of whether districts are component units of another financial reporting entity, are joint ventures of several reporting entities (such as consolidated educational agencies), or meet the definition in GASB Codification, Section 2100 as separate reporting entities, many school districts prepare separate financial statements to accomplish one or more of the following:

- Support state or federal aid applications
- Report financial activities to parent, taxpayer, and citizen groups
- Prepare a financial report for use in an official statement for bond issuance purposes

Although school districts are a common type of government, they face a number of unique issues that make them distinct from states, cities, counties, or other local governmental entities.

These issues often result in internal control and operational challenges that district management must address::

- *Attendance reporting*: Most school districts receive state aid on the basis of average daily membership (ADM), average daily attendance (ADA), or a similar pupil count method. ADM and ADA data typically are determined at individual school sites and then reported to a central attendance unit. That unit prepares reports for state aid and, in many cases, for federal aid, such as impact aid. Incorrect attendance reporting can lead to the allocation of too much or too little aid.
- *Student activity funds*: Most school districts have cash funds or bank accounts at individual schools under the control of school principals

or club advisors. These funds may be excluded from the district's normal accounting controls. These funds present a unique control challenge to school districts given their decentralized nature and the production of financial records and reports by non-accounting personnel.

- *U.S. Department of Education requirements*: Federal reporting requirements and others mandated by state-level education agencies are typically more detailed than the account code structures of cities and other local governments. Thus, district accounting systems must have the ability to account for transactions at a level of detail beyond that required by other governments. This issue is particularly complex for school district payroll systems, given the plurality of funding sources for district personnel and reporting requirements for personnel costs.
- *School lunch programmes*: Most school districts participate in the U.S. Department of Agriculture (USDA) free or reduced-price food programmes. These programmes require school districts to segregate food service programmes from other programmes. School districts that receive federal commodities during the year should recognize the fair value as revenue in the period when all eligibility requirements are met (typically, when the commodities are received). (Guide to Implementation of GASB Statement 34 and Related Pronouncements Q&A, Q152) Because the federal agricultural commodity programme involves purpose restrictions in the use of the resources, the value of inventory remaining on hand at fiscal year-end should be reflected as a reservation of fund balance/ restriction of net assets. USDA-donated commodities may also pose accounting and reporting problems because of restrictive federal rules regulating the use of these commodities.
- *Site-based management initiatives*: Over the past decade, many states and school districts have implemented site-based management initiatives. These initiatives have been designed to delegate to individual schools greater levels of authority to determine the use of financial resources. As a result, local administrators may control and report on the use of financial resources, even though they may lack financial management skills. This issue creates a challenge to district management in controlling financial resources and ensuring that reported results are correct.
- *Educational accountability*: Educational accountability has become a key policy issue at both state and national levels and has resulted in a number of recent reforms. Several educational accountability reforms have required school districts to collect and present school-level financial information. In addition, school-level financial

information is often related to non-financial information (*e.g.*, student achievement) in published reports and is used for comparison purposes. As a result, school districts must increasingly focus on ensuring that financial information reported by schools is accurate and consistent across the district.

In conclusion, school districts, like other governmental entities, must annually compile financial data and report on their financial position. Accounting and reporting standards for this information are set forth by a number of oversight agencies, including GASB, FASB, and AICPA. A major change in reporting requirements for governments was recently established by GASB Statement 34. This accounting standard requires governmental agencies, including school districts, to increase their financial reporting to include government wide financial statements as well as the traditional fund reporting. Although this new reporting model does not change the basic internal control expectations for governments, GASB Statement 34 presents new financial reporting challenges for school districts.

12

Standard Costing and Variance Analysis

STANDARD COSTING

You know that management accounting is managing a business through accounting information. In this process, management accounting is facilitating managerial control. It can also be applied to your own daily/monthly expenses, if necessary. These measures should be applied correctly so that performance takes place according to plans. Planning is the first tool for making the control effective.

The vital aspect of managerial control is cost control. Hence, it is very important to plan and control costs. Standard costing is a technique which helps you to control costs and business operations. It aims at eliminating wastes and increasing efficiency in performance through setting up standards or formulating cost plans.

MEANING OF STANDARD

When you want to measure some thing, you must take some parameter or yardstick for measuring. We can call this as standard. What are your daily expenses? An average of $50! If you have been spending this much for so many days, then this is your daily standard expense. The word standard means a benchmark or yardstick.

The standard cost is a predetermined cost which determines in advance what each product or service should cost under given circumstances. In the words of Backer and Jacobsen, "Standard cost is the amount the firm thinks a product or the operation of the process for a period of time should cost, based upon certain assumed conditions of efficiency, economic conditions and other factors."

DEFINITION

The CIMA, London has defined standard cost as "a predetermined cost which is calculated from managements standards of efficient operations and the relevant necessary expenditure." They are the predetermined costs on technical estimate of material labour and overhead for a selected period of time and for a prescribed set of working conditions. In other words, a standard cost is a planned cost for a unit of product or service rendered. The technique of using standard costs for the purposes of cost control is known as standard costing.

It is a system of cost accounting which is designed to find out how much should be the cost of a product under the existing conditions. The actual cost can be ascertained only when production is undertaken. The predetermined cost is compared to the actual cost and a variance between the two enables the management to take necessary corrective measures.

ADVANTAGES

Standard costing is a management control technique for every activity. It is not only useful for cost control purposes but is also helpful in production planning and policy formulation. It allows management by exception.

In the light of various objectives of this system, some of the advantages of this tool are given below:

- *Cost control:* Every costing system aims at cost control and cost reduction. The standards are being constantly analyzed and an effort is made to improve efficiency. Whenever a variance occurs, the reasons are studied and immediate corrective measures are undertaken. The action taken in spotting weak points enables cost control system.
- *Efficiency measurement*: The comparison of actual costs with standard costs enables the management to evaluate performance of various cost centers. In the absence of standard costing system, actual costs of different period may be compared to measure efficiency. It is not proper to compare costs of different period because circumstance of both the periods may be different. Still, a decision about base period can be made with which actual performance can be compared.
- *Eliminating inefficiencies*: The setting of standards for different elements of cost requires a detailed study of different aspects. The standards are set differently for manufacturing, administrative and selling expenses. Improved methods are used for setting these standards. The determination of manufacturing expenses will require time and motion study for labour and effective material control devices for materials. Similar studies will be needed for finding other expenses. All these studies will make it possible to eliminate inefficiencies at different steps.
- *Finding of variance:* The performance variances are determined by comparing actual costs with standard costs. Management is able to spot out the place of inefficiencies. It can fix responsibility for deviation in performance. It is possible to take corrective measures

at the earliest. A regular check on various expenditures is also ensured by standard cost system.

- *Management by exception*: The targets of different individuals are fixed if the performance is according to predetermined standards. In this case, there is nothing to worry. The attention of the management is drawn only when actual performance is less than the budgeted performance. Management by exception means that everybody is given a target to be achieved and management need not supervise each and everything. The responsibilities are fixed and every body tries to achieve his/her targets.
- *Right decisions*: It enables and provides useful information to the management in taking important decisions. For example, the problem created by inflating, rising prices. It can also be used to provide incentive plans for employees etc.

LIMITATIONS OF STANDARD COSTING

- It cannot be used in those organizations where non-standard products are produced. If the production is undertaken according to the customer specifications, then each job will involve different amount of expenditures.
- The fixing of responsibility is not an easy task. The variances are to be classified into controllable and uncontrollable variances. Standard costing is applicable only for controllable variances.
- The process of setting standard is a difficult task, as it requires technical skills. The time and motion study is required to be undertaken for this purpose. These studies require a lot of time and money.
- There are no inset circumstances to be considered for fixing standards. The conditions under which standards are fixed do not remain static. With the change in circumstances, if the standards are not revised the same become impracticable.

For instance, if the industry changed the technology then the system will not be suitable. In that case, as suggested, have to change or revise the standards. A frequent revision of standards will become costly.

SETTING STANDARDS

Normally, setting up standards is based on the past experience. The total standard cost includes direct materials, direct labour and overheads. Normally, all these are fixed to some extent. The standards should be set up in a systematic way so that they are used as a tool for cost control. Various Elements which Influence the Setting of Standards

SETTING STANDARDS FOR DIRECT MATERIALS

There are several basic principles which ought to be appreciated in setting standards for direct materials. Generally, when you want to purchase some material what are the factors you consider. If material is used for a product, it is known as direct material. On the other hand, if the material cost cannot be assigned to the manufacturing of the product, it will be called indirect material.

Therefore, it involves two things:

1. Price of the material
2. Quality of material

When you want to purchase material, the quality and size should be determined. The standard quality to be maintained should be decided. The quantity is determined by the production department. This department makes use of historical records, and an allowance for changing conditions will also be given for setting standards.

A number of test runs may be undertaken on different days and under different situations, and an average of these results should be used for setting material quantity standards.

The second step in determining direct material cost will be a decision about the standard price. Material's cost will be decided in consultation with the purchase department. The cost of purchasing and store keeping of materials should also be taken into consideration. The procedure for purchase of materials, minimum and maximum levels for various materials, discount policy and means of transport are the other factors which have bearing on the materials cost price.

It includes the following:

- Carrying cost
- Cost of materials
- Ordering cost

The purpose should be to increase efficiency in procuring and store keeping of materials. The type of standard used—ideal standard or expected standard—also affects the choice of standard price.

SETTING DIRECT LABOUR COST

If you want to engage a labour force for manufacturing a product or a service for which you need to pay some amount, this is called wages. If the labour is engaged directly to produce the product, this is known as direct labour. The second largest amount of cost is of labour. The benefit derived from the workers can be assigned to a particular product or a process. If the wages paid to workers cannot be directly assigned to a particular product, these will be known as indirect wages.

The time required for producing a product would be ascertained and labour should be properly graded. Different grades of workers will be paid different rates of wages. The times spent by different grades of workers for manufacturing a product should also be studied for deciding upon direct labour cost.

The setting of standard for direct labour will be done basically on the following:

- Labour rate per hour
- Standard labour time for producing

Standard labour time indicates the time taken by different categories of labour force which are as under:

- Semi–skilled labour
- Skilled labour
- Unskilled labour

For setting a standard time for labour force, we normally take in to account previous experience, past performance records, test run result, work-study etc. The labour rate standard refers to the expected wage rates to be paid for different categories of workers. Past wage rates and demand and supply principle may not be a safe guide for determining standard labour rates. The anticipation of expected changes in labour rates will be an essential factor.

In case there is an agreement with workers for payment of wages in the coming period, these rates should be used. If a premium or bonus scheme is in operation, then anticipated extra payments should also be included. Where a piece rate system is used, standard cost will be fixed per piece. The object of fixed standard labour time and labour rate is to device maximum efficiency in the use of labour.

SETTING STANDARDS OF OVERHEADS

The next important element comes under overheads. The very purpose of setting standard for overheads is to minimize the total cost. Standard overhead rates are computed by dividing overhead expenses by direct labour hours or units produced. The standard overhead cost is obtained by multiplying standard overhead rate by the labour hours spent or number of units produced.

The determination of overhead rate involves three things:

1. Determination of overheads
2. Determination of labour hours or units manufactured
3. Calculating overheads rate by dividing A by B

The overheads are classified into fixed overheads, variable overheads and semi-variable overheads. The fixed overheads remain the same irrespective of level of production, while variable overheads change in the proportion of production. The expenses increase or decrease with the increase or decrease in output.

Semi-variable overheads are neither fixed nor variable. These overheads increase with the increase in production but the rate of increase will be less than the rate of increase in production. The division of overheads into fixed, variable and semi-variable categories will help in determining overheads.

DETERMINATION OF STANDARD COSTS

How should the ideal standards for better controlling be determined?

Determination of Cost Center

J. Betty, *"A cost center is a department or part of a department or an item of equipment or machinery or a person or a group of persons in respect of which costs are accumulated, and one where control can be exercised."* Cost centers are necessary for determining the costs.

If the whole factory is engaged in manufacturing a product, the factory will be a cost center. In fact, a cost center describes the product while cost is accumulated. Cost centers enable the determination of costs and fixation of responsibility. A cost center relating to a person is called personnel cost center, and a cost center relating to products and equipments is called impersonal cost center.

Current Standards

A current standard is a standard which is established for use over a short period of time and is related to current condition. It reflects the performance that should be attained during the current period. The period for current standard is normally one year.

It is presumed that conditions of production will remain unchanged. In case there is any change in price or manufacturing condition, the standards are also revised. Current standard may be ideal standard and expected standard.

Ideal Standard

This is the standard which represents a high level of efficiency. Ideal standard is fixed on the assumption that favourable conditions will prevail and management will be at its best. The price paid for materials will be lowest and wastes etc. will be minimum possible. The labour time for making the production will be minimum and rates of wages will also be low.

The overheads expenses are also set with maximum efficiency in mind. All the conditions, both internal and external, should be favourable and only then ideal standard will be achieved. Ideal standard is fixed on the assumption of those conditions which may rarely exist. This standard is not practicable and may not be achieved.

Though this standard may not be achieved, even then an effort is made. The deviation between targets and actual performance is ignorable. In practice, ideal standard has an adverse effect on the employees. They do not try to reach the standard because the standards are not considered realistic.

Basic Standards

A basic standard may be defined as a standard which is established for use for an indefinite period which may a long period. Basic standard is established for a long period and is not adjusted to the preset conations. The same standard remains in force for a long period. These standards are revised only on the changes in specification of material and technology productions. It is indeed just like a number against which subsequent process changes can be measured.

Basic standard enables the measurement of changes in costs. For example, if the basic cost for material is ₹ 20 per unit and the current price is ₹25 per unit, it will show an increase of 25% in the cost of materials. The changes in manufacturing costs can be measured by taking basic standard, as a base standard cannot serve as a tool for cost control purpose because the standard is not revised for a long time. The deviation between standard cost and actual cost cannot be used as a yardstick for measuring efficiency.

Normal Standards

As per terminology, normal standard has been defined as a standard which, it is anticipated, can be attained over a future period of time, preferably long enough to cover one trade cycle. This standard is based on the conditions which will cover a future period of five years, concerning one trade cycle. If a normal cycle of ups and downs in sales and production is 10 years, then standard will be set on average sales and production which will cover all the years.

The standard attempts to cover variance in the production from one time to another time. An average is taken from the periods of recession and depression. The normal standard concept is theoretical and cannot be used for cost control purpose. Normal standard can be properly applied for absorption of overhead cost over a long period of time.

Organization for Standard Costing

The success of standard costing system will depend upon the setting up of proper standards. For the purpose of setting standards, a person or a committee should be given this job. In a big concern, a standard costing committee is formed for this purpose.

The committee includes production manager, purchase manager, sales manager, personnel manager, chief engineer and cost accountant. The cost accountant acts as a co-coordinator of this committee.

Accounting System

Classification of accounts is necessary to meet the required purpose, *i.e.* function, asset or revenue item. Codes can be used to have a speedy collection of accounts. A standard is a pre-determined measure of material, labour and overheads. It may be expressed in quality and its monetary measurements in standard costs.

REVISION OF STANDARDS

For effective use of this technique, sometimes we need to revise the standards which follow for better control. Even standards are also subjected to change like the production method, environment, raw material, and technology. Standards may need to be changed to accommodate changes in the organization or its environment. When there is a sudden change in economic circumstances, technology or production methods, the standard cost will no longer be accurate. Standards that are out of date will not act as effective feed forward or feedback control tools. They will not help us to predict the inputs required nor help us to evaluate the efficiency of a particular department. If standards are continually not being achieved and large deviations or variances from the standard are reported, they should be carefully reviewed. Also, changes in the physical productive capacity of the organization or in material prices and wage rates may indicate that standards need to be revised. In practice, changing standards frequently is an expensive operation and can cause confusion. For this reason, standard cost revisions are usually made only once a year. At times of rapid price inflation, many managers have felt that the high level of inflation forced them to change price and wage rate standards continually. This, however, leads to reduction in value of the standard as a yardstick. At the other extreme is the adoption of basic standard which will remain unchanged for many years. They provide a constant base for comparison, but this is hardly satisfactory when there is technological change in working procedures and conditions.

VARIANCE ANALYSIS

I will use this example throughout this Exercise:

Standard cost of Product A	$
Materials (5kgs x $10 per kg)	50
Labour (4hrs x $5 per hr)	20
Variable o/hds (4 hrs x $2 per hr)	8
Fixed o/hds (4 hrs x $6 per hr)	24
	102

Budgeted results		**ACTUAL Results**	
Production:	1,200 units	Production:	1,000 units
Sales:	1,000 units	Sales:	900 units
Selling price:	$150 per unit	Materials:	4,850 kgs, $46,075
		Labour:	4,200 hrs, $21,210
		Variable o/hds:	$9,450
		Fixed o/hds:	$25,000
		Selling price:	$140 per unit

A variance is the difference between an actual result and an expected result. The process by which the total difference between standard and actual results is analysed is known as variance analysis. When actual results are better than the expected results, we have a favourable variance (F). If, on the other hand, actual results are worse than expected results, we have an adverse (A).

VARIABLE COST VARIANCES

Direct Material Variances

The direct material total variance is the difference between what the output actually cost and what it should have cost, in terms of material. From the example the material total variance is given by:

	$
1,000 units should have cost (x $50)	50,000
But did cost	46,075
Direct material total variance	3, 925 (F)

It can be divided into two sub-variances

The Direct Material Price Variance

This is the difference between what the actual quantity of material used did cost and what it should have cost.

	$
4,850 kgs should have cost (x $10)	48,500
But did cost	46,075
Direct material price variance	2,425 (F)

The Direct Material Usage Variance

This is the difference between how much material should have been used for the number of units actually produced and how much material was used, valued at standard cost

1,000 units should have used (x 5 kgs)	5,000 kgs
But did use	4,850 kgs
Variance in kgs	150 kgs (F)
Valued at standard cost per kg	x $10
Direct material usage variance in $	$1,500 (F)

The direct material price variance is calculated on material purchases in the period if closing stocks of raw materials are valued at standard cost or material used if closing stocks of raw materials are valued at actual cost (FIFO).

Direct Labour Total Variance

The direct labour total variance is the difference between what the output should have cost and what it did cost, in terms of labour.

	$
1,000 units should have cost (x $20)	20,000
But did cost	21,210
Direct material price variance	1,210 (A)

Direct Labour Rate Variance

This is the difference between what the actual number of hours worked should have cost and what it did cost.

4200hrs should have cost (4200hrs x $5)	$21000
But did cost	$21210
Direct labour rate variance	$210(A)

The Direct Labour Efficiency Variance

The is the difference between how many hours should have been worked for the number of units actually produced and how many hours were worked, valued at the standard rate per hour.

	$
1,000 units should have taken (x 4 hrs)	4,000 hrs
But did take	4,200 hrs
Variance in hrs	200 hrs
Valued at standard rate per hour	x $5
Direct labour efficiency variance	$1,000 (A)

When idle time occurs the efficiency variance is based on hours actually worked (not hours paid for) and an idle time variance (hours of idle time x standard rate per hour) is calculated.

VARIABLE PRODUCTION OVERHEAD TOTAL VARIANCES

The variable production overhead total variance is the difference between what the output should have cost and what it did cost, in terms of variable production overhead.

	$
1,000 units should have cost (x $8)	8,000
But did cost	9,450
Variable production o/hd expenditure variance	1,450 (A)

The Variable Production Overhead Expenditure Variance

This is the difference between what the variable production overhead did cost and what it should have cost

	$
4,200 hrs should have cost (x $2)	8,400
But did cost	9,450
Variable production o/hd expenditure variance	1,050 (A)

The Variable Production Overhead Efficiency Variance

This is the same as the direct labour efficiency variance in hours, valued at the variable production overhead rate per hour.

Labour ef ficiency variance in hours	200 hrs (A)
Valued @ standard rate per hour	x $2
Variable production o/hd efficiency variance	$400 (A)

FIXED PRODUCTION OVERHEAD VARIANCES

The total fixed production variance is an attempt to explain the under– or over–absorbed fixed production overhead.

$$\text{Remember that Overhead Absorption Rate} = \frac{\text{Budgeted Fixed Production Overhead}}{\text{Budgeted Level of Activity}}$$

If either the numerator or the denominator or both are incorrect then as suggested, have under- or over-absorbed production overhead:

- If actual expenditure ± budgeted expenditure (numerator incorrect) » expenditure variance
- If actual production/hours of activity » budgeted production/hours of activity (denominator incorrect) » volume variance.
- The workforce may have been working at a more or less efficient rate than standard to produce a given output » volume efficiency variance (similar to the variable production overhead efficiency variance).
- Regardless of the level of efficiency, the total number of hours worked could have been more or less than was originally budgeted (employees may have worked a lot of overtime or there may have been a strike and so actual hours worked were less than budgeted) » volume capacity variance.

THE FIXED PRODUCTION OVERHEAD VARIANCES

Fixed Production Overhead Variance

This is the difference between fixed production overhead incurred and fixed production overhead absorbed (= the under–or over–absorbed fixed production overhead)

	$
Overhead incurred	25,000
Overhead absorbed (1,000 units x $24)	24,000
Overhead variance	1,000 (A)

Fixed Production Overhead Expenditure Variance

This is the difference between the budgeted fixed production overhead expenditure and actual fixed production overhead expenditure

	$
Budgeted overhead (1,200 x $24)	28,800
Actual overhead	25,000
Expenditure variance	3,800 (F)

Fixed Production Overhead Volume Variance

This is the difference between actual and budgeted production volume multiplied by the standard absorption rate per unit.

	$
Actual production at std rate (1,000 x $24)	24,000
Budgeted production at std rate (1,200 x $24)	28,800
	4,800 (A)

Fixed Production Overhead Volume Efficiency Variance

This is the difference between the number of hours that actual production should have taken, and the number of hours actually worked (usually the labour efficiency variance), multiplied by the standard absorption rate per hour.

Labour efficiency variance in hours	200 hrs (A)
Valued @ standard rate per hour	x $6
Volume efficiency variance	$1,200 (A)

Fixed Production Overhead Volume Capacity Variance

This is the difference between budgeted hours of work and the actual hours worked, multiplied by the standard absorption rate per hour

Budgeted hours (1,200 x 4)	4,800 hrs
Actual hours	4,200 hrs
Variance in hrs	600 hrs (A)
x standard rate per hour	x $6
	$3,600 (A)

Key

The fixed overhead volume capacity variance is unlike the other variances in that an excess of actual hours over budgeted hours results in a favourable variance and not an adverse variance as it does when considering labour efficiency, variable overhead efficiency and fixed overhead volume efficiency. Working more hours than budgeted produces an over absorption of fixed overheads, which is a favourable variance.

SELLING PRICE VARIANCE

The selling price variance is a measure of the effect on expected profit of a different selling price to standard selling price. It is calculated as the difference between what the sales revenue should have been for the actual quantity sold, and what it was.

	$
Revenue from 900 units should have been (x $150)	135,000
But was (x $140)	126,000
Selling price variance	9,000 (A)

Sales Volume Variance

The sales volume variance is the difference between the actual units sold and the budgeted quantity, valued at the standard profit per unit.

In other words it measures the increase or decrease in standard profit as a result of the sales volume being higher or lower than budgeted.

Budgeted sales volume	1,000 units
Actual sales volume	900 units
Variance in units	100 units (A)
x standard margin per unit (x $ (150 - 102))	x $48
Sales volume variance	$4,800 (A)

Key

Don't forget to value the sales volume variance at standard contribution marginal costing is in use.

REASONS FOR VARIANCES

Material price:

- (F)–unforseen discounts received, greater care taken in purchasing, change in material standard
- (A)–price increase, careless purchasing, change in material standard.

Material usage:

- (F)–material used of higher quality than standard, more effective use made of material

- (A)– defective material, excessive waste, theft, stricter quality control

Labour rate:

- (F)–use of workers at rate of pay lower than standard
- (A)–wage rate increase

Idle time:

- Machine breakdown, non-availability of material, illness

Labour efficiency:

- (F)–output produced more quickly than expected because of work motivation, better quality of equipment or materials
- (A)–lost time in excess of standard allowed, output lower than standard set because of deliberate restriction, lack of training, sub-standard material used.

Overhead expenditure:

- (F)–savings in cost incurred, more economical use of services.
- (A)–increase in cost of services used, excessive use of services, change in type of services used

Overhead volume:

- (F)–production greater than budgeted
- (A)–production less than budgeted

INTERDEPENDENCE BETWEEN VARIANCES

The cause of one (adverse) variance may be wholly or partly explained by the cause of another (favourable) variance:

- Material price or material usage and labour efficiency
- Labour rate and material usage
- Sales price and sales volume

THE SIGNIFICANCE OF VARIANCES

The decision as to whether or not a variance is so significant that it should be investigated should take a number of factors into account:

- The type of standard being used
- Interdependence between variances
- Controllability
- Materiality

MATERIALS MIX AND YIELD VARIANCES

The materials usage variance can be subdivided into a materials mix variance and a materials yield variance if the proportion of materials in a mix is changeable and controllable.

The mix variance indicates the effect on costs of changing the mix of material inputs. The yield variance indicates the effect on costs of material inputs yielding more or less than expected. Standard input to produce 1 unit of product X:

		$
Material A	20 kgs x $10	200
Material B	30 kgs x $5	150
		350

In period 3, 13 units of product X were produced from 250 kgs of material A and 350 kgs of material B.

Solution: individual prices per kg as variance valuation cases

Mix Variance

		Kgs
Standard mix of actual use:	A: 2/5 x (250+350)	240
	B: 3/5 x (250+350)	360
		600
		===

	A	B
Mix should have been	240 kgs	360 kgs
But was	250 kgs	350 kgs
Mix variance in kgs	10 kgs (A)	10 kgs (F)
x standard cost per kg	x $10	x $5
Mix variance in $	$100 (A)	$50 (F)
	=====	===
	50 (A)	

Total mix variance in quantity is always zero.

Yield variance

	A	B
13 units of product X should have used	260 kgs	390 kgs
but actual input in standard mix was	240 kgs	360 kgs
Yield variance in kgs	20 kgs (F)	30 kgs (F)
x standard cost per kg	x $10	x $5
	$200 (F)	$150 (F)
	=====	=====
	$350 (F)	
	====	

Solution: budgeted weighted average price per unit of input as variance valuation base. Therefore, Budgeted weighted average price =$350/50 = $7 per kg

- Mix variance

	A	B
13 units of product X should have used	260 kgs	390 kgs
but did use	250 kgs	350 kgs
Usage variance in kgs	10 kgs (F)	40 kgs (F)

x individual price per kg–budgeted weighted average price per kg	$ (10 - 7)	x $3
	$ (5 - 7)	____
	x ($2)	$30 (F)
	$80 (A)	===
	===	$50 (A)
	===	

- Yield variance

	A	B
Usage variance in kgs	10 kg (F)	40 kg (F)
x budgeted weighted average Price per kg	x $7	x $7
	$70 (F)	$ 280 (F)
	===	====
	$350 (F)	====

SALES MIX AND QUANTITY VARIANCES

The sales volume variance can be subdivided into a mix variance if the proportions of products sold are controllable.

Sales Mix Variance

This variance indicates the effect on profit of changing the mix of actual sales from the standard mix.

It can be calculated in one of two ways:

1. The difference between the actual total quantity sold in the standard mix and the actual quantities sold, valued at the standard margin per unit.
2. The difference between actual sales and budgeted sales, valued at (standard profit per unit - budgeted weighted average profit per unit)

Sales Quantity Variance

This variance indicates the effect on profit of selling a different total quantity from the budgeted total quantity.

It can be calculated in one of two ways:

1. The difference between actual sales volume in the standard mix and budgeted sales valued at the standard margin per unit.
2. The difference between actual sales volume and budgeted sales valued at the budgeted weighted average profit per unit.

13

Documentation and Preparation of Vouchers

DEFINITION OF DOCUMENT

A document is a bounded physical or digital representation of a body of information designed with the capacity to communicate. A document may manifest symbolic, diagrammatic or sensory-representational information. To document is to produce a document artifact by collecting and representing information. In prototypical usage, a document is understood as a paper artifact, containing information in the form of ink marks. Increasingly documents are also understood as digital artifacts. Colloquial usage is revealed by the connotations and denotations that appear in a Web search for document.

From these usages, one can infer the following typical connotations:

- Writing that provides information person's thinking by means of symbolic marks.
- A written account of ownership or obligation.
- To record in detail; "The parents documented every step of their child's development".
- A digital file in a particular format.
- To support or supply with references; "Can you document your claims?".
- An artifact that meets a legal notion of document for purposes of discovery in litigation.
- Document is the practical construct for describing matter in different forms which retain information for a reasonable period of time wherein it can be perceived by a sentient observing entity.

The variety usage reveals that the notion of document has rich social and cultural aspects besides the physical, functional and operational aspects:

- Document is just a practical concept which presently would be defined narrowly based on human understanding and perception of the external world.
- Document in its wider connotation could include matter in all its

forms, even a universe could be perceived as a document on a wider scale.

- The practical construct requires the retention of information but the relevance of the information
- The information must also be with reference to the observing entity be retained for a reasonable period of time wherein it can be observed. Fleeting images which cannot be seen are almost as if never observed.

CONCEPTUALIZATION IN ANALYTICAL PHILOSOPHY

The notion of document admits both an empirical and analytical characterization. The analytical characterization hinges on the semantic character of the word document, as well as the use of a primitive notion of document in accounts of larger communication constructs such as discourses, or related constructs such as language games. The nominal 'document', like other nominals, exhibits familiar patterns of polysemy.

For example, "document" might be used on an occasion to denote a certain body of information independently of how that information is physically rendered, or it might be used to denote a particular physical instantiation of a body of information. This kind of polysemy bears some similarity to what Nunberg, 1979 termed "container/contents polysemy". These patterns of polysemy exhibited by 'document' matter for the following reason.

A certain document qua body of information will have different properties than a document qua physical rendering of a body of information. Importantly, the latter would have the property of being a static, physically bounded thing.

The former would have the properties of being able to evolve over time, being susceptible of certain changes to information content, and being capable of supporting multiple physical instantiations that have allowable differences in information content. This distinction is relevant to the discussion of aspects and history of documents below.

EMPIRICAL CHARACTERIZATION

In light of the polysemy of the core concept of document, it is useful to note a number of examples ranging from instances commonly understood as prototypical documents, to instances that are understood as documents only in specialized or rare situations.

- *Prototypical Documents*: Letters, memos, legal forms, owners manual
- *Documents of Record*: Newspapers, magazines
- *Books*: Textbooks, novels, cookbooks, encyclopedias, comic books
- *Canonical Documents*: Code of law, statute, constitution, religious text
- *Transactional Documents*: Cheques, contracts, medical prescriptions, receipt, forms, Postage stamps

- *Functional Documents*: Portable Document Format files, PostScript files, XML files, e-mail
- *Non–Prototypical Documents*: Post-it notes, fortune cookie strips, maps, paintings, milk cartons, cereal boxes
- *Non–Classical Digital Documents*: Web pages, blogs, wikis
- *Boundary Examples*: The Pioneer plaque on the Pioneer 11 spacecraft, designed by astronomer Carl Sagan, and using information assumed to be universal is an extreme example of a document that is intended to communicate with aliens. Conversely, the recorded and printed signals of the SETI project would constitute documents if they were discovered to contain alien communication.

SOCIAL ASPECTS OF DOCUMENTS

Documents play a key role in the construction of social reality and therefore play a part in accounts of every important aspect of human society and culture. An example of this type of account is in the seminal account of the role of print in political evolution, Imagined Communities. More direct examples include the works of Marshall McLuhan.

Many key social aspects of documents arise from their historically unchanging character. This aspect leads to a definition of a document as a talking thing, whose strengths and weaknesses both arise from its relative immutability with respect to oral forms of communication.

The relative immutability of documents has thus historically been important for establishing a record of transient events, or for preserving information whose precise linguistic form is of ritual or practical importance. Note though, that historically many societies have accorded greater authority to disciplined oral traditions as more reliable than parallel written ones.

With this caveat in mind, the following social aspects of information may be noted:

- *Social Value*: The information in documents as well as documents themselves are often valuable; the information because of the influence represented, and the document itself when it is believed to be a rare or unique and authentic representation of the information it contains.
- *Manifestation of authority*: Documents are often produced to provide a record that will be considered authoritative in the future, particularly with respect to government. Consider receipts, titles, and deeds as examples of proof of ownership, and passports or driver's licenses as proof of identity.
- *Conventional*: Documents inherit a key feature of language-based communication in general: they are denoted as documents by convention. Virtually any medium can constitute a document provided the people involved can agree on the meaning represented. Hence cave drawings, hieroglyphics, scrolls of sheepskin, sheets of

papyrus, ink on paper, magnetic tape and electronic files are all documents under certain accounts.

- *Manifestation of economic labour*: Historically, the effort required to produce a document has been significant, so only the most important documents were created. The Illuminated manuscript of the pre-Gutenberg era demonstrates the cost have become richer.
- *Manifestation of business processes*: Documents play many roles in the internal management of a business as well in the interfaces between businesses and their suppliers, employees, and customers. Current trends towards longer value chains and increased regulation increase the number of documents that must be generated and processed.
- *Instruments of Governance and Law*: The unchanging aspect of documents is crucial to the consistent communication of policy and administration of law to citizens. Documents that play such roles include constitutions, corporate annual reports and religious texts.
- *Analytical philosophical character*: The notion of document plays a role in political philosophy, as well as in the philosophy of law
- *Role in Religion*: Documents play a key role in religion, and constitute canonical content. Document-related terms such as dogma and doctrine have today acquired pejorative connotations primarily due to historical events associated with religious documents.
- *Cultural Significance*: Documents play a central role in art of all varieties. In the movie Office Space for instance, central plot elements are frustration with bureaucratic process involving the fictional "TPS reports" and a malfunctioning printer.
- *Metaphoric Significance*: Metaphors based on documents permeate our thinking, ranging from the obvious to the highly allegorical.

FUNCTIONAL CHARACTERISTICS

Documents also manifest several, more localized characteristics that determine how we use them in everyday life:

- *Manifest nature*: Information is physical, *i.e.* it always must exist in a tangible form, even when digital. IBM computer scientist Rolf Landauer is credited with this observation and working out its implications. By virtue of being realizations of chunks of information, documents are necessarily physical in all their forms.
- *Contextuality and Situatedness*: All communication takes place in a context, which includes at least the shared understanding of the parties communicating. Explicit and implicit references to the context can convey a large amount of meaning by building on the shared understanding, but that meaning is lost to another party that does not share that context. For example, Shakespeare in the original would be incomprehensible to modern readers simply because of the evolution of language and spelling since the seventeenth century,

and modern readers normally read modernized versions. Similarly, hypertext documents exist in a context which is lost if printed, leading to a different offline reading context.

- *Evolvability*: When we think of a document as a definitive source containing the best known information about a topic there is need to change that information as more is learned. This is frequently done by revising the document into a new version or edition. Typically, older versions are archived to facilitate understanding how the document has changed. In modern contexts, when technologies such as wikis or software source code are under discussion, this evolvability can require very sophisticated version control technologies.
- *Renderability*: Every abstract entity that is understood to be a document in some context can be rendered, often in more than one way. A rendition of a document refers to a particular physical or electronic representation of the information from the document. For example, a portable document format representation and a web page may contain the same information but have substantially different properties and appearances. We think of them as different renditions of the same document. We might similarly consider different translations of a document to be the same document although differences in language context and structure may make it impossible to express precisely the same meaning in both languages.
- *Affordances*: Documents in digital and physical forms manifest various "affordances". The affordances of a particular rendition of a document determine its uses. For example, paper has the affordances of allowing flipping and easy tactile manipulation, while digital forms are easier to edit.

CLASSICAL ROLES AND WORKFLOWS IN DOCUMENT PRODUCTION

There are a number of roles in which people are involved in the creation and distribution of traditional paper documents; some, but not all documents are processed by people acting in each role, each of which may be performed by an individual or a group.

Books are a well known example of documents that require an extensive publication process, but many other documents undergo similar processes to at least some of those from book publication. Each of these roles is considered to improve or add value to a document. These roles are generally understood as being clustered in various phases in the production of a classical document, including authorship, editing and prepress. Roles and workflows in the production of modern digital documents are more variable and are discussed in the part on future documents.

- An author selects the content to be communicated and performs the initial organization and recording of the content. A document in this state is often called a manuscript.
- A reviewer reads the content and evaluates it with respect to the intended audience. Reviewers often recommend only the best documents to be published. Documented reviews are frequently published as guidelines for document consumers as well.
- An editor helps to organize and express the content so that the meaning is clear and understandable, and follows the conventions of the symbolic representation such as spelling and grammar.
- A publisher orchestrates the process of producing a document, often decides whether a document is worth the effort of publishing, and collects and disseminates the profits from sales of a produced document.
- A printer formats the document into a comfortable form such as a bound book. Printing can be a very complex and elaborate process, including
  - *Pagination:* function performed by an individual who takes on the tasks of organizing text, fonts, images, headings, footnotes, chapters and parts to accommodate the physical constraints of a printed page aesthetically.
  - *Pre–Press*: function performed by print shops in preparing paper documents for production.
  - *Imposition*: organizing desired pages on a larger media such that when folded and trimmed the pages will be upright and in order.
  - *Printing*: marking paper with ink or toner
  - Folding pages into parts
  - Binding pages together and covering
  - Trimming
  - Packaging
- A distributor manages inventory and physical distribution of printed documents to retailers.
- A retailer manages a local inventory and sales to consumers, and often is familiar with the content and can make appropriate recommendations.
- A librarian organizes, tracks borrowing of, and archives documents.

A publication process enables a consumer to purchase or borrow, read and learn from documents. Consumers are often the intended audience of the publication process.

DOCUMENT PRODUCTION TECHNOLOGY

Document production technology has evolved significantly through history. While a great deal can be said about ancient production technologies including papyrus, palm leaves, stone tablets and marking devices ranging from quills to chisels, the modern form of the document has evolved largely under the influence of printing technologies.

The Illuminated manuscript of Europe is a useful prototypical instance of the document at the end of its evolution before the widespread use of printing. The associated technology was largely a human one. Other cultures at this stage used other forms of pre-print era documents.

The history of printing can be traced as follows:

- Bronze Age civilizations made extensive use of seals for commercial and transactional purposes. The particular case of the signet ring was of particular importance, and is still in use in place of signatures in East Asian countries like Korea, where it is common for individuals to carry a seal.
- Chinese Woodblock printing was the first widespread technology that automated important parts of the document production process.

The Gutenberg Printing Press enabled the mass production of faithful copies of documents, and hence the widespread dissemination of information. The widespread access to information enabled fundamental changes to society in religion, government, law, business, and entertainment.

Prior to the press the huge effort required to faithfully hand-copy severely limited the number of documents available, and hence access to the information contained therein. The effort to set type and prepare a document for reproduction was still high, but many high fidelity copies could be produced.The development of Lithography constituted the next great advance in document production technology and continues today to dominate the economic landscape of document production, an economic sector estimated to be of the order of $1 trillion.

Lithography brought economies of scale and extremely high quality and low cost to documents. The typewriter improved the accessibility of document production technologies and enabled it to enter mainstream workplaces. Carbon paper enabled a modest number of copies to be produced concurrently with the original. A brief era of photography-based technologies flourished in parallel with the age of typewriters. The Xerox Copier became a major milestone in document production by eliminating the typesetting effort required by a printing press.

The Xerographic technology could produce durable and economical copies of a paper document easily and quickly. Modern digital printers from Xerox and other companies such as HP, Canon and Ricoh, can produce more than 240 black and white or 170 copies of a page each minute, and work with up to 6 colours and dry and wet inks. This technology supports a $100 billion market in digital printing, particularly in domains where lithography has clear limitations. Computers enabled information to be stored electronically in databases and electronic files on magnetic tapes, drums, and disks. This led to a radical disruption of all document production technologies. Initially most of this information was printed onto paper by teletypes, but computer printers rapidly became faster and more sophisticated.

Computers, by controlling lasers in xerography, micro-nozzles in inkjet systems, and tiny solenoids in mechanical systems, became capable of being serially embedded in the document production process. Computers are also critical to modern lithography.

A whole interaction style with computers was developed around the metaphor of working with documents and folders on a desktop, to the point that the word document is now commonly associated with the information stored in a computer file according to the metaphor. Today, electronic paper is viewed as one potential future evolutionary physical form of the prototypical document, as it can present the electronic document with the readability of printed paper.

DOCUMENT LIFE CYCLE MANAGEMENT TECHNOLOGY

Technology to manage documents has evolved in parallel with documents themselves. Of particular importance are practices concerning the preservation, archival, destruction and management of documents.

These constitute what is known as the "document life cycle":

- *Physical preservation*: Documents in both traditional physical forms and in digital physical forms such as magnetic media must be physically preserved. This aspect of document management deals with such issues as the aging of paper and obsolescence of magnetic media.
- *Storage*: This aspect includes management of scarce resources such as shelf space and disk space, and associated technologies such as optimal space utilization. Modern libraries such as the University of Nevada and the University of Michigan often use complex space-saving technologies such as robotic retrieval systems for stacks and moving bookshelves. In the digital realm, the entire discipline of compression technologies can be viewed as concerned with the storage of documents.
- *Cultural Preservation*: This function, traditionally ascribed to librarians involves the selection, arrangement and storage of documents in safe places. The importance of this part of document life cycle management can be seen in the impact of historical events such as the destruction of books in ancient China and the burning of the library at Alexandria. Today, library and information science has evolved into an important academic discipline.
- *Bibliometrics*: This aspect of document management involves

functions of indexing, generating statistics and taxonomies, and improving the usability of large collections of documents. The modern history of this management technology dates back to Melvil Dewey and the Dewey Decimal System. Today, the science of bibliometrics is largely concerned with managing the impact of electronic technologies. This aspect must also deal with ISBN numbers, Library of Congress data and other standards.

- *Digital Content Management*: The explosion of digital content has resulted in technologies to manage large collections of digital information generated by organizations. Such systems must manage access control and privileges, multiple electronic format, interface with printing infrastructures and enable collaborative work flows around documents.
- *Digital–Physical Interaction Management*: As long as both paper and digital documents continue to have value, the modern management technologies to manage their interaction will continue. Key to this management is the management of large scale and systematic scanning of physical documents.
- *Destruction*: With the increased cost of identity theft, corporate scandals and privacy concerns, the destruction of both paper and electronic documents has become increasingly important to manage. Technologies such as shredders play a role, as do verifiable processes of destruction of electronic documents to ensure compliance with privacy laws.
- *Security*: Shannon's information theory has led to an entire discipline that concerns itself with the security of documents, and associated technologies such as encryption, as well as more physical security features such as watermarks and making currency documents safe from counterfeiting.
- *Transportation*: The entire postal system, as well as modern courier systems, is largely built on the need to move documents physically from one location to the other.

THE DOCUMENT ECONOMY

The economics of the production and management of documents indirectly impacts every economic sector. While the total economic value of the document economy is hard to estimate, the economic sectors with business models directly dependent on documents include:

- *Document Authoring Technology*: This sector supports a huge variety of digital and physical production technologies, ranging from Microsoft Word to LaTeX to advanced layout software.
- *Education*: The production and processing of documents is so critical that entire educational disciplines have evolved around writing,

editing, layout and design of documents. The information sciences are also part of the document economy.

- *Electronic Document Management*: Managing documents within organizations and in public and personal contexts supports a huge industry in content management systems, ranging from free public infrastructure such as wikipedia to proprietary enterprise applications such as Docushare and Documentum.
- *Physical Document Management*: Large manufacturing sectors producing everything from 3-ring binders to filing cabinets and office desks exist largely due to the need to process documents.
- *Media*: The paper industry exists to support the document economy.
- *Print equipment*: From lithography and xerography to pencils and crayons, an extraordinarily diverse set of equipment industries depend on documents.
- *Document Services*: In large organizations, the life of documents in the work flows and processes of daily activity represent an enormous locus of value addition and cost reduction, which has led to a burgeoning industry in managed document services, ranging from specialized niches to managed office printing.
- *Retail Production*: From large chains such as Kinko's in the United States to small copy shops and offset print shops, documents support a large production sector for the end user.
- *Publishing*: All publishing, ranging from offset-based newspaper and magazine printing, to highly customised modern publishing using publish-on-demand digital print technology, is part of the document economy. The publishing industry includes major sub-areas such as the writer's market, small, medium and large publishing houses, small and large distributors and a vast network of independent and chain bookstores, online retailers, a large used-documents market and subscription-based markets.
- *Document Transportation*: The international postal system, as well as the commercial package transportation systems represented by companies such as DHL and UPS have economic models based largely on the demand for document transportation.

FUTURE OF DOCUMENTS

Since the advent of the digital era, documents have been rapidly evolving, and may require fundamental reconcept-ualization. Efforts at this reconceptualization include Vannevar Bush's initial conceptualization of hypertext.

The impact of digital technology can be understood in terms of several key aspects:

- *Blurring the notion of document boundary*: Hypertext and Web content make it hard to determine what is being denoted by the term document. While the early days of the Web resulted in documents that mimicked their physical ancestors, Web content rapidly took on new characteristics. Reconceptualization of the notion of "boundary" is a key intellectual challenge.

- *Increasing structure and openness*: The document is going from an opaque container of information to a much more open, structured document. XML is underlying most document formats today. In the future, it will become even more queriable, with the actual elements of this document being tagged—*e.g*. HR-XML.
- *Dynamic nature*: Web analogs of traditional paper documents like a newspaper column have taken on a dynamic character due to the impact of technology enabling the addition of comments from readers. The document will increasingly become "virtual", bringing up-to-date information from various sources in one container—as such,it will be kept evergreen.
- *Paper and electronic are reconciling*: Paper has traditionally been a gap in document processing workflows. Technologies such as OCR, OMR, 2D Barcodes and Anoto pattern technology are helping get its content back into the electronic world. In the future however, Not only will that transition be seamless, but it will also be possible to track it while in the "physical" world through RFID and MemorySpot.
- *Hybrid automated/human authorship*: authorship workflows for digital documents have evolved to include the computer in a key role. Dynamic Web pages may be viewed as the joint output of a human author and a software system. Sophisticated examples of this phenomenon can be found in recent evolutions in paper documents as well. Variable data technology, for instance, allows creators of direct mail marketing documents to vary the content of every piece in a print run using technologies such as DesignMerge or Xmpie.
- *Prosumer workflows*: Content repositories such as Wikipedia radically alter traditional document production workflows by blurring roles such as author and editor.
- *Customizability*: Digital technology allows users to actively participate in the construction of documents they see, realizing the postmodern notion of construction of meaning in an unexpectedly literal way.
- *Long Tail Economics*: Technologies such as blogs have allowed document production economics to operate with such radically cheap cost structures that single individuals can derive an income from a global audience with low capital expenses. This has led to an explosion of niche content.
- *Blurring of Documents and Interfaces*: Technologies such as Ajax or Apollo blur the distinction between documents and user interfaces

to "intelligent" technologies, leading to a whole class of smart documents that can go beyond the passive nature of traditional documents.

- *Fluidity and Dynamic Microstructure*: Distinct from the impact of hypertext on the notion of document is the fluid potential of modern documents at the microlevel, which allows an enormous variety of word and sentence level dynamic phenonomenology.

DOCUMENT MANAGEMENT SYSTEM

A document management system is a computer system used to track and store electronic documents and/or images of paper documents. The term has some overlap with the concepts of content management systems. It is often viewed as a component of enterprise content management systems and related to digital asset management, document imaging, workflow systems and records management systems.

Beginning in the 1980s, a number of vendors began developing systems to manage paper-based documents. These systems managed paper documents, which included not only printed and published documents, but also photos, prints, etc. Later, a second style of system was developed, to manage electronic documents, *i.e.*, all those documents, or files, created on computers, and often stored on local user file systems.

The earliest electronic document management systems were either developed to manage proprietary file types, or a limited number of file formats. Many of these systems were later referred to as document imaging systems, because the main capabilities were capture, storage, indexing and retrieval of image file formats.

These systems enabled an organization to capture faxes and forms, save copies of the documents as images, and store the image files in the repository for security and quick retrieval. EDM systems evolved to where the system was able to manage any type of file format that could be stored on the network. The applications grew to encompass electronic documents, collaboration tools, security, and auditing capabilities.

COMPONENTS

Document management systems commonly provide storage, versioning, metadata, security, as well as indexing and retrieval capabilities.

Here is a description of these components:

- *Metadata*: Metadata is typically stored for each document. Metadata may, for example, include the date the document was stored and the identity of the user storing it. The DMS may also extract metadata from the document automatically or prompt the user to add metadata. Some systems also use optical character recognition on scanned images, or perform text extraction on electronic documents. The resulting extracted text can be used to assist users in locating documents by identifying probable keywords or providing for full text search capability, or can be used on its own. Extracted text can also be stored as a component of metadata, stored with the image, or separately as a source for searching document collections.

- *Integration*: Many document management systems attempt to integrate document management directly into other applications, so that users may retrieve existing documents directly from the document management system repository, make changes, and save the changed document back to the repository as a new version, all without leaving the application. Such integration is commonly available for office suites and e-mail or collaboration/groupware software. Integration often uses open standards such as ODMA, LDAP, WebDAV and SOAP to allow integration with other software and compliance with internal controls.
- *Capture*: Capture primarily involves accepting and processing images of paper documents from scanners or multifunction printers. Optical character recognition software is often used, whether integrated into the hardware or as stand-alone software, in order to convert digital images into machine readable text. Optical mark recognition software is sometimes used to extract values of check-boxes or bubbles. Capture may also involve accepting electronic documents and other computer-based files.
- *Indexing*: Track electronic documents. Indexing may be as simple as keeping track of unique document identifiers; but often it takes a more complex form, providing classification through the documents' metadata or even through word indexes extracted from the documents' contents. Indexing exists mainly to support retrieval. One area of critical importance for rapid retrieval is the creation of an index topology.
- *Storage*: Store electronic documents. Storage of the documents often includes management of those same documents; where they are stored, for how long, migration of the documents from one storage media to another and eventual document destruction.
- *Retrieval*: Retrieve the electronic documents from the storage. Although the notion of retrieving a particular document is simple, retrieval in the electronic context can be quite complex and powerful. Simple retrieval of individual documents can be supported by allowing the user to specify the unique document identifier, and having the system use the basic index to retrieve the document. More flexible retrieval allows the user to specify partial search terms involving the document identifier and/or parts of the expected metadata. This would typically return a list of documents which

match the user's search terms. Some systems provide the capability to specify a Boolean expression containing multiple keywords or example phrases expected to exist within the documents' contents. The retrieval for this kind of query may be supported by previously-built indexes, or may perform more time-consuming searches through the documents' contents to return a list of the potentially relevant documents.

- *Distribution*: A published document for distribution has to be in a format that can not be easily altered. As a common practice in law regulated industries, an original master copy of the document is usually never used for distribution other than archiving. If a document is to be distributed electronically in a regulatory environment, then the equipment tasking the job has to be quality endorsed AND validated. Similarly quality endorsed electronic distribution carriers have to be used. This approach applies to both of the systems by which the document is to be inter-exchanged, if the integrity of the document is highly in demand.
- *Security*: Document security is vital in many document management applications. Compliance requirements for certain documents can be quite complex depending on the type of documents. For instance, in the United States, the Health Insurance Portability and Accountability Act requirements dictate that medical documents have certain security requirements. Some document management systems have a rights management module that allows an administrator to give access to documents based on type to only certain people or groups of people. Document marking at the time of printing or PDF-creation is an essential element to preclude alteration or unintended use.
- *Workflow*: Workflow is a complex problem and some document management systems have a built-in workflow module. There are different types of workflow. Usage depends on the environment the electronic document management system is applied to. Manual workflow requires a user to view the document and decide who to send it to. Rules-based workflow allows an administrator to create a rule that dictates the flow of the document through an organization: for instance, an invoice passes through an approval process and then is routed to the accounts payable department. Dynamic rules allow for branches to be created in a workflow process. A simple example would be to enter an invoice amount and if the amount is lower than a certain set amount, it follows different routes through the organization. Advanced workflow mechanisms can manipulate content or signal external processes while these rules are in effect.

- *Collaboration*: Collaboration should be inherent in an EDMS. In its basic form, a collaborative EDMS should allow documents to be retrieved and worked on by an authorized user. Access should be blocked to other users while work is being performed on the document. Other advanced forms of collaboration allow multiple users to view and modify a document at the same time in a collaboration session. The resulting document should be viewable in its final shape, while also storing the markups done by each individual user during the collaboration session.
- *Versioning*: Versioning is a process by which documents are checked in or out of the document management system, allowing users to retrieve previous versions and to continue work from a selected point. Versioning is useful for documents that change over time and require updating, but it may be necessary to go back to or reference a previous copy.
- *Searching*: Finds documents and folders using template attributes or full text search. Documents can be searched using various attributes and document content
- *Publishing*: Publishing a document is sometimes tedious and involves the procedures of proofreading, peer or public reviewing, authorizing, printing and approving etc. Those steps ensure prudence and logic thinking. Any careless handling may result in the inaccuracy of the document and therefore mislead or upset its users and readers. In law regulated industries, some of the procedures have to be completed as evidenced by their corresponding signatures and the date(s) on which the document was signed. Refer to the ISO divisions of ICS 01.140.40 and 35.240.30 for further information. The published document should be in a format that is not easily altered without a specific knowledge or tools, and yet it is read-only or portable.

STANDARDIZATION

Many industry associations publish their own lists of particular document control standards that are used in their particular field. The following is the list of some of the relevant ISO documents. Divisions ICS 01.140.10 and 01.140.20.

The ISO has also published a series of standards regarding the technical documentation, covered by the division of 01.110:

- ISO 2709: 1996 Information and documentation—Format for information exchange
- ISO 15836: 2009 which replaces ISO 15836:2003 Information and documentation—The Dublin Core metadata element set
- ISO 15489: 2001 Information and documentation—Records management

- ISO 21127: 2006 Information and documentation—A reference ontology for the interchange of cultural heritage information
- ISO 23950: 1998 Information and documentation—Information retrieval—Application service definition and protocol specification.
- ISO/CD 10244 Document management—Business process/workflow baselining and analysis associated with EDMS technologies
- ISO 32000—portable document format

DOCUMENTATION

Documentation may refer to the process of providing evidence or to the communicable material used to provide such documentation. Documentation may also refer to tools aiming at identifying documents or to the field of study devoted to the study of documents and bibliographies.

Subfields of documentation include:

- Medical documentation
- Technical documentation
- Legal documentation
- Administrative documentation
- Historical documentation

Documentation In Computer Science:

The following are different types of documentations usually seen in the Computer Science field:

- Architectural and Design documentation.
- Technical Documentation.
- User Documentation.
- System Documentation.
- Marketing Documentation.

There are various types of Documentation Tools which are available for this purpose.Documentation understood as document is any communicable material used to explain some attributes of an object, system or procedure. It is often used to mean engineering documentation or software documentation, which is usually paper books or computer readable files that describe the structure and components, or on the other hand, operation, of a system/ product.

A professional whose field and work is documentation used to be termed a documentalist. Normally, documentalists are trained or have a background in both a specific subject and in the field of documentation. A person who more or less exclusively writes technical documentation is called a technical writer.

Technical writers are similarly trained or have a background in technical writing, along with some knowledge of the subject(s) they are documenting. Often, though, they collaborate with subject matter experts, such as engineers. Common types of computer hardware/software documentation include online help, FAQs, how-tos, and user guides. The term RTFM is often used colloquially in regard to such documentation, especially to computer hardware and software user guides. A common type of software document frequently written by software engineers in the simulation industry is the SDF. While developing the software for a simulator, which can range from embedded avionics devices to 3D terrain databases by way of full motion control systems, the engineer keeps a notebook detailing the development lifecycle of the project.

The notebook can contain a requirements part, an interface part detailing the communication interface of the software, a notes part to detail the proof of concept attempts to track what worked or didn't work in solving certain problems, and a testing part to detail how the software will be tested to prove conformance to the requirements of the contract.

The end result is a detailed description of how the software is designed, how to build and install the software on the target device, and any known weaknesses in the design of the software. This document will allow future developers and maintainers of the trainer to come up to speed on the software design in as short a time as possible and have a documented reference when modifying code or searching for bugs.

PRINCIPLES

While associated ISO standards are not easily available publicly, a guide from other sources for this topic may serve the purpose. David Berger has provided several principles of document writing, regarding the terms used, procedure numbering and even lengths of sentences, etc.

The following is a list of guides dealing with each specific field and type:

- Documentation in health care
- Thesis writing
- Papers for academic journal publishing

PROCEDURES AND TECHNIQUES

The procedures of documentation vary from one sector, or one type, to another. In general, these may involve document drafting, formatting, submitting, reviewing, approving, distributing, repositing and tracking, etc., and are convened by associated SOPs in a regulatory industry.

JOURNAL VOUCHER PREPARATION AND APPROVAL

INTRODUCTION

roper preparation and adequate support for Journal Vouchers (JV) is important to ensure JVs accurately record financial events and detailed audit trail documentation exists. Proper preparation and adequate support for JVs is the joint responsibility of Agency Office of the Chief Financial Officer (OCFO), and Centers' OCFO personnel. The accurate and timely preparation of financial statements and other financial reports is often dependent upon accurate, timely and fully supported JVs.

NASA Agency OCFO and each of the Centers shall take due care and diligence to fully comply with each of the following requirements:

- Internal controls;
- Use of JVs;
- Supporting documentation;
- Approval thresholds; and
- Management oversight and review.

Applicability. The requirements in this stage are applicable to all NASA organizational elements that prepare and approve JVs.

For the purposes of this NPR, a transaction is considered to be a journal voucher when:

- The General Ledger accounts to be debited and credited are selected and entered by the user;
- A transaction is corrected with a regular SAP document;
- Embedded system logic is not used to determine the general ledger accounts to be posted, or;
- When transactions meeting the criteria in 1.1.3.1.a to 1.1.3.1.c above are reversed or when a reversing document is a correction.

Automated distributions of summary amounts such as the distribution of payroll charges provided by the Department of Interior (DOI) based on the automated labour distribution information are not within the scope of this stage.

AGENCY REQUIREMENTS

Operational Controls. Operational internal controls shall be in place to ensure the proper recording of JVs. JVs may be prepared at the NASA Center level or at the Agency level. The Center CFO and the Director of the NASA Shared Services Center (NSSC) are responsible for developing center level operating procedures that ensure full compliance with the requirements of this stage.

General Requirements. All JVs shall be:

- Sequentially numbered in the Center's JV log and systematically numbered by the core financial system when posted by the reporting unit.
- Classified as a correction entry or a source entry based on user ID. Each SAP user has a duplicate user ID that starts with ER. These are to be used when recording transactions to identify those JVs and transactions that are correcting errors. Normal user IDs should be used on source JVs. Additional types of JVs may be added by the Agency OCFO in order to ensure greater management control and oversight of the JV process.

- Adequately documented to support the validity and amount of the JV transaction.
- Reviewed, and approved before posting at the appropriate level of management by the appropriate Agency or Center CFO or designee to ensure proper recording of entries at the posting account, appropriation, and fund levels.
- Annotated with the name, title, date, office symbol, and signature of both the preparer and the approver. In an electronic environment, the name, title, and office symbol may be represented by a user identification. A separate table shall be maintained to correlate user ID to identifying information.
- Maintained in sequential order in a central location in either hard copy, electronic form or both. The Center OCFO and the Agency OCFO must each maintain a summary log of all JVs that identifies the JV numbers and dollar amounts. The log must also reference the SAP document number that was recorded for the JV, the SAP document that was corrected and the source document information supporting the entry.

Segregation of Duties. In order to maintain the proper segregation of duties, the functions of preparation and approval of JVs must be performed by different individuals. Once the JV is prepared, the preparer submits the JV together with the supporting documentation to the approving official for approval.

When the approver has approved and initialed the JV, the preparer enters the JV into the core financial system. The preparer must then give the approving official a copy of the system printout showing how the JV was posted. Centers must have adequate internal controls in place to ensure that JVs are posted exactly as they were approved. This should be accomplished as part of the periodic monitoring and control processes.

ROLES AND RESPONSIBILITIES

Director for Financial Management, Agency OCFO shall:

- Review and, if appropriate, approve Center JVs exceeding $50 Million that are submitted by Center CFOs.
- Review and, if appropriate, discuss with the Agency DCFO and approve all prior period adjustment JVs.

Financial Management Division Branch Chief, Agency OCFO shall:

- As needed, request Agency level JVs and supporting documentation from the Center CFOs.
- Review the Agency level JVs and supporting documentation submitted by the Center CFOs for completeness and accuracy.

Center CFO shall:

- Together with the Center DCFO review and, if appropriate, approve

Center JVs with dollar amounts greater than $25 Million and equal to or less than $50 Million

- Review Center JVs with amounts greater than $50 million and, if appropriate, forward to The Director for Financial Management, Agency OCFO for approval.
- Prepare Agency level JVs and supporting documentation as requested by the Financial Management Division Branch Chief, Agency OCFO.

Center Deputy Chief Financial Officer shall:

- Together with the Center CFO review and, if appropriate, recommend approval of Center JVs with dollar amounts greater than $25 Million and equal to or less than $50 Million.
- Together with the Center Reporting Branch Chief review and, if appropriate, approve Center JVs with dollar amounts greater than $10 Million and equal to or less than $25 Million.

Center Reporting Branch Chief shall:

- Together with the Center Reporting Branch Chief review and, if appropriate, recommend approval of Center JVs with dollar amounts greater than $10 Million and equal to or less than $25 Million.
- Review and, if appropriate, approve Center JV equal to or less than $10 Million.

USE OF JOURNAL VOUCHERS

JV Groupings. NASA has two primary types of JVs:

1. Correcting entries, and
2. Source entries.Correcting Entries.

Correcting entry JVs adjust for errors detected subsequent to posting including errors identified during the financial statement reporting and review process. This type of accounting entry includes specific amounts, accounts, and/or transactions related to the required correction. In some cases, correcting entries are required to adjust for errors on previously prepared JVs. In those instances, correcting entries should both reverse the incorrect entries and record the correct amount.

In some cases, both entries can be made with one JV properly documented by a single set of supporting documentation. Regardless of whether a single JV is prepared, or multiple JVs are prepared, the correcting JV shall include a copy of the original JV, documentation supporting the correct amount and a narrative explanation detailing the reason why the original entry is incorrect and why the correcting entry is necessaryAll error corrections shall be recorded in SAP using ER user IDs so they can be identified by the Agency OCFO on a NASA-wide basis. This applies when transactional corrections or other document types are used for error correction. Where feasible, error correction JV transactions shall be linked to the original transactions that were corrected.

In cases where corrections are processed through interfaces and an ER user ID cannot be used, the Center shall still employ the approval process and will log the transactions in a manner that will allow them to be identified and sent to the Agency OCFO on a monthly basis.JVs record those accounting entries that, due to system limitations or timing differences have not been otherwise recorded.

By nature, source-entry JVs are usually summarized at the entity level by general ledger account. The source-entry accounting transaction shall be supported by documentation for the summarized amounts and identify the location of the transaction-level supporting detail. These documents shall be recorded in SAP using normal user IDs. Source entry JVs generally are used for month-end closing and year-end processing and closing purposes. Source-entry JVs also may include postings of information provided through data calls, such as those required to record values for property, plant, and equipment recognition; if so, such JVs must be supported by documentation for the summarized amounts and identify the location of the transaction-level supporting detail. Presentation.

Both correcting and source entry JVs normally will be summarized amounts for which documentation is required. In these situations, the summarized accounting entry represents the amount to record the sum of the detailed transactions. In all such cases, the summarized accounting entry shall include documentation of the effect of the detailed transactions and identify the location of the transaction-level supporting detail. JV Reversal Transactions.

When JVs are reversed, the transactions must be prepared, approved, recorded, and documented in accordance with all of the requirements applicable to the original JV except when the JVs are reversed automatically as part of the routine JV reversal process. In those instances, documentation and approval for the original JVs will be considered as the documentation and approval for the reversing entry.Sub-groupings.

Both correcting and source entry JVs are further subdivided into audit-recommended JVs and customer-requested JVs. Audit-Recommended JVs. If, as a result of their audit, auditors recommend a JV adjustment be made, the auditors shall be asked to provide copies of the appropriate work papers or relevant information from the work papers to support the recommended JV adjustment.

The JV approving official shall perform an analysis of the recommendation using the auditors' work papers and other relevant information to determine if the recommended adjustments should be made. If the JV approving official identified determines that the auditors' recommended adjustments are required, a correcting JV shall be prepared. If the JV approving official determines that the audit recommended adjustments are not required, no adjustment shall be made. All auditor recommended adjustments must be approved by the Center CFO or DCFO and the Director Financial Management, Agency OCFO.

Any determination regarding JV preparation shall:

- Document why the adjustment is, or is not, required;
- Indicate how the JV approving official determined the audit recommendation should, or should not, be followed;
- Identify the audit recommendation serving as the basis for the actions taken;
- Include documentation of the decision to prepare or not prepare a JV, along with other pertinent information as the documentation for that voucher.

Customer-Requested JVs. When NASA personnel prepare proposed JVs to enter adjustments or corrections, the approving officials at NASA Centers or Headquarters must determine that they comply with this JV preparation guidance.

Evidence to support the adjustment must include, at a minimum, supporting documentation which has been reviewed and approved by the JV approving official and any related analysis performed by the JV approving official to ascertain that the adjustment is fully supported and in accordance with this JV preparation and approval guidance.

SUPPORTING DOCUMENTATION

Documentation. Proper documentation, in either hard copy, electronic form or both is necessary to support all JV entries. This documentation must be sufficient for the approving official and auditors to clearly understand the reason for preparing the JV and to be able to determine that it is proper and accurate. A request for a JV entry not supported by accurate or proper documentation shall be denied with a demand for additional information required to process the JV, along with any applicable authoritative guidance to support the need for the JV.

The supporting documentation, whenever practical, should be attached to a copy of the JV. In some cases, however, due to the large number of detailed transactions summarized in the voucher, it may not be practical to attach all of the documentation. In those cases, specific and detailed information summarizing the content and identifying the location of the supporting documentation shall be attached to the voucher.

The specific types of JV and the explanations of what is considered sufficient documentation. Note: Regardless of what method of documentation is used for any category of JV, *i.e.*, whether it is a detailed listing, a narrative explanation, or a calculation supporting the amount, the dollar amount(s) on the JV shall be clearly and readily identifiable in the supporting documentation. Identified Errors and Reasonableness Checks/Timing Differences due to Monthly/Annual Closing. When the JV approving official has identified errors through analysis, reasonableness checks, quality control procedures, subsequent activity occurring after a period closes, or other means, a correcting JV shall be prepared. In the event an auditor identified an apparent error or omission and provided the documentation for the JV, the JV approving official will be a management official at the appropriate authorizing level, consistent with the entity internal control structure.

Evidence to support either an "authorized official" or "auditor identified" correcting JV shall include a detailed listing of identified errors, narrative explaining why the original entry is incorrect, why the correcting entry is necessary, a related analysis documenting the calculation of the correct amount, and the sources of the data used in the analysis. Reconciliation of Trial Balance and Budget Execution Reports.

When the JV approving official has determined during a reconciliation of data between two or more sources that a discrepancy exists, a correcting JV may be necessary. JV entries included in this category often are made to reconcile trial balances or other source data reported by NASA Headquarters or Centers to NASA's budget execution reports. Evidence to support this type of JV includes reference to specific documents, other source data, and a complete analysis that supports the correct amount.

If a JV is necessary, the voucher shall document why the discrepancy exists in the data, it shall contain evidence to support the proposed correction, and a description of the methodology used to validate the entries on the JV.Reversing Entries for Prior Reporting Period. When monthly or yearly accruals or correcting entries have been made for reporting purposes, they may need to be reversed in the following reporting period. The JV reversing entries shall include documentation regarding the original accrual or correcting entry and an explicit statement that the JV is a reversing entry. Data Call Entry.

Frequently, during the financial statement preparation process, source-entry information is provided by data calls where data are not recorded on a detailed transaction basis. For example, transactions at the detail levels from sources external to the OCFO may not be available in the core financial systems or information required from external Government agencies to prepare the financial statements are available only in summarized forms.

If this occurs, JVs shall be prepared to record the summarized data call amounts, so these amounts can be recorded in the general ledger trial balance. The data call entry shall be supported by documentation for the summarized amount and shall identify the source or location of the transaction-level supporting detail and/or information for the entry. Data call information, in most cases is not contained in the core financial systems and is provided by sources outside of the CFO's office.

Examples of an independent source include the NASA logistics data calls, environmental liability data calls, and accrual information from the

Department of Labour and the Office of Personnel Management. Evidence to support the JV includes the transmission record of the data.

Examples of data call entries include:

- Property, plant and equipment;
- Operating materials and supplies;
- Environmental liabilities;
- Contingent liabilities; and
- Employee benefits data, Federal Employees Compensation Act data, and other information from other Federal sources.

Other Accruals. A number of typical month-end and year-end adjusting entries are made, and subsequently may be reversed at the beginning of the next period to accrue amounts for payroll, workers compensation, judgment fund liabilities, unfunded leave, and other transactions. The supporting documentation for these other accrual JVs shall include a narrative explaining the basis for the accrual, a worksheet documenting the calculation of the amounts being recorded, and the basis for any subsequent reversal.

Prior Period Adjustments. All JVs that adjust amounts reported in audited financial statements issued for a previous fiscal year, regardless of amount and type, must be approved by the Center CFO and the Director Financial Management, Agency OCFO.

APPROVAL THRESHOLDS

Journal Vouchers Prepared and Posted at the Center Level. Approval of the JV also constitutes acceptance of the supporting documentation. The organizational level within the Center or NSSC, at which JVs must be approved, varies by the dollar amount of the voucher as shown by the following table.

Table. Approval Thresholds for Center Generated JVs

JV Dollar Amount	JV Approving Official
0 to $10 Million	Center Reporting Branch Chief
Over $10 Million to $25 Million	Center Reporting Branch Chief
and Center DCFO	
Over $25 Million to $50 Million	Center DCFO and Center CFO
Over $50 Million	Center CFO and Director for Financial
Management, Agency	OCFO

Prior period adjustments - JVs that are adjusting beginning balances Center CFO and Director for Financial Management, Agency OCFO All JVs regardless of the type or amount that adjust amounts reported in audited financial statements issued for a previous fiscal year must be approved by the Director for Financial Management, Agency OCFO.

All auditor recommended adjustments must be approved by the Center CFO or DCFO and the Director for Financial Management, Agency OCFO.

Within each of the foregoing thresholds, other approval thresholds with lower dollar values than those specified may be established to accommodate the organizational level of those preparing the JV. The Center CFO shall designate in writing the approval threshold structure—dollar thresholds and position of approving officials within the Center. In the event that the approval authorities must be delegated to an individual other than the one identified, that delegation must also be documented in writing and signed by the Center CFO. Journal Vouchers Posted at the Agency Level. The Agency OCFO, Financial Management Division, Data Analysis Branch Chief in coordination with the External Reporting Branch Chief will, as needed, request Centers CFOs submit JVs that will be posted at the Agency Level. These JVs must be submitted with all applicable supporting documentation and approvals. Upon receipt of the requested JV the FMD, Data Analysis Branch Chief in coordination with the External Reporting Branch Chief will review the supporting documentation for completeness and the JV for accuracy.

When the JV is determined to be accurate and all required documentation is present the Branch Chiefs will forward the JV to the FMD Director or his/her designee for approval. If the JV is over $100 million, the FMD Director will discuss the JV with the Agency DCFO prior to posting in SAP.

MANAGEMENT OVERSIGHT AND REVIEW

Managerial Controls. Adequate managerial internal controls shall be maintained at each level of management to ensure proper oversight of JV preparation. The Center CFO's and the Director of the NSSC must ensure the validity and accuracy of the JVs processed as part of their normal monthly financial management monitoring process by ensuring that adequate documentation exists to support the JV entry before it is recorded. All corrections made by the Competency Center or by the Agency OCFO on behalf of the Centers or Agency OCFO are subject to this process.

The Competency Center and/or the Agency OCFO will only make corrections/adjustments once this documentation is received. Copies of the documentation of the corrections will be attached to the Service Request and originals maintained in the Centers' logs and records. Service requests shall be established for activities performed either by the Competency Center or the Agency OCFO.

COMMERCIAL PAYMENT VOUCHERS AND SUPPORTING DOCUMENTS

AN OVERVIEW

Purpose

This stage prescribes the policy for the preparation of commercial payment vouchers and the supporting documentation. It highlights the forms most often used for contracts, receiving reports, and vouchers. It provides guidance on their usage, certification, and distribution to the paying office.

Scope

A properly certified voucher is the authority for Disbursing Officers to make payments of government obligations. The certifying officer must review evidence sufficient to support a determination that the payment is proper. Preparation and certification of a payment voucher by the entitleme1nt office advises the disbursing office that the contractual conditions for payment have been met.

14

Personnel Management and Industrial Relations

AN OVERVIEW

The relationship between the employers and employees and trade unions is called Industrial Relations. Harmonious relationship is necessary for both the employers and employees to safeguard the interests of both the parties of production. To maintain good relationship with the employees is the main function of every organization so as to ensure industrial peace and higher production.

Personnel management is mainly concerned with the human relations in the industry because the main theme of personnel management is to get the work done by the human power and it fails in its objectives if good industrial Revelations are not maintained. In other words, good industrial relations means industrial peace which is necessary for better and higher production.

Definitions: Industrial relations have been defined by some of the thinkers a follows:

- "Industrial relations and personnel management are almost synonymous term with the only difference the former places emphasis on the aspect of employer relationship rather than on the executive policies and activities that are set up to foster good relations." - E.F.L. Brec
- "Industrial relations is that part of management which is concerned with the man power of the enterprise- whether machine operator, skilled worker or manager".
- 'Industrial relationship is the composite result of the attitudes and approaches the employers and employees towards each other with regard to planning, supervision, direction and coordination of the activities of an organization with a minimum of human efforts and friction, with an animating sprite of cooperation and with proper regard for the genuine well-being of all the members of the organization."

TEAD AND MATCAL

It is clear from the analysis of the definitions that employment relations are generally called industrial relations. It is a relationship between employer and employees employer and employee and trade unions and employees.

Impact of Industrial Relations on Industrial Peace

An economy organised for planned production and distribution, aiming at the realization of social justice and welfare of the masses, can function effectively only in an atmosphere of industrial peace.

If the twin objectives of rapid national development and increased social justice are to be achieved, there must be harmonious relationship between management and labour.

The impact of good industrial relations on production may be seen from the following facts:

- *Reduces Industrial disputes*: Good industrial relations reduce the industrial disputes. Disputes are reflections of the basic human urges or motivations to secure adequate satisfaction or expression which are fully cured by good industrial relations. Strikes, lock-outs, go slow tactics, gherao and grievances are some of the reflections of industrial unrest which do not spring up in an atmosphere of industrial peace. It helps promoting cooperations and increasing production.
- *High Morale*: Good industrial relations improve the morale of the employees. Employees work with great zeal with the feeling in mind that the interest of employer and employees is one and the same i.e. to increase production. Every worker feels that he is a co-owner of the industry. The employer in his turn must realise that the gains of industry are not for him alone but they should be showed equally and generously with his workers. In other words, complete unity of the thought and action is the main achievement of industrial peace of workers into the society and their ego is satisfied. It naturally affects production, because a mighty cooperative efforts alone can produce great results.
- *Mental Revolution*: The main object of industrial relations ins a complete mental revolution of workers and employers. The industrial peace lies ultimately in a transformed outlook on the part of both. It is the business of leadership in the ranks of workers employees and government to work out a new relationship in consonance with a spirit of true democracy. Both should think themselves as a partners of the industry and the role of worker in such a partnership should be recognized. On the other hand, workers must recognize employer authority. It

will naturally have impact on production because they recognize the interest of each other.

- *New Programmes*: New programmes for workers development are introduced in an atmosphere of peace such as training facilities, labour welfare facilities etc. It increases the efficiency of workers resulting in higher and better production at lower costs.
- *Reduced Wastage*: Good industrial relations are maintained on the basis of cooperation and recognition of each other. It will help increase production. Wastages of man material and machines and reduced to the minimum and thus national interest is protected.

Thus form the discussion it is evident that good industrial relations is the basis of higher production with minimum cost and higher profits. It also results in increased efficiency of workers. New and new projects are introduced for the welfare of he workers and to promote the morale of the people at work.

The conflicts and disputes between employer and employees on any industrial matter are known as industrial disputes.

Industrial Disputes

The disputes between employer and employer both and vitiate the industrial atmosphere and peace. Whether these tactics are successful or unsuccessful, unpleasantness is created between both the parties. The worst result ins the loss of production and decline in natural income. Industrial dispute is defined by *Section 2 (x)* of the *Industrial Disputes Act 1947* as follows:-

Industrial disputes is "Any dispute or difference between the employers and employees, or between employs workmen, or between workmen and workmen, which is connected with the employment or unemployment or the terms of employment or with the conditions of labour of any person:".

There must be following ingredients of an industrial dispute:

- There must be a relationship of employer and employee.
- The worker must be on the roll list of the industry.
- The demands of the workers must have been rejected by the employer.
- The dispute may be between two employers or between two employees.
- The dispute may be connected with employment or terms of employment or with labour conditions of any person.
- The industrial unit must be a going concern. It must not be dead.

The new industrial set-up has given birth to the capitalistic economy which divided the industrial society into two groups of labour and capitalists.

Causes of Industrial Disputes

The interests of these two groups are not common which created industrial disputes.

The main resources of industrial disputed may be classified into four groups:

1. Economic
2. Managerial
3. Political
4. Others

ECONOMIC CAUSES OF INDUSTRIAL DISPUTES

Really, the most common causes of industrial disputes are economic causes.

These are follows:

- *Wages*: The wage-increase was the prime most cause of dispute both after the first and second world wars. A large number of strikes were organised during this time because of the rise in cost of living. The real wages of the workers declined faster and they were dissatisfied with their present wages and struggled for the improvement in wages. By having a cursory glance on the history of industrial dispute, it becomes clear that cause of most of the industrial disputes was wages.
- *Dearness Allowance and Bonus*: Increase in cost of living was the main cause of the demand of dearness allowance by the workers to equate their wages with the rise of prices. Bonus also play an important role as a cause of industrial dispute. Both the quantum and the method of bonus payment has led to a number of disputes.
- *High Industrial Profits*: During and after the world wars, prices of the commodities went up and the industrialists earned a huge profits. In order to get share in the prosperity of the industry, it naturally led to the resentment on their part. The increased profits also led to the demands of higher wage and bonus. Now, in the changing world, concept of labour has changed considerably. They think themselves as a partner of the industry and demand their share in the profits.
- *Working Conditions and Working Horus*: The working conditions in Indian industries are not hygienic. There is not ample provision of water, heating, lighting, safety etc. Working hours are also greater. The demand of palatable working conditions and shorter hours of work led to labour disputes.
- *Modernization and Automation of Plant and Machine*ry: The attempt at modernization and introduction of automatic machinery to replace labour has been the major cause of disputes of India. Workers go on strike, off and on, to resist rationalization. A strike in cotton textile industry in Kanpur in 1955 for 80 days long is an example of such disputes. Workers in life-insurance corporation went on strike recently against introducing computers in the corporation.

- *Weakness of Trade Unions*: Weaknesses of trade unions encourages the employers to deny certain basic needs of the workers such as medical, education and housing facilities etc. This led to resentment on the part of workers who resorted to direct action.

VISION FOR THE NATIONAL SKILL DEVELOPMENT INITIATIVE IN INDIA

At present the capacity of skill development in India is around 3.1 million persons per year. The 11th Five Year Plan envisions an increase in that capacity to 15 million annually. India has target of creating 500 million skilled workers by 2022. Thus, there is a need for increasing capacity and capability of skill development programmes.

High inclusivity: The skill development initiatives will harness inclusivity and reduce divisions such as male/female, rural/urban, organized/unorganized employment and traditional/contemporary workplace. Dynamic and demand-based system planning: The skill development initiatives support the supply of trained workers who are adjustable dynamically to the changing demands of employment and technologies. This policy will promote excellence and will meet the requirements of knowledge economy. Choice, competition and accountability: The skill development initiative does not discriminate between private or public delivery and places importance on outcomes, users? choice and competition among training providers and their accountability. Policy coordination and coherence: The skill development initiatives support employment generation, economic growth and social development processes.

Skill development policy will be an integral part of comprehensive economic, labour and social policies and programmes. A framework for better coordination among various Ministries, States, industry and other stakeholders will be established. The operational strategies will be adopted: Folding the future in: If we start from our current position, we are likely to extrapolate. Folding the future in allows us to innovate. Innovation is, therefore, an important element of the strategy.

Skills framework must move to a system of equivalence to diplomas and degrees: National Vocational Qualification Framework (NVQF) will be created with an open/flexible system which will permit individuals to accumulate their knowledge and skills, and convert them through testing and certification into higher diplomas and degrees. NVQF will provide quality assured various learning pathways having standards, comparable with any international qualification framework. NVQF will support lifelong learning, continuous upgradation of skills and knowledge.

Skills must be bankable: The process of skill acquisition especially for the poor and needy persons will be made bankable. The effort would be to complement public investment with institutional/ bank finance. Co-created solutions and forging partnerships: We have to accept a very asymmetric India as a starting point. Partnerships will be consciously promoted between Government, industry, local governments, civil society institutions and all potential skill providers.

Institutional mechanism and standing platforms will be created to ensure sustainability. Game-changing delivery/innovation: Availability of public institutions above the high school level, after class hours for skill development by the Private Sector, without disturbing the normal working, will be explored. Necessary regulations would be brought in by the local management authority of the particular educational institution.

CORE OPERATING PRINCIPLES

Government financial support must complement private investment: The Central Ministries must focus on areas where private investment in skilled development is unlikely to be available or forthcoming. The Government would aim at useful public-private partnerships.

States as key actors: The States being the key actors in Skill Development would set up over arching integrated framework for action for Skill Development through State level Skill Development Missions. Deployment of funds: The funds would be deployed more for activities than for buildings and other hard assets.

However, upgradation of machinery and equipment, teaching and learning aids will be a continuous process. Creation of infrastructure in latest technology, need-based new initiatives, creation of infrastructure in rural, remote and difficult areas will continue. Focus of modular courses, open architecture and short term courses: With fast changing skills in the labour market, focus would be on short, relevant and effective courses that would get candidates into the workplace. They will be welded through NVQF to maintain dynamism and open to feedback. Separate financing from delivery: Today Government funds are only available for government delivery. National Skill Development Corporation will support private skill development initiatives.

Following financing options will be explored:

- *Link financing to outcomes*: Today public and private training is financed largely on inputs viz., number of courses, number of students, faculty, etc. Efforts would be made to move towards Government financing linked to placement ratios and outcomes.
- *Focus funding on candidates:* The focus would be on funding the candidates rather than institutions to create choice. This could be structured as a scholarship, skill voucher, outcome based reimbursement, etc. Create infrastructure for on-the-job-training and encourage apprenticeships: The enabling infrastructure for large number of formal apprentices needs to be built that includes modification to the Apprentices Act, 1961. Publicise rating and

outcome information on training institutions: A framework of accreditation and infrastructure for information dissemination around measurable criteria on institutions will be created. Ratings of public and private institutions would be put on public domain. Effective assessment and credible certification: Quality assured learning, credible assessment and certification will be developed. This will allow employers to use the certificate as a proxy to fast track job applicants.

Restructure employment exchanges as career guidance centres: Employment Exchanges will be restructured as career guidance centres to channelize candidates into jobs, apprenticeships and training.

Expand formal employment: Formal employment is not only fiscally attractive but more amenable to financing innovations. This will require a review of existing State and Central legislations which encourage informal and unorganized employment.

Approach to Deliverables

Diversity of skills: There is a need to identify, catalog and project the range and depth of skills e.g. traditional, industrial-era and post-industrial era skills to understand and present the vast array of skills that individuals can choose from. Talent pool: The ultimate measure is the "500 Million" skilled people. Skill inventory along with its various levels and grades will be created. Employment outcomes Skill training must ensure a job for those who seek it. The placement ratio will be monitored and placed in the public domain by agencies involved in skill training.

THE MISSION STATEMENT, AIMS AND OBJECTIVES

MISSION

The policy envisions the establishment of a National Skill Development Initiative with the following mission: National Skill Development Initiative will empower all individuals through improved skills, knowledge, nationally and internationally recognized qualifications to gain access to decent employment and ensure India's competitiveness in the global market.

Aims: The aim of skill development in the country is to support achieving rapid and inclusive growth through:

- Enhancing individuals? employability (wage/ self employment) and ability to adapt to changing technologies and labour market demands.
- Improving productivity and living standards of the people.
- Strengthening competitiveness of the country.
- Attracting investment in skill development. Objectives of National Policy on Skill Development:

The objectives of the national policy on skill development are to:

- Create opportunities for all to acquire skills throughout life, and especially for youth, women and disadvantaged groups.
- Promote commitment by all stakeholders to own skill development initiatives.
- Develop a high-quality skilled workforce/entrepreneur relevant to current and emerging employment market needs.
- Enable the establishment of flexible delivery mechanisms that respond to the characteristics of a wide range of needs of stakeholders.
- Enable effective coordination between different ministries, the Centre and the States and public and private providers.

Scope of the National Skill Development Policy

The coverage of the National Policy on Skill Development includes the following:

- Institution-based skill development including ITIs/ITCs/vocational schools/technical schools/ polyte-chnics/ professional colleges, etc.
- Learning initiatives of sectoral skill development organised by different ministries/departments.
- Formal and informal apprenticeships and other types of training by enterprises
- Training for self-employment/entrepreneurial development
- Adult learning, retraining of retired or retiring employees and lifelong learning
- Non-formal training including training by civil society organizations
- E-learning, web-based learning and distance learning.

Institutional Arrangements

Prime Minister's National Council on Skill Development, under the Chairmanship of Prime Minister has been set up as an apex institution for policy direction and review. The Ministers for Human Resource Development, Finance, Industries, Rural Development, Housing and Urban Poverty Alleviation, Labour and Employment and Micro Small & Medium Enterprises are members.

Deputy Chairman, Planning Commission, Chairperson of the National Manufacturing Competitiveness Council, Chairperson of the National Skill Development Corporation and 6 experts in the area of skill development are other members.

Principal Secretary to the Prime Minister is the Member Secretary to the Council. National Skill Development Coordination Board: A National Skill Development Coordination Board has been set up under the Chairmanship of Deputy Chairman, Planning Commission. Secretaries of Ministries of

Human Resource Development, Labour and Employment, Rural Development, Housing and Urban Poverty Alleviation and Finance are members. Chairperson/Chief Executive Officer of the National Skill Development Corporation, Secretaries of four States by rotation, for a period of two years, and three distinguished Academicians/Subject Area Specialists are other members.

Secretary, Planning Commission is Member Secretary of the Board. National Skill Development Corporation: The National Skill Development Corporation is a non-profit company under the Companies Act 1956 with an appropriate governance structure. The head of the Corporation is a person of eminence/reputed professional in the field of Skill Development.

The Corporation would constitute Sector Skills Councils with following functions:

- Identification of skill development needs including preparing a catalogue of types of skills, range and depth of skills to facilitate individuals to choose from them.
- Development of a sector skill development plan and maintain skill inventory.
- Determining skills/competency standards and qualifications.
- Standardization of affiliation and accreditation process.
- Participation in Affiliation, accreditation, examination and certification.
- Plan and execute Training of Trainers.
- Promotion of academies of excellence.
- Establishment of a well structured sector specific Labour Market Information System (LMIS) to assist planning and delivery of training.

National Council for Vocational Training

NCVT will be strengthened and re-engineered with a broader mandate and representation.

The main functions include:

- Design, development and maintenance of NVQF which inter alia includes:
  - Setting up a framework for competency standards, structure of courses, credit structure, accumulation and certification.
  - Setting up a framework for affiliation and accreditation of institutions.
  - Quality control mechanism.
- Labour market information system and dissemination of information at the national level.
- Monitoring and evaluation on the effectiveness and efficiency of national skill development efforts through appropriate reporting and communication mechanism.

SOCIAL PARTNERS IN SKILL DEVELOPMENT

Partnerships will be consciously promoted between Government, industry, trade unions, local governments, civil society institutions and all skill providers. It will also include, training providers, professional societies, Self Help Groups, Cooperatives and NGOs/civil society institutions. Creation of an institutional mechanism and regular consultation with stake holders will form the corner stone of Skill Development Initiative.

Roles and Responsibilities of Stake Holders

Roles and Responsibilities of Government (Central /State or Local Level)

- Setting up priority and policy planning-statistics gathering
- Providing regulatory framework and enabling environment for stake holders.
- Devising financing mechanism, reward and promotional framework.
- Capacity building of social partners.
- Setting up of monitoring, evaluation and disse-mination of information.
- Facilitating international cooperation.
- Setting up of a qualification framework and quality assurance mechanism.
- Preparation of work plans to meet sector specific skill sets.

Roles and Responsibilities of Employers/Industries

- Owning Skill Development activities.
- Identification of competencies and setting up of competency standards,
- Skill demand analysis and curriculum development.
- Facilitating training of trainers.
- Delivery of training, monitoring and evaluation.
- Participation in examination and certification.
- Participation in affiliation and accreditation process
- Sharing of work place experience, machinery and equipment.
- Support by way of physical, financial and human resources.
- Facilitating employment of trained graduates.
- Supporting skill development initiatives of other public and private agencies.
- Implementing apprenticeship schemes.
- Investing in skill development activities.

Roles and Responsibilities of Trade Unions

- Assist in developing competency standards.
- Assist in course designing, examination and certification.
- Raising awareness about the benefit of training, skill development plans and activities among the workers
- Promote skill upgradation and lifelong learning among the workers.
- Running special skill development institutes for skill development of workers.
- Promoting investment on skill development among the employers.
- Facilitate improving status of VET trained graduates.

Roles and Responsibilities of Civil Society Organizations

- Raising awareness about skill development plans and activities among the public.
- Facilitate improving status of VET trained graduates.
- Implementing skill development programmes of the Government.
- Assist in developing competency standards.
- Assist in course designing, examination and certification.
- Promote lifelong learning among the public.
- Promoting dignity of labour among the public.
- Sharing experience of learning with others.

EXPANSION OF OUTREACH, EQUITY AND ACCESS

The current capacity for skill development in the country is 3.1 million. India has set a target of skilling 500 million people by 2022 to meet the challenges of India @ 75.

Expansion of outreach Skill Development Initiative needs considerable amount of expansion of capacity and innovative delivery approaches and Public Private Partnerships.

A few of them are:

- Innovative approaches will be adopted to raise the capacity of the system extensively over a limited period.
- Incentive mechanisms will be developed to encourage the private sector to participate in skill development.
- The expansion of public training institutions will be promoted, particularly, in rural, border, hilly and difficult areas, where the private sector may find it difficult to invest.
- Innovative delivery models such decentralized delivery, mobile training, distance learning, e-learning and web-based learning will be used.

- Skill development centres at village and block level will be promoted to provide skill development opportunity as well as to act as one-stop kiosks with information On the local labour market/ employment, vocational learning opportunities and support schemes.
- Panchayats, municipalities and other local bodies will be involved in skill development and employment generation at the local level in collaboration with SHGs, cooperatives and NGOs.
- The coverage of vocations will be expanded.
- At present about 23,800 establishments are covered under the Apprenticeship Training Scheme imparting training to 2.58 lakh apprentices. Over the next five years, this will be increased to about 1 lakh establishments covering about 1 million apprentices. The existing Apprentices Act, 1961 will be revisited to meet desired target.

Equity and Access

- Equal access to skill development is essential for all social groups particularly women and disadvantaged part of society, to help them in securing decent employment and moving out of poverty. Removing barriers to access and addressing their specific needs are key elements in achieving inclusive growth.
- Entry barriers such as educational qualification, transportation, loss of wages, language etc. will be addressed. While enhancing the opportunity of skill development for all, entry assessments will be deployed to channelize people with different profiles and needs into appropriate skill development programmes.
- The effort will be combined with a major initiative in raising awareness among the target groups about the benefit of skill development, employment and learning opportunities and also about support schemes that enable them to participate in training.
- In addition to vocational skills, the provision of soft (or life) skills - including basic literacy, numerous, occupational safety and health, hygiene, basic labour rights, team work and confidence building - will be made as an integral component of the curricula. This will also help in empowerment of vulnerable groups.

Vocational Training for Women Skill development for employability will be used as an agent of change in promoting women's employment. Women face a multitude of barriers in accessing skills and productive employment, remaining on the job due to effect of globalization or otherwise and advancing to higher level jobs, as well as returning to the labour market after a period of absence spent, for example, in raising children.

- A policy of non-discrimination will be pursued vigourously to provide equal access for women to skill development and employment.

- This Policy will aim to raise women's participation to at least 30% by the end of the 11th Plan.
- Proactive measures that overcome barriers and facilitate participation, such as hostels for women, scholarships, transport, training materials and loans, will be made available on a large scale.
- The Women's Vocational Training Programme will be expanded and the institutional network providing training facilities exclusively for women, so that they can obtain skills with high wage and self-employment potential, will be greatly expanded.
- In order to promote skills and employability of women, the sectors which employ a large number of women will be identified. These may include construction, home- based traditional crafts or piece rate work, financial and health service as well as agricultural sectors.
- Gender stereotyping in vocational courses will be eliminated to encourage women's participation in non-traditional occupations, including existing and emerging technological fields.

REGIONAL IMBALANCE OPPORTUNITIES

- Infrastructure and programmes for skill development are particularly scarce in rural and difficult areas and thus the problem of access to training is most acute in these areas. Specially the women are increasingly the main workers in rural households, as their husbands migrate but often equipped with only traditional and outdated skills and knowledge.
- Skill development in rural areas contributes to improve productivity and working conditions in the agricultural sector while at the same time enabling rural workers, particularly young people, to access emerging employment opportunities beyond the agricultural sector.
- The outreach and quality of skill development in rural areas will be improved so as to enable rural workers to acquire and upgrade technologies; improve linkages to value chains; increase agricultural production; expand access to market and engage in off-farm activities which can generate supplemental income.
- In view of the limited training infrastructure, a range of infrastructure facilities, including schools, community centres and local government buildings, will be utilized as training venues. Institutes for entrepreneurship training such as Rural Development & Self-employment Training Institutes (RUDSETI) will be further promoted. The Government itself will set up public institutions and will also promote the establishment of private sector training institutions through a package of suitably designed incentives such as provision of land and financial assistance. The convergence with national employment programmes, such as National Rural

Employment Guaranteed Scheme (NREGS), will be promoted as an opportunity for imparting skills training in rural areas. Training facilities need to be updated regularly so as to meet changing demands.

- Village- or block-based skill development centres will be set up to serve the needs of local communities. Facilitated by the district offices and panchayats, these skill development centres will play a pivotal role in identifying local employment opportunities and providing, or organizing, adequate training and post-training support according to the specific needs of local areas. The centres will also function as information centres for training and employment opportunities as well as various support schemes. These efforts will be combined with the creation of incentive mechanisms in motivating, particularly youth to participate in training and removal of other barriers in accessing training.
- Various mobile training arrangements will be deployed to reach out to remote and difficult areas.
- Skill development for self-employment will be an important component in these skill development efforts in rural areas. Post-training support, including mentoring for access to markets, credit and appropriate technologies, is an important part of skill development strategy for self-employment.
- Training modules will incorporate specific needs of target groups, e.g. literacy, the level of education and the local language. The delivery of training will be flexible in terms of hours and duration to encourage participation, particularly among women.
- In general, there is a regional imbalance in training opportunities and some parts of the country are quite deficient in skill development institutions. In order to provide more equitable access across the country, special efforts will be mounted to establish training facilities in deficient regions.

Disadvantaged Groups

- The reservations applicable to these groups will be strictly enforced, with appropriate gender composition.
- Existing schemes for benefiting these groups will be reviewed, strengthened and made more effective.
- Efforts will be made to mobilize capabilities and expertise of civil society organizations.
- New innovative schemes and measures will also be devised to ensure full and effective participation by these groups, as well as the accrual of real benefits from skill development initiatives.

Minorities

- Skill development opportunities for minority groups will be expanded, particularly in Minority Concentrated Areas (MCAs).
- Existing schemes benefiting these groups will be reviewed, strengthened and made more effective.
- Efforts will be made to mobilize capabilities and expertise of civil society organizations.
- Formalization of non-formal skill acquisition and transfer will also be promoted in traditional art and craft sectors.

Persons with Disabilities

- The current level of participation of persons with disabilities in skill programmes is very low, despite guidelines of reserving 3% of the seats for them. The guidelines apply only to the government sector.
- People with varying degrees of physical and mental disabilities will be provided with appropriate adjustment training and skills training to bring them in the economic mainstream and make them productive citizens.
- This Policy aims to expand the facilities for people with disabilities and to provide reasonable accommodation that enables them to access the facilities through suitable transport and building designs.
- The number of Vocational Rehabilitation Centres will be doubled in the 11th Plan and expanded further in subsequent Plans. Similar efforts will also be made at the State level to improve access and outreach.
- Training will be integrated with efforts to secure appropriate employment opportunities. Programmes of public awareness and community participation will be strengthened to promote demand for vocational training by people with disabilities as well as to facilitate their inclusion in the labour market.

The School Drop-outs and Child Labour

- School education would be strengthened to reduce the school drop outs. The quality of school education will influence the effectiveness of skill development programme as a whole. This will lay solid foundation for young people to acquire employable skills and engage in continuous skill upgradation throughout their working life.
- School education will be used as a tool to increase vocational awareness among the young people.
- School drop-outs (leaving the schools before completing XII standard), child labour and out-of-school youth need to be given

alternative education coupled with skill development opportunities to bring them into the economic and social mainstream.

- Short term, market oriented, demand-driven programmes will provide a flexible delivery framework suited to the characteristics and circumstances of the target group.
- Multi-skilling, multi-entry and exit, and linkages to skill upgradation opportunities in the future, will characterize such programmes. The scheme of Modular Employable Skills (i.e. short-term employable skills) will be expanded greatly to cater to the large size of the group.
- Formal educational requirements in accessing training will be reviewed in order to facilitate easy access.

Economically Challenged: Persons Below Poverty Line

- Skill development for employability is an important strategy in the fight against poverty. The poor will have a priority claim and easy access to opportunities for skill development.
- This Policy aims at mitigating the impact of these economic barriers at different stages, as well as actively promote access of the poor to educational and skill development opportunities through specially designed schemes and measures. Such measures as special coaching for competing in admission tests, provision of non-formal skill development opportunities and the expanded provision of scholarships, books and soft-loans will be developed and implemented.
- Efforts will be made to better integrate skill development into broader poverty reduction programmes and to strengthen the existing skill development components of such programmes.

QUALITY AND RELEVANCE

Quality and relevance of skill development are key to India's global competitiveness as well as improving an individual's access to decent employment. For enterprises to compete in the global economy, the quality of training must reach world standards and be relevant to the needs of national and international markets. To increase the relevance with future employment market including promotion of self employment, soft skills and entrepreneurship skills will be made integral part of skill development. The demographic advantage that the country enjoys, coupled with prospects of global shortages in skills as the world population ages, means that the country could be supplying skills to the world.

Quality Assurance is Based on Five Key Functions

- Validation of Qualifications for ensuring that qualifications reflect market needs and workplace requirements and are expressed in the form of competencies with clear assessment criteria;

- Validation of Training Process for ensuring that proper tools, techniques, methodologies and material, as suggested in the curriculum/standards are used by the resource persons;
- Quality Assured Assessment of Learners for ensuring that assessment is based on national standards (competencies) and uses valid and reliable assessment methods;
- Accreditation of Training Providers and Training Institutions for ensuring that training is delivered by competent and qualified trainers in well-resourced and managed institutions;
- Research and Information for linking the supply of skilled workers to trends in well-researched Labour Market Information (LMI) covering both the organised and unorganised sectors of the economy.

The objective of enforcing quality and relevance in skill development will be realised through improving infrastructure, improving quality of trainer and developing National Vocational Qualification Framework.

Quality of Infrastructure

- Extensive use of Information & Communication Technology will be promoted for learning or increasing the impact of learning.
- Optimum use of existing physical infrastructure will be ensured in multiple shifts or otherwise.
- Industries will be encouraged to provide their spare capacity to supplement skill development activities.
- Physical infrastructure will be created, expanded and upgraded according to skill requirement of specific sectors of economy.

Quality of Trainer

- Innovative ways of recruiting trainers will be adopted including the employment of former trainees who have gained workplace experience and of practitioners of a craft, trained as master craft persons.
- Innovative skill development schemes, in which trainees acquire theoretical learning at the institution while obtaining practical skills in the workplace, will be devised.
- Retired employees mainly from defence forces will be retrained to meet the requirement of trainers.
- Award and incentive mechanisms, including reward and career progression systems, will be reviewed and institutionalized to improve the status of trainers.
- A system of granting Accredited Trainer Status for a limited period, to all vocational trainers of programmes, leading to National Vocational Qualifications will be developed.

- Special efforts will be made to improve the gender balance among trainers.

NATIONAL VOCATIONAL QUALIFICATIONS FRAMEWORK

To stimulate and support reforms in skills development and to facilitate nationally standardised and acceptable, international comparability of qualifications, a "National Vocational Qualifications Framework" will be established.

All the existing Institutions/Councils/Boards under different Ministries, involved in skill development will be encouraged to follow National Vocational Qualification Framework.

This framework will have the following features:

- Competency based qualifications and certification on the basis of nationally agreed standards and criteria;
- Certification for learning achievement and qualification;
- A range of national qualification levels - based on criteria with respect to responsibility, complexity of activities, and transferability of competencies;
- The avoidance of duplication and overlapping of qualifications while assuring the inclusion of all training needs;
- Modular character where achievement can be made in small steps and accumulated for gaining recognizable qualification;
- Quality Assurance regime that would promote the portability of skills and labour market mobility;
- Lifelong learning through an improved skill recognition system; recognition of prior learning whether in formal, non-formal or informal arrangements;
- Open and flexible system which will permit competent individuals to accumulate their knowledge and skill through testing & certification into higher diploma and degree;
- Different learning pathways - academic and vocational - that integrate formal and non-formal learning, notably learning in the workplace, and that offer vertical mobility from vocational to academic learning;
- Guidance for individuals in their choice of training and career planning;
- Comparability of general educational and vocational qualifications at appropriate levels;
- Nationally agreed framework of affiliation and accreditation of institutions.
- Multiple certification agencies/institutions will be encouraged within NVQF.

LABOUR MARKET INFORMATION SYSTEMS

- Improving the relevance and reducing skill mismatch of skill development requires establishment of Labour Market Information System (LMIS) and Human Resource Planning (HRP) for the reliable and realistic assessment of economic trends and labour market needs.
- Sector specific LMIS will be established at national and state levels, and area specific ones at local levels with the help of Sector Skill Councils (under National Skill Development Corporation) to undertake labour market analysis.
- Human Resource Planning exercises will be undertaken to gauge the anticipated supply and demand of skilled workers by different skill levels, economic sectors and geographical areas, over different periods.
- The information so generated by the LMIS and HRP exercises will be collated and disseminated widely to government, employers, training providers, trainees and prospective trainees at national, state and local levels, to enable them to take appropriate decisions.
- NCVT will be responsible for dissemination of information at the national level with inputs from SSCs and State Governments.
- Employment Exchanges will be strengthened and upgraded under the National Employment Service to provide counselling, guidance and placement services to the employment seekers. They will also channel the candidates into jobs, apprenticeship and training. Efforts will be made to expand formal employment.

SKILL DEVELOPMENT FOR THE UNORGANISED SECTOR

Approximately 93 per cent of the country's workforce is in the unorganized sector. The sector cuts across all economic activities and includes rural and urban areas. It contributes to about 60 per cent of the country's GDP. Strengthening the skill base of the unorganized sector will improve productivity, working conditions, labour rights, social security and living standards.

Separate institutional mechanism will be explored which will interalia plan, implement and monitor the skill development efforts for the unorganised sector. The mode of informal apprenticeship and learning will be recognized and accommodated in the NVQF to help in horizontal and vertical mobility. Target Groups The target groups in the unorganized sector include own-account workers, workers and apprentices in micro enterprises; unpaid family workers; casual labourers; home-based workers; peripatetic workers and migrant labourers; out of school youth and adults in need of skills; farmers and artisans in rural areas, among others. In order to encourage participation in skill development, entry barriers such as educational qualification, transportation, loss of wages, problem of language, etc. will be suitably addressed.

- Various avenues/institutions including schools and public/private training institutions/civil society organizations/NGOs etc. will be encouraged to conduct skill development programmes for the unorganised sector.
- Mobile training vans will also be deployed in rural and remote areas where training infrastructure is awfully deficient.
- Skill development centres will conduct skill development programmes primarily to support services and unorganised sector.
- Public training institutions will be given greater managerial and academic autonomy to design and offer programmes that meet the requirements of local economy and specific target groups.
- Flexible delivery strategy and patterns that suit the needs of the target groups, such as part/full time and on/off site training, will be adopted.
- Training will be predominantly short-term to encourage participation.
- Arrangements will be made for the testing and certification of skills acquired in non-formal and informal arrangements. These certificates will be integrated with NVQF.

Informal Apprenticeship

- Skill development programmes will be devised in existing/traditional skills and knowledge. Mechanisms will be evolved to upgrade them into modern skill areas.
- Skills of local trainers will be upgraded in modern techniques, technologies and pedagogy. They will be trained and developed into master craftsmen. Opportunities for linking these arrangements to formal training institutions will be explored to extend expertise, pedagogical support and tools & equipment.
- Dual-type apprenticeships will be encouraged.
- Social protection mechanism for apprentices will be devised. Special efforts will be made to eliminate child labour, to improve access for girls, people with disabilities and other vulnerable groups.

Literacy and Soft Skills

Skill development initiatives for the unorganized sector will include a definite component on literacy, basic education and soft skills .

Skill Development for Self-employment

- The focus will be given to entrepreneurship skill development for the unorganized sector.

- Institutes for entrepreneurship development, technology incubation centres and other such institutional arrangements will be utilized to support successful adoption of entrepreneurship of unorganized sector workers.

Lifelong Learning and Recognition of Prior Learning

- Competency standards and certification systems will be developed for unorganized sector work and incorporated in the national testing and certification system.
- Mechanisms will be developed for vocational counselling and career guidance;
- Information regarding employment trends and training opportunities will also be provided to motivate young people and workers to acquire and continuously upgrade their skills and knowledge.

Replication of Successful Models

Various successful models have been tried in India and around the world. In designing skill development strategies and programmes for the unorganised sector, successful models will be studied and adopted to suit local conditions.

FINANCING SKILL DEVELOPMENT

Skill development brings return to the individual, the employing enterprise and the economy as a whole. Therefore, all stakeholders, the Government both at Centre and States, the enterprise - public and private, and the direct beneficiary - the individual, would share the burden of mobilizing financial or in-kind resources for skill development. To fulfil the mandate envisaged in this policy apart from adequate central outlay, the Planning Commission will also provide a specific budgetary provision for skill development in the State plans. In addition, private sector investment in skill development will be encouraged through innovative methods.

A National Skill Development Corporation (NSDC) has been established with Central Government commitment of ₹ 1,000 crore. ₹ 15,000 crore is envisaged to be generated from other Governments, public sector entities, private sector, bilateral and multilateral sources.

RESPONDING TO THE FUTURE

Occupational patterns are changing; new jobs and job titles, job enlargement, job enrichment, and new flexible work arrangements are emerging. Employment demands are shifting towards higher skill categories. 8.1.1 It is imperative, therefore, for India to move up the skill-ladder and produce a larger number of people with higher education and generic training for new types of knowledge work, both in high skill services and high technology industrial production. Knowledge professionals will need support from middle-skilled workers in new knowledge and technology areas. The skill development system will need to meet this challenge. The response time is limited as the rate of change is high and accelerating.

Promoting Excellence

To promote excellence, a significant number of well performing institutions will be assisted to develop into institutions of excellence. These institutions will be generously resourced, equipped with internationally comparable facilities and high quality faculty and able to offer high quality programmes in current and emerging technology areas.

These institutions will be networked with a number of training institutions in their vicinity and serve as lead institutions in supporting their development.

EXPERIMENTATION, INNOVATION AND RESEARCH

- Policy encourages the creation of a National Skill Development Initiative that is highly dynamic and nimble-footed. This will always be extrapolating the future requirements.
  It will have to be constantly responsive to changes in the immediate as well as global environments, learn from them, and experiment with new approaches and structures. A culture of innovation will drive the future system.
- Research will be a key strategy for managing change and benefiting from it. Since experimentation and innovation flourishes in a vibrant and self-confident environment, flexibility and operational autonomy will be extended to deserving institutions.
- Research in international developments and in organizational practices and pedagogical approaches will be an on-going activity. Standing institutional arrangements will be established for the purpose and research will be funded both in these arrangements and in outside research institutions.

Policy Review

Skill development is placed in a highly dynamic environment and thus it is imperative that this Policy undergoes a periodic review and target revision to maintain its relevance. The National Policy on Skill Development will be reviewed every five years and revised appropriately to take account of progress in implementation and emerging trends in the national and international environment.

Research and the promotion of good practices are vital activities that will enable this Policy and the Skill Development Initiative to meet emerging needs.

The implementation of the Policy will be continuously monitored to provide the basis for review.

Outcomes of Skills Development Policy

- Demand driven system guided by labour market signals thereby reducing skills mismatch: Labour Market Information and Human Resource Planning
- Expansion of outreach using established as well as innovative approaches.
- National Vocational Qualifications Framework which will interalia include opportunities for horizontal and vertical mobility between general and technical education, Recognition and certification of competencies irrespective of mode of learning.
- System to deliver "competencies? In line with nationally and internationally recognised standards.
- Focus on new emerging occupations
- Life long learning- focus both on pre-service and in - service training
- Equity consideration - adequate participation of women, disabled persons and disadvantaged groups including economically backward & minorities- enhancing their access to training; improving employability and increasing employment opportunities
- Stress on research, planning and monitoring
- Involvement of social partners- responsibility for management and financing of the system would be shared with all stakeholders and provide greater space for Public Private Partnership.
- Promoting excellence
- Use of modern training technologies including distance learning, e-learning, web based learning etc.
- Skill upgradation of trainers, their quality assurance, and improvement of status.

GOVERNMENT OF INDIA

Ministry of Labour and Employment

National Policy On Safety, Health And Environment At Work Place

- Preamble
  - The Constitution of India provide detailed provisions for the rights of the citizens and also lays down the Directive Principles of State Policy which set an aim to which the activities of the state are to be guided.
  - These Directive Principles provide
    a. For securing the health and strength of employees, men and women;
    b. That the tender age of children are not abused;

c. That citizens are not forced by economic necessity to enter avocations unsuited to their age or strength;
d. Just and humane conditions of work and maternity relief are provided; and
e. That the Government shall take steps, by suitable legislation or in any other way, to secure the participation of employee in the management of undertakings, establishments or other organisations engaged in any industry.

- On the basis of these Directive Principles as well as international instruments, Government is committed to regulate all economic activities for management of safety and health risks at workplaces and to provide measures so as to ensure safe and healthy working conditions for every working man and woman in the nation. Government recognizes that safety and health of workers has a positive impact on productivity and economic and social development. Prevention is an integral part of economic activities as high safety and health standard at work is as important as good business performance for new as well as existing industries.
- The formulation of policy, priorities and strategies in occupational safety, health and environment at work places, is undertaken by national authorities in consultation with social partners for fulfilling such objectives. A critical role is played by the Government and the social partners, professional safety and health organizations in ensuring prevention and in also providing treatment, support and rehabilitation services. Government of India firmly believes that without safe, clean environment as well as healthy working conditions, social justice and economic growth cannot be achieved and that safe and healthy working environment is recognized as a fundamental human right. Education, training, consultation and exchange of information and good practices are essential for prevention and promotion of such measures.
- The changing job patterns and working relationships, the rise in self employment, greater sub-contracting, outsourcing of work, homework and the increasing number of employees working away from their establishment, pose problems to management of occupational safety and health risks at workplaces. New safety hazards and health risks will be appearing along with the transfer and adoption of new technologies. In addition, many of the well known conventional hazards will continue to be present at the workplace till the risks arising from exposure to these hazards are brought under adequate control. While advancements in technology have minimized or eliminated some hazards at workplace, new risks can emerge in their place which needs to be addressed.

- Particular attention needs to be paid to the hazardous operations and of employees in risk prone conditions such as migrant employees and various vulnerable groups of employees arising out of greater mobility in the workforce with more people working for a number of employers, either consecutively or simultaneously.
- The increasing use of chemicals, exposure to physical, chemical and biological agents with hazard potential unknown to people; the indiscriminate use of agro-chemicals including pesticides, agricultural machineries and equipment; industries with major accident risks; effects of computer controlled technologies and alarming influence of stress at work in many modern jobs pose serious safety, health and environmental risks. The fundamental purpose of this National Policy on Safety, Health and Environment at workplace, is not only to eliminate the incidence of work related injuries, diseases, fatalities, disaster and loss of national assets and ensuring achievement of a high level of occupational safety, health and environment performance through proactive approaches but also to enhance the well-being of the employee and society, at large. The necessary changes in this area will be based on a coordinated national effort focused on clear national goals and objectives.
- Every Ministry or Department may work out their detailed policy relevant to their working environment as per the guidelines on the National Policy.

Goals

The Government firmly believes that building and maintaining national preventive safety and health culture is the need of the hour. With a view to develop such a culture and to improve the safety, health and environment at work place, it is essential to meet the following requirements: Providing a statutory framework on Occupational Safety and Health in respect of all sectors of industrial activities including the construction sector, designing suitable control systems of compliance, enforcement and incentives for better compliance.

Providing administrative and technical support services. Providing a system of incentives to employers and employees to achieve higher health and safety standards Providing for a system of non-financial incentives for improvement in safety and health. Establishing and developing the research and development capability in emerging areas of risk and providing for effective control measures. Focusing on prevention strategies and monitoring performance through improved data collection system on work related injuries and diseases. Developing and providing required technical manpower and knowledge in the areas of safety, health and environment at workplaces in different sectors. Promoting inclusion of safety, health and environment, improvement at workplaces as an important component in other relevant national policy documents. Including safety and occupational health as an integral part of every operation.

Objectives

The policy seeks to bring the national objectives into focus as a step towards improvement in safety, health and environment at workplace.

The objectives are to achieve:

- Continuous reduction in the incidence of work related injuries, fatalities, diseases, disasters and loss of national assets.
- Improved coverage of work related injuries, fatalities and diseases and provide for a more comprehensive data base for facilitating better performance and monitoring.
- Continuous enhancement of community awareness regarding safety, health and environment at workplace related areas.
- Continually increasing community expectation of workplace health and safety standards.
- Improving safety, health and environment at workplace by creation of "green jobs" contributing to sustainable enterprise development.

Action Programme

The following action programme is drawn up and where necessary time bound action programme would be initiated, namely:

Enforcement

- By providing an effective enforcement machinery as well as suitable provisions for compensation and rehabilitation of affected persons;
- By effectively enforcing all applicable laws and regulations concerning safety, health and environment at workplaces in all economic activities through an adequate and effective labour inspection system;
- By establishing suitable schemes for subsidy and provision of loans to enable effective implementation of the policy;
- By ensuring that employers, employees and others have separate but complementary responsibilities and rights with respect to achieving safe and healthy working conditions;
- By amending expeditiously existing laws relating to safety, health and environment and bring them in line with the relevant international instruments;
- By monitoring the adoption of national standards through regulatory authorities;
- By facilitating the sharing of best practices and experiences between national and international regulatory authorities;

- By developing new and innovative enforcement methods including financial incentives that encourage and ensure improved workplace performance;
- By making an enabling legislation on Safety, Health and Environment at Workplaces;
- By setting up safety and health committees wherever deemed appropriate;

National Standards

By developing appropriate standards, codes of practices and manuals on safety, health and environment for uniformity at the national level in all economic activities consistent with international standards and implementation by the stake holders in true spirit; By ensuring stakeholders awareness of and accessibility to applicable policy, documents, codes, regulations and standards;

Compliance

- By encouraging the appropriate Government to assume the fullest responsibility for the administration and enforcement of occupational safety, health and environment at workplace, provide assistance in identifying their needs and responsibilities in the area of safety, health and environment at workplace, to develop plans and programmes in accordance with the provisions of the applicable Acts and to conduct experimental and demonstration projects in connection therewith;
- By calling upon the cooperation of social partners in the supervision of application of legislations and regulations relating to safety, health and environment at work place;
- By continuous improvement of Occupational Safety and Health by systems approach to the management of Occupational Safety and Health including developing guidance on Occupational Safety and Health management systems, strengthening voluntary actions, including mechanisms for self-regulatory concept and establishing auditing mechanisms which can test and authenticate occupational safety and health management systems;
- By providing specific measures to prevent catastrophes, and to coordinate and specify the actions to be taken at different levels, particularly in the industrial zones with high potential risks;
- By recognising the best safety and health practices and providing facilitation for their adoption.

  By providing adequate penal provisions as deterrent for violation of laws for the time being in force;
- By encouraging all concerned to adopt and commit to "Responsible

Care" and / or "Corporate Social Responsibility" to improve safety, health and environment at workplace performance;

- By ensuring a suitable accreditation machinery to recognise institutions, professionals and services relating to safety, health and environment at workplace for uniformity and greater coverage as also authenticating safe management system;
- By encouraging employers to ensure occupational safety and health management systems, establish them in efficient manner to improve workplace safety and health;
- By specifically focusing on such occupational diseases like pneumoconiosis and silicosis; developing a framework for its prevention and control as well as develop technical standards and guidelines for the same;
- By promoting safe and clean technology and progressively replacing materials hazardous to human health and environment;

Awareness

- By increasing awareness on safety, health and environment at workplace through appropriate means;
- By providing forums for consultations with employers' representatives, employees representa-tives and community on matters of national concern relating to safety, health and environment at work place with the overall objective of creating awareness and enhancing national productivity;
- By encouraging joint labour-management efforts to preserve, protect and promote national assets and to eliminate injuries and diseases arising out of employment;
- By raising community awareness through structured, audience specific approach;
- By continuously evaluating the impact of such awareness and information initiatives;
- By maximizing gains from the substantial investment in awareness campaigns by sharing experience and learning;
- By suitably incorporating teaching inputs on safety, health and environment at work place in schools, technical, medical, professional and vocational courses and distance education programme;
- By securing good liaison arrangements with the International organisations;
- By providing medical criteria wherever necessary which will assure insofar as practicable that no employee will suffer diminished health, functional capacity, or life expectancy as a result of his work place activities and that in the event of such occupational diseases having been contracted, is suitably compensated;

- By providing practical guidance and encouraging employers and employees in their efforts to reduce the incidence of occupational safety and health risks at their places of employment and to impress upon employers and employees to institute new programmes and to improve existing programmes for providing safe and healthful working conditions, requiring employers to ensure that workers and their representatives are consulted, trained, informed and involved in all measures related to their safety and health at work;

Research and Development

- By providing for research in the field of safety, health and environment at workplace, including the social and psychological factors involved, and by developing innovative methods, techniques including computer aided Risk Assessment Tools, and approaches for dealing with safety, health and environment at workplace problems which will help in establishing standards;
- By exploring ways to discover latent diseases, establishing causal connections between diseases and work environmental conditions, updating list of occupational diseases and conducting other research relating to safety, health and environmental problems at workplace;
- By establishing research priorities as per national requirements; exploring partnerships and improving communications with various national and international research bodies; By ensuring a coordinated research approach and an optimal allocation of resources in Occupational Safety and Health sector for such purposes;

Occupational Safety and Health Skills Development

- By building upon advances already made through employer and employee initiative for providing safe and healthy working conditions;
- By providing for training programmes to increase the number and competence of personnel engaged in the field of occupational safety, health and environment at workplace;
- By providing information and advice, in an appropriate manner, to employers and employees organisations, with a view to eliminating hazards or reducing them as far as practicable;.
- By establishing occupational health services aimed at protection and promotion of health of employee and improvement of working conditions and by providing employee access to these services in different sectors of economic activities;
- By integrating health and safety into vocational, professional and labour related training programmes as also management training including small business practices;

- By adopting Occupational Safety and Health training curricula in workplace and industry programmes;

Data Collection

- By compiling statistics relating to safety, health and environment at work places, prioritising key issues for action, conducting national studies or surveys or projects through governmental and non-governmental organisations;
- By reinforcing and sharing of information and data on national occupational safety, health and environment at work place information amongst different stake holders through a national network system on Occupational Safety and Health;
- By extending data coverage relevant to work-related injury and disease, including measures of exposure, and occupational groups that are currently excluded, such as self-employed people;
- By extending data systems to allow timely reporting and provision of information;

  By developing the means for improved access to information;

Review

An initial review and analysis shall be carried out to ascertain the current status of safety, health and environment at workplace and building a national Occupational Safety and Health profile.

National Policy and the action programme shall be reviewed at least once in five years or earlier if felt necessary to assess relevance of the national goals and objectives.

CEASE

There is a need to develop close involvement of social partners to meet the challenges ahead in the assessment and control of workplace risks by mobilising local resources and extending protection to such working population and vulnerable groups where social protection is not adequate. Government stands committed to review the National Policy on Safety, Health and Environment at Workplace and legislations through tripartite consultation, improve enforcement, compilation and analysis of statistics; develop special programmes for hazardous operations and other focus sectors, set up training mechanisms, create nationwide awareness, arrange for the mobilisation of available resources and expertise.

The National Policy and programme envisages total commitment and demonstration by all concerned stake holders such as Government and social partners. Our goals and objectives will be that through dedicated and concerted efforts consistent with the requirements of safety, health and environment at work place and thereby improving the quality of work and working life.

Index

G

I

L

M

O

P

R

S

T

V

X